AMERICAN LABOR

FROM CONSPIRACY
TO
COLLECTIVE BARGAINING

THE PROBLEM OF
GROUP RESPONSIBILITY
TO SOCIETY

John Herman Randall, Jr.

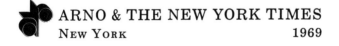

ARNO & THE NEW YORK TIMES

New York   1969

Reprint edition 1969 by Arno Press, Inc.

Library of Congress Catalog Card No. 72–89760

Manufactured in the United States of America

THE PROBLEM OF
GROUP RESPONSIBILITY
TO SOCIETY

THE PROBLEM OF

GROUP RESPONSIBILITY

TO SOCIETY

AN INTERPRETATION OF THE HISTORY OF
AMERICAN LABOR

SUBMITTED IN PARTIAL FULFILLMENT OF THE REQUIREMENTS
FOR THE DEGREE OF DOCTOR OF PHILOSOPHY, IN THE
FACULTY OF PHILOSOPHY, COLUMBIA UNIVERSITY

JOHN HERMAN RANDALL, JR., A.B., M.A.

NEW YORK

1922

VITA

John Herman Randall, Jr., was born in Grand Rapids, Michigan, February 14, 1899. Attended school in Grand Rapids and New York City. Received B.A., June, 1918, and M.A., June, 1919, from Columbia University. Since 1920 Instructor in Philosophy in Columbia University.

CONTENTS

INTRODUCTION

PART I

THE AIMS AND MOTIVES OF LABOR ORGANIZATIONS IN THE UNITED STATES

PART II

GROUP RESPONSIBILITY

INTRODUCTION

I. THE PROBLEM OF GROUP RESPONSIBILITY

WHEN we look abroad upon the world today, at the close of a war fought because of the conflicting and irresponsible ambitions of the various groups of mankind; when we behold the dissensions, the strife of interests and impulses, the selfish nationalisms and the bitterness and hostility which mark the present "peace"; when we look within the nations to class wars, prejudices, and hatreds, and observe group warring against group, capital against labor, skilled labor against unskilled, craft against craft, and see strikes of the utmost seriousness to the common welfare threatened and fought with a reckless disregard of social consequences surpassed only by the irresponsible profiteering and manipulation of the manufacturers and producers of necessities; in a word, when we look upon the seething, boiling mass of contemporary civilization some two years after the world was supposedly absolutely at one in the accomplishment of a single aim, we are disposed to agree with Mr. Graham Wallas that the amalgam seems to have dropped out of present-day society, leaving all its various discordant elements free to pursue their reckless and unthinking courses to their mutual destruction. When we look closer at the industrial conflict in those nations, like Britain and the United States, where the industrial revolution has advanced furthest, and observe the refusal of the workers of the community to perform their wonted tasks, even when tempted by wages higher than they have ever before known, we may also agree with Mr. H. J. Laski that the very mainspring of the industrial system of the last century, the willingness of the worker to produce as much as he possibly can for a low wage, seems to have broken; and with Mr. Arthur Gleason that large sections of the workers refuse any longer to operate the system of private enterprise and private profits. Our agreement will be all the more probable if we realize that the war, far from being the direct cause of all our present discontents, has but hastened a state of affairs which long ago was foreseen as the inevitable result of our reckless disregard of the social consequences of our ways.

Most of us have not yet awakened from the bewilderment these sudden and stupefying events have induced, and are still hoping to "get things back to normal," "to restore pre-war conditions." But there are some who have realized that even the election of a second McKinley can not bring things back to where they were before the war, even as the restoration of Louis XVIII could not undo the work of the Revolution, spread far and wide through the European fabric by the armies of Napoleon. Such men, and they are growing in number every day, are busy asking themselves, "Why?" What is the cause of all this unsettling scramble? Whither are we as a civilization tending? And they are patiently seeking, in the very framework and structure of our modern society, the answer to these questions.

The most striking difference between the society of today and that of the pre-industrial period lies in the far-reaching and intricate economic structure which has taken the place of the old simple agricultural community. In the old society the single family was the economic unit; all essentials were produced in the household itself, and there was very little need to bother about the families who lived in the next valley. Whatever exchange of commodities took place was limited to the village; and there was really small reason why if one of these self-sufficient communities had been shut off by impenetrable walls from the rest of mankind, it could not, with never a thought of the others, have thriven and prospered greatly.

The industrial revolution has been changing all that. It has taken these little communities, spread at random over the surface of the land, and made of them one enormous and intricate machine for the satisfaction of human needs. One by one the various functions which the farmer used to perform for himself have been absorbed by highly specialized industries; and each further specialization has made the rest of the community more and more dependent upon those who control the physical means and the technical skill necessary for the performance of their chosen function in industrial life. Men formerly cut their fuel in the neighboring forest; now they are dependent upon the distant coal-mine. Men formerly grew wool, spun it, wove it into cloth, and sewed it into garments, all in their own household; now they are dependent upon the Western sheep-raiser, the New England mill, the New York tailor. Today even the farmer, and still more the city-dweller, would be utterly helpless if any breakdown in the great industrial machine forced him to rely upon himself for the necessities of life. Each of the functions necessary to the carrying on of life has been assumed by a specialized type of worker, and all depend upon the intricate system of transportation and exchange whereby products are transferred from those who have made them to those who can use them.

This growing interdependence of society, this welding into one great organism of what formerly were separate and rather unrelated units, has long been a commonplace of the economist; but it has been forced home to every man by the experience of the war. Those who had not realized the extent to which society had become one great machine embracing every man learned that it was no longer possible to direct the national purpose to some great common end without including in that end every productive factor in the industrial system. No longer was it possible to regard the army as the fighting-machine par excellence; even more important than the soldiers in the trenches was the great industrial system behind the lines which made possible those soldiers. The war revealed a society so unified by its very differentiation, so completely interdependent, one part upon another, that only as a unit, as a completely integrated whole, could it prosecute the common purpose. It was no longer simply a question of calling an army to the colors; it was rather a problem of mobilizing an entire nation. Thus it was impressed upon every man in every calling that his particular work was an integral and necessary part of the efficient functioning of the great organization fighting the enemy.

This industrial system has its invaluable advantages in enabling a large population to live in comfort where in the old society there was but a scanty subsistence for a meagre people; but upon them it is not pertinent to dwell. It has one great disadvantage: the very delicacy of structure necessary to produce the wonders of modern industry exposes society to a thousand and one dangers undreamed of in former days. Every disturbance, however slight, is caught up in a vast network of relations and transmitted throughout the whole system; a single failure of a single cog will throw out of gear the entire machine. In the lower organisms it is possible to destroy most of the animal without injuring it permanently; but in the higher mammals a slight injury in the right place will render the whole body helpless. Just so the older society could endure almost complete devastation, and those portions left untouched could continue relatively unchanged; in modern society there are small groups of individuals whose destruction would bring about the disintegration of the community. In the city of New York there are any number of groups upon whom has devolved the performance of a particular function which they alone are able to fulfill. Should anything occasion the withdrawal of the transportation industry, or the means of getting food to the city; should the public service utilities, the purveyors of light and heat, suddenly fail, the whole city would find itself in desperate straits.

The essential requisite for any highly functionalized society is that all the various parts, all those individuals who perform a particular task in the great machine, should fulfill their functions with a minimum of friction and a maximum of efficiency and harmony. Where the life of the whole cannot tolerate any interruption or any inefficiency in the providing of those services upon which it depends for its continuance, it is of prime importance that there be some power, some force, some principle of cohesion compelling the elements making up society to work together for the common good. Only when they are thoroughly habituated to performing their part in the great engine of society will it function at all; recalcitrancy on the part of any group immediately upsets the delicate balance and, unless speedily overcome, ruins the whole machine. For that reason the fundamental problem of social organization today as never before is at bottom one of education; it is the development of social ways of acting, of character and responsibility, individual and collective. The well-ordered state is that whose institutions foster the formation of habits of social coöperation, and provide channels through which the energies of man can be so liberated that they directly enhance the life of the whole. Without in any sense accepting the static and permanently stratified nature of Plato's *Republic*, we must take the harmonizing and ordering principle of Platonic Justice as both the ideal end and the indispensable condition of any state which is to serve the good life; and we can strive to attain that form of political organization which will permit and require of the members of society an individual and group responsibility for the efficient performance of their necessary functions in the life of the whole.

Nevertheless, this force binding and welding into one organic union the manifold elements making up the modern industrial state has been and is today conspicuously absent. Despite the close interdependence of the modern economic structure, which makes well-nigh imperative such a harmonious and coöperative functioning, it seems, as one surveys the bitter struggles at present in progress both between and within nations in every corner of the globe, as if Mr. Wallas were right in asserting that the amalgam has dropped out of present-day society. The simple facts of the case are that those cohesive forces which under the old agricultural society were fairly adequate to secure the comparatively slight coöperation then necessary between the various classes of society, the authority of religion, the power of the king's army, and perhaps above all the time-honored habituation to ancient custom and the inertia of a stable community, have, with the rapid growth of the Great Society, largely lost their force and disappeared; and as yet there has arisen little to take their place. A society which depends for its very existence upon the harmonious coöperation of all its members is at the prey of groups whose purposes are far more apt to be the callous pursuit of their own private interests, and so far the sense of mutual dependence has not proved strong enough to control the anti-social motives.

The necessity of securing coöperation between those who do not as yet realize the extent of their mutual dependence, of building up, as John Stuart Mill phrased it, individual and collective moral character, is in no sense a new one. It was recognized by Greek thinkers, and it is to the glory of Greece that in her political life she achieved something of that harmonious functioning which has been the envy and the inspiration of succeeding ages. But it is a problem which modern economic conditions have made peculiarly urgent, and it is also a problem whose very existence has been obscured by the economic and political theories upon which modern civilization rests and in accordance with which it acts. That theory, assailed at its birth even by those thinkers who gave it greatest popularity, from Bentham down, has nevertheless managed to retain, with slight modifications, its position at the basis of our legal structure and our economic system; and it is at present receiving renewed homage even from the theorists, who had of late years almost all deserted it. The philosophy practically followed in the law courts and the marts of trade today, the same, with one modification, as that delivered by the Fathers a century ago, can, perhaps, be best described as individualism tempered by democracy; and its chief characteristic is just this lack of recognition of the organic nature of modern society, this refusal to think in terms and concepts which imply a community of units functioning in the life of the whole, this emphasis on the conflicting rights and powers of individuals and of another entity, the state, set over against them, and this failure to acknowledge the mutual and reciprocal duties of its members in the common pursuit of life.

True, there has of late years occurred somewhat of a collectivist reaction; it was inevitable that the palpable inadequacies and the gross failures of the individualistic system when brought into contact with a highly industrialized society should develop some antagonistic theory. But when the collectivists tried to foster among the citizens of the state a sense of responsibility for the welfare of the whole, when they tried to get all men to come together to utilize the machinery of the state for the purpose of achieving social ends, they failed lamentably; and they failed because the structure of society is by no means so simple as they had supposed. No longer can men be regarded as the isolated units, the simple citizens, which both the individualistic and the collectivistic theory presupposes; the functionalization of the economic system has proceeded at such a pace that in place of individuals there are now for the most part groups, and it is to these groups that men today owe their primary allegiance. The business man or manufacturer, when he votes or participates in any way in political life, thinks first, not of the good of society in general, but of his own economic and group interests; and even more is it true that the average worker finds that economic group to which he belongs, and in which he feels that he is playing a real part, to be a much more real thing than some distant and rather shadowy legislature representing the state, or society as a whole. When men today turn to the state, it is merely as one of the means through which they can effect the purposes of the group with which their interests are bound up.

And so it is that those qualities of loyalty and fidelity to one's fellows, of civic pride and responsibility, without which no society can endure, have for the most part been developed within certain specified and limited groups; while these groups themselves have taken their places in the framework of the old individualistic system of relationships with very little more sense of social solidarity and responsibility than the older biological units possessed. Within the groups, the individualistic philosophy has generally been superseded by something more adequate and more effective, more suited to actual conditions; in the hard school of experience men have been forced to learn to coöperate with one another, to stand by each other and fulfill their mutual duties. Participation in group life has been a most valuable educative process, leading through prolonged self-discipline to a very real sense of solidarity and reciprocal responsibility. There has been developed a group spirit, an *esprit de corps*, a set of group standards and ideals which no member would willingly violate. Yet between groups, in the relations which the groups hold to one another and especially to that group which represents the power of society as a whole, the state, just as in the further relations into which national groups enter with their fellows, there has been developed little corresponding sense of a larger social responsibility. The labor unionist will faithfully subordinate his own private interests to the interests of his union; the corporation official is inspired often by a real devotion to the company, and will stand by it through thick and thin. But of neither union nor corporation can it be said that it is actively aware of the duty which it owes to the whole in which it functions. So far as the relations between groups are concerned, modern society is still conducted upon an individualistic basis; and though the exigencies of industrial organization have enlarged the terms in the older theory from the single employer and the single workman to the great corporation and the powerful trade union, the essence of the relation between them remains unchanged. The present-day community, despite the socialized character of its industrial structure, is still endeavoring to function upon the basis of group-individualism.

But not only is the spirit which actually obtains in the manifold struggles and competitions of the industrial field fundamentally opposed to the needs and conditions of social life; of late years that spirit has come consciously to the fore in the writings of social theorists, and both legal philosophers like M. Duguit and Mr. Laski and economic idealists like the syndicalists and the guild-socialists have adopted group-individualism as the philosophy which is to solve the problems of social organization. Under the name of "pluralism" the tacit assumptions upon which the unionist and the monopolist have been acting have been rationalized into a theory of society and opposed to the tenets of state socialism or collectivism. A brief analysis will make clear the fundamental similarity between this social theory and the older conception of individualism.

The essence of the old individualism which reigned during the nineteenth century is briefly as follows: Society is composed of a number of equal units, each separate and distinct from all the others, each endowed with a private and individual will or purpose to further his own ends, each indifferent to the ends of all the rest. These units possess one and only one purpose in common, the desire to remain free from interference by the other units. This end is served by an organization called the State, which, however it may have originated, at present embodies this general will or purpose of, first, protecting the units from agression from outside the community, and, secondly, of curtailing with blindfolded and impartial justice the activities of each unit in such a way that no one will be encroached upon any more than he encroaches upon others. Since the function of the state is fundamentally to limit the will and rights of each unit, it is to the interests of the units that the state function no more than is absolutely necessary. To this end each unit preserves against the state certain rights; that is, certain powers of enforcing its will upon other wills when it wills something not prohibited by law.[1]

Now this conception makes of society, not a whole in which each of the parts performs its own function smoothly, but an aggregate of conflicting wills whose interests are all, above a certain minimum, antagonistic. Over against these individual wills is placed a higher will of the state, to restrain them, combat them, and keep them within bounds. This higher will of the state is assumed to be the general or social will; not the

[1] This analysis follows in general the lines of M. Duguit's.

will of all the members, for no such entity can possibly exist, but the will which purposes the general good. Only upon such an assumption can the acts of the state in restraining its members be justified, for only in order to achieve the general good have they surrendered absolute independence. As it practically works out, the all-important function of determining this general will is left to the majority which can enforce its desires, and the determination of the will of the majority is again left to those powerful and interested groups who are willing to put forward the efforts necessary to secure success in a modern election. Thus, under color of the fiction (necessary though it be on the given premises) that the acts of the state embody the real will of all the people, certain powerful groups are enabled to impose, by force or by threat of force, their will and interest upon their fellows. And, theoretically at least, the larger the minority the more justification does the state have in employing force to uphold the majesty of the law. Such, for example, was the theory of our Civil War.

The modern pluralists recognize this situation, that sovereignty, which is the power to make the other fellow do what you want, does not reside in the people as a whole, nor in the majority, nor in the state, but is to be found wherever there exists the power to enforce the will of a group. Some, like Mr. Laski, seem quite satisfied with this conclusion, and regard with imperturbable equanimity the reintroduction, in theory as in fact, of the *bellum omnium contra omnes* of Hobbes. Others, more disturbed at the prospect of powerful economic groups, each with special interests and with the power to enforce them, desire a federal state upon an economic and industrial basis, overlooking, perhaps, how a divergence in economic interest came near wrecking in the Civil War the most successful federal state. These latter thinkers desire a state which, in the words of Professor John Dewey, as one of the many organizations functioning in society, shall check and regulate the other groups and preserve a proper harmony between them. And these men are bringing in, together with their Benthamite passive policeman state, the whole structure of the individualistic social philosophy, merely substituting therein groups for single human beings.

The entire system is there. The old individualism depended upon the primacy of self-interest and the consequent conflict of wills. Now while psychology has thrown grave doubts upon the validity of this as a universal motive with the human being, it certainly seems as though groups which acted with disinterested benevolence were rare. We are familiar with the "soulless corporation"; and, for the matter of that, labor unions are not famed for the generous regard which they show either to their fellow unions or to those dependent upon their toil. Nor are national groups calculated to impress by their disdain of their own interests. Indeed, experience would lead to the conclusion that only when groups found their interests clearly and unmistakably identical, as with unions engaged in a common struggle against their employers or with allied nations in wartime, are they able to transcend their purely individual aims. Thus strikes are commonly praised as developing solidarity amongst labor, and the recent war was formerly supposed to have brought the Allied and Associated Powers to a mutual brotherly understanding. But the disappearance of more petty quarrels hardly compensates for the existence of struggles of such magnitude.

This conflict of will, the basis of individualism, once assumed, the other elements all follow logically. It is again necessary to bring in some organization with a superior will and power to enforce harmony amongst conflicting groups. The problem becomes once more the enforcing of responsibility from above; and instead of our harmoniously functioning state we are confronted with the alternatives of, on the one hand, a bureaucratic and efficient autocracy wisely but firmly keeping every group in its proper place and necessarily supported by a strong military force, the Prussian ideal, which, curiously enough, seems to have been approximated in present-day Soviet Russia; or, on the other hand, of a weak and ineffectual congress merely placing the stamp of legal approval on the balance of power produced by the conflicting groups themselves, the ideal of the Holy Roman Empire and the Germanic Confederation. And since, as the pluralists have pointed out, there do exist in an industrial society, unlike Russia, innumerable economic groups which possess the power of not only resisting the state, but, should self-defense follow its usual slippery path, of becoming predatory upon society, it is probable that the second alternative would in practice result.

This, then, is the situation to which social thinkers would have men look forward; strange contrast, indeed, to the society of harmonious coöperation which the intricacy of the modern industrial machine demands! In such a society, where every group were free to place its individual interests and desires above the welfare of the community, where the most powerful and the most strategically located unions were able to bring the entire nation to the verge of starvation to effect a slightly higher rate of remuneration, the delicate organization built up by a century of industrial growth would rapidly disintegrate; and such a collapse of the very bases of civilization might well mean the extinguishing of everything which man has prized and cherished in his long pilgrimage through history, if indeed it did not presage his total disappearance from the face of the earth.

Thus modern social theory has indeed performed a great service in pointing out the changed situation which the industrialization of society has brought about. It has shown one-half of the new condition which functional organization has effected; overlooking the increased need of coöperation, it has portrayed in striking colors the growth of new *imperia in imperio*, of powerful and irresponsible groups within the state. This is a fact of political and economic life which assuredly any social philosophy which cares to commune with actual conditions must assume as part of the data with which it has to work. It is at least a portion of that natural basis whose disregard has led previous social theory to become increasingly unreal and unfruitful of solution for the difficult problems of social organization. But when it goes on to ask men not only to recognize the extent of group-individualism, but also to accept it as permanent and to idealize it as best they may; when it asks them to construct a new philosophy extolling, in the optimistic spirit of Adam Smith, the marvellous way in which the self-interest of the various groups making up society works together for the greatest good of the greatest number, or deploring in the Ricardian spirit of disillusionment the sad but inevitable laws of group activity which necessitate that society remain a bloody field of combat: then it is for men to point out that it has left untouched the primary problem of social organization, and confronts in silence the demand of the modern industrial system for a society in which the same relations of functional service which obtain within groups shall also subsist between them. It has after all made little or no advance upon its immediate predecessor toward securing that harmonious and coöperative liberation of human energies, and it has fallen far below those wondrous Greeks, who, despairing perhaps of the tumultuous realities of political struggle, were yet able to erect on high for the inspiration of future ages their splendid vision of what the ideal state should be. That problem remains for the modern age, as it remained for the Benthamite liberal, as it remained for the political thinker of whatever age or clime; and in redoubled insistence it presses upon the world today as the problem of securing *virtuous* individuals and *virtuous* groups, *virtuous* in the fine old Greek sense of fulfilling to the best of their abilities that function which it is theirs to perform in the community, and in that service to their fellows of developing ever new sources of power and potentialities of spirit.

To one who with an unprejudiced eye surveys the industrial havoc which the war spread throughout Central and Eastern Europe, and who realizes the precarious situation in which even the Western powers, England and France, have been placed as a result of the interference of relatively external causes with the industrial and economic structure that has grown up with modern society; to one who has any understanding of the forces motivating groups of labor today, and realizes that it is not only in England that what Mr. Gleason points out is true, that the workers care much more about other ends than they do about securing the maximum of production even for high wages—that Mr. Laski voiced much more than a half-truth when he said that the profit motive inspiring the modern industrial system seems dangerously near to breaking down—to such a one it seems entirely within the range of possibility that the present technique of industry—the machine technique of the industrial revolution—might itself have to give way to a society of agriculture and handicraft, even as it has in certain localities of Central and Eastern Europe. It is undoubtedly true that the average member of Western civilization finds this a ludicrous, a ridiculous prospect. Only a lunatic could possibly doubt the inevitability of the industrial revolution and the machine process continuing and growing till the earth itself is extinguished in cosmic blackness.

So, indeed, it must have seemed, while the barbarians were even then at their very gates, to the citizens of that proud empire they worshipped as Eternal Rome. But it was not the incursion of the Teuton tribes that extinguished Hellenistic civilization; that was only the external symptom of a long process of internal decay. Who can say whether such a process be not even now at work in our society—our society which but recently ridiculously elevated its hope in progress into a cosmic principle? It might surprise the self-complacent member of Western civilization to realize that the majority of the human race, the millions of China and of India, do not today accept this basic axiom of the West, and would greatly rejoice if the European and his machines should disappear entirely from the earth. Nay, in the very heart of European society there are great numbers who would rejoice at the entire overthrow of the machine, which to them stands only for drudgery and servitude.

Samuel Butler depicted in his *Erewhon* a society which, perceiving that the machine had become its master, forthwith rejected it entirely in favor of more "primitive" habits of life. In the Victorian age in which the work was penned it was received as an amusing whimsicality. But Butler was in earnest, and there are those today, after the rude shattering of the Victorian faith in progress, who regard his words as somewhat prophetic. But it appears more probable that if such an unheard-of state of affairs should come to pass, it would be not because man refused to allow the machine to become his master, but because he proved unable to master himself.

It will do no harm, and it may be productive of much good, for men to stop to ask themselves why the continuance of the machine process is inevitable. Assuredly no man can stop it; but if, as the apostles of progress would have it, such mighty forces rest on the lap of the gods, what knowledge have we that we presume to know the inscrutable minds of the divinities? It might well be that in this world where so many things are born and run their course and die, the industrial revolution might share the common lot, and have even now advanced far in its old age.

Ah, but man will not permit it! Man will control his destiny; somehow he will conquer and find his way out!

Why? Such an attitude might have been possible ten years ago; but this false optimism was irretrievably shattered by the war. Many and wise men foresaw that cataclysm, and strove to avert it; but the collective wisdom of mankind proved impotent against its collective passion and folly. The cynic can today plead a well-nigh irrefutable case. Nor does the world seem to have learned much from its mistakes; so far as one can judge it appears content to proceed in the same old muddle-headed fashion to a repetition of its disasters. And if our present system of machine production should disappear, it is at least an open question whether humanity, purified and made clean by such a terrific purge, released from all those things which have constituted for it progress, might not enjoy a greater measure of collective well-being.

I do not, however, share these opinions, nor these expectations, gloomy or joyful. I believe that the machine process, when properly made the servant of man, is an inestimable and priceless boon. And I believe that man will find his way out of his present discontents to a larger measure of social well-being. But I also believe that if a way out is found, it will be found, not by trusting to a beneficent providence, nor yet to a cosmic process of evolution, but solely through the patient and persistent application of human intelligence to the solution of the manifold problems facing human society. And I believe that if through any reason that intelligence slackens in its application, it is entirely possible that the destiny of man may be quite different from that contemplated by the optimistic apostles of perfectibilitarianism.

In this particular and specific problem of the securing of a society whose functioning shall not tear it to pieces, whose centripetal shal outbalance its centrifugal tendencies, no one contemplates the eventual avoiding of a pluralistic community, or the reduction of social life to a single-minded adherence to a single purpose, however inclusive. That might indeed be a desirable end, though that question remains highly dubious; but it certainly is an end never to be attained. Mankind is too different, too richly endowed with manifold and conflicting tendencies, ever to make possible the attainment of a single-minded society, or ever to avoid the generous complexity of its variegated interests and desires. Yet the disclaimer of any such aim does not involve the simultaneous rejection of any possible adjustment between conflicting interests and impulses. To conserve individuality it is not necessary to evoke a *bellum omnium centra omnes*, nor to preserve initiative is it requisite to institute a state of complete anarchy. What society does need is sufficient unity of purpose, sufficient harmonization and reconciliation of conflicting interests, to enable it to work together for the attainment of those varying ends. Conflicting impulses have always been in the world, and will always be; but in the old agricultural society there was, on the whole, enough of common purpose to hold the state together and prevent its disruption. The Great Society has as yet hardly achieved this binding principle; and it needs, intensely and profoundly needs, a motive sufficient to cause its component members to work together with a reasonable degree of efficiency and to prevent them from running amuck and bringing the whole social structure toppling down upon their heads. The examination of this problem, the discovery of some such cohesive principle, it is the purpose of this volume to undertake.

There are two general modes of approach to the problem, and both of them shed much light on the conditions necessary for a solution. The one is that which has been assumed by the Hobbists and their sympathizers: it phrases the end to be obtained as political obedience, and seeks by the aid of force and penalties imposed by the state to create a wholesome respect for constituted authority. It aims to secure social coherence through a sense of fear engendered by a firm central government. The other mode of approach would like to discard fear entirely as the basis of political obligation, and seeks rather to build up from the bottom a habit of social coöperation resting upon consent and voluntary performance of duty. This is the ideal of the philosophical anarchist, of a Godwin or a Proudhon, who would found society solely upon the basis of voluntary associations; but it is also the ideal hesitatingly approached by Liberalism, that Liberalism that appeals to reason and decries the exercise of compulsion. The one method empha-

sizes obedience, the other, obligation; the one aims at binding society
together by bonds of steel applied from without, the other at fostering
and developing within society itself a desire and a will which shall weld
into one all discordant elements. Obviously, both methods have under-
lain all states up to the present; there has not existed one which was not
supported by a measure of executive force, yet likewise there has existed none which has not ultimately rested upon the passive assent, if
not the active consent, of its members. The second type of society,
that in which every citizen is imbued with a desire to act wholly in accord with political virtue, is, of course, ideally preferable to a society
held in restraint by external force; every Utopia is peopled by just such
virtuous citizens. Yet somehow actual states have tended to resemble
more the first type; men have needed restraint and fear to hold them
in check, and it is quite futile to blame faulty conditions and arrange-
ments for the failings of those men who, after all, are responsible for
producing that social structure. The theorists of the second type have
been almost exclusively idealists; they have elevated into universal
terms what they desired to see in the state. Those of the first have correspondingly been political realists, aiming solely at describing communities as they are. Rare indeed have been those who have envisaged
the problem as one of education, of so molding social machinery that
it would cultivate a spirit of active coöperation among the members of
the state, and advance gradually from enforced to voluntary cohesion.

The answer of the advocate of force and authority to the particular
problem of group responsibility facing contemporary society is simple.
There exist powerful groups within the bosom of the state, too powerful to be extirpated. Let the state then recognize their existence, as it
does not at present; but let it hold them to strict accountability for
their actions. Let it carefully limit and define the fields of their activity,
and proscribe with rigid penalties any overstepping of the legal restrictions it imposes. Let it place stringent regulations about the monopoly
and extend to all industries the power enjoyed now by the Interstate Commerce Commission over the railroads, or by any public service
commission over the public utilities within its jurisdiction. Let it also
prohibit strikes, by injunction or by courts of compulsory arbitration;
and let it, if need be, call out the troops or mobilize the strikers in case
of disobedience of the government's mandates.

Upon the feasibility of this solution the discussion need not enter
here. Everything put forward by the pluralists has been evidence of
the extreme difficulty the modern state experiences in enforcing its will

against functional groups. Unquestionably, if sovereignty be the power to force others to do your will, the modern trust or the modern trade union certainly possesses a considerable measure of sovereignty; and with the existence of many such *imperia in imperio* within its jurisdiction the industrial state is apt to find itself in the plight of the Capetian kings before their great feudatories. Mr. Laski is undoubtedly right in saying, "The fact is that a unity produced by terror is at best but artificial; and where the deepest convictions of men are attacked terror must prove ultimately worthless."[1] The most absolutistic government can endure only so long as it is tolerated by its subjects; the aim of a state resting primarily upon force must be, so far as possible, to obtain the support of its citizens. If the modern state is to rely upon its police power to secure the efficient functioning of its members, it must utilize that power to foster habits of group responsibility. It must endeavor to bring home to the component groups the duty they are under of contributing their share to the life of the whole.

Thus even the rigid authoritarian faces grave difficulties in the pursuit of his solution to the problem, and is ultimately forced to acknowledge that his is but one method of education in group responsibility. And the measure of his success is just that degree in which the educative process makes unnecessary the use of force to compel political obedience. It is upon this common ground that he can meet the advocate of the development of a voluntary sense of group responsibility, of an attitude of mind predisposing toward harmonious coöperation rather than discordant individualism.

The latter, equally with the authoritarian, recognizes the necessity of requiring social functioning from the various groups upon which the community depends; but he believes that that unity can come to pass only when there has grown up a real cohesive force, a real principle of social responsibility permeating every nook and cranny of the state. He feels that society cannot attain that smoothness of functioning which modern industrial organization demands and without which it cannot continue until the component groups have become habituated to directing their energies not in purely private, but also in social channels. He uses force, not as the bond which is to prevent the disruption of the entire system, but as a means of guiding and controlling this educative process. With Plato he holds that the perfect state must be schooled in self-discipline until its parts are dominated by the harmonizing and coöperative principle of Justice.

[1] Laski, *Authority in the Modern State*, p. 34.

In so recognizing that the coercive force of the government can in no sense be conceived as ultimate, he does not minimize the difficulty of his problem. Rather is it the pure authoritarian who assumes a too easy solution to the attainment of group responsibility. He imagines that injunctions and courts of arbitration, laws against strikes and the mobilization of troops can of themselves provide a proper lubrication for the industrial machine. He believes the wise government to be that which is continually proclaiming in strident tones, "Off with his head!" The advocate of educative measures perceives clearly the difficulties in the way of such an attempted solution; but he also sees enormous difficulties in his own path. He looks abroad upon society today, with all its warring classes and groups, its pluralistic purposes and its indifference to larger responsibilities, and he does indeed feel the magnitude of the task before him. But he realizes that no solution will stand which is built upon the sand of military power, and he knows that the future of civilization and of the human race depends upon an answer being found. Therefore it is that he envisages the problem in terms of education and will, of building up those habits of response to the needs of society which constitute the essense of political virtue.

The obstacles in the way of creating and fostering this sense of responsibility are great. How, for instance, is it possible to expect that a public service industry (and all are rapidly approaching this category; he is wise indeed who can even today draw the line) will have as its primary aim the service of the public, when it has been created and is controlled by men whose motive is avowedly private profit? And if it is difficult to develop a sense of social responsibility in a group whose function is directly productive, how much more so is it in the case of the union, where social responsibility means first of all responsibility to a group whose interests are in many respects fundamentally opposed to theirs! Such considerations raise the further question of whether the solution will not entail fundamental changes in the administrative system of modern industry that its productive technique may be preserved.

Before, however, these questions can be even intelligently propounded, there is required a careful examination of the prevailing conditions, social, economic and human, from which any solution to the problem must start. There are many evidences that society is at present dominated by what was been called the habit and attitude of group-individualism, and the task is to change this attitude, to develop out of it, if possible, a truly social vision. Such a change in attitude, in purpose, in philosophy, implies an exact knowledge of the possibilities inherent in the present situation, and of the causes which have made that situation what it is. What conditions have led to the present dominance of the habits of group-individualism? Is this the sole motive underlying the action of industrial groups, and what grounds are there, in their past history, to suppose that any other can be made prominent? What have been the conditions that have militated against the development of habits of social responsibility?

The question then is primarily one of understanding the motives of human beings in the industrial machine, and of so ordering conditions that these motives may be modified and turned into other and social channels. What are the springs of action of the trade unionist, his aims, his desires, his beliefs, his theories? What conditions have produced them, and not others, in his life? Why is he not commonly predisposed to look beyond his own group in his policies and actions? And what is there in the mind of the trade-unionist to lead one to suspect that under other conditions he will find his aim in coöperating with the whole body of society as well as with his fellow unionists?

All these questions necessitate an examination of the motives and theories underlying the various efforts men have made at industrial organization, and the reaction between them and the growing economic machine. Such a task it is the aim of the succeeding section to attempt, always with the end in view of discerning the bearing of this record upon the problem which the last section will endeavor to clarify. With this in mind it is proposed to examine the ideals and aspirations which have lifted the workers above their sordid surroundings and held out to them the promise of a better day to come. For the record of the progress of the aims and purposes of American labor organizations is the story of repeated attempts of certain groups to bring about a more harmonious state, and of their repeated failure to make their way against the deadening grip of the habits, the attitudes, the philosophy whence they themselves sprang and which dominated the life of the nation whose spirit they were renouncing. From their brief moments of success there can, mayhap, be gleaned hope for the eventual development of group responsibility out of group individualism; from their manifold failures there can be discerned, if men but will, those elements in the system of organized social life which have prevented the emergence of the sense of group obligation which the preservation of the nation from disintigration demands. Only in the light of such knowledge of the wanderings of the human spirit can man approach the most difficult problem of social organization.

PART I

THE AIMS AND MOTIVES OF LABOR ORGANIZATIONS IN
THE UNITED STATES

2. THE PLACE OF SOCIAL THEORY AND PROGRAMS IN THE AMERICAN LABOR MOVEMENT

BEFORE we can proceed to an examination of the theories and the philosophy underlying the movement of the American workers toward organization, we must make clear just what we mean to do in such a process. In what sense, indeed, can we speak of any particular philosophy, any particular view of society, as claiming the allegiance of the American working man? Onlookers have felt, and, as a perusal of the columns of almost any of our metropolitan journals will convince, still feel today that the only aim of labor organizations is the purpose of certain agitators to fill their own pocketbooks and live upon the fat of the land. Even those who realize that this ideal would scarcely appeal to the thousands of workmen who, assuredly not under compulsion, elect to undergo the terrible hardships of a prolonged strike rather than to continue to do an honest day's work for generous wages in a model and hygienic factory, are prone to explain the motives of the labor movement solely in terms of greed and laziness. In what sense, then, can we claim that the actions of labor unions are governed by any theories or preconceived notions, or have their basis in a social ideal and a definite plan for attaining that end?

In the first place, if by social theory we understand a fully elaborated, carefully worked out and scientifically stated explanation of the present system of social organization; if we expect a detailed Utopia, graphically delineated, an apocalyptic vision of the good time coming, then assuredly we cannot claim that any such system is to be discovered animating American labor; though there have indeed been individual leaders who have worked out such philosophies. In this respect America differs from most European countries. Such a definite *Weltanschauung* is to be discovered in the history of German Social Democracy; in Karl Marx the German workman discovered not only the inspired prophet of the new day, but even an authoritative Bible to serve as a guide in all the affairs of economic life. To this day those who owe their inspiration to Marx have been for the most part dogmatic and doctrinaire; and these are sins which have never been imputed to the American labor movement. Its philosophy, if philosophy it has, has been unsystematic, fragmentary, and in general subordinated to the economic realities of daily life.

Nor, again, if by the social theory underlying American labor we mean any one habit of thinking, any one set of mind and orientation which can be traced throughout its history and which is unchallenged today, can we fairly attribute such an attitude to American labor. It has been dominated by various aims and various ideals at various times in its history, and even at the same period there have always been conflicting theories and programs struggling for the place of influence, each called forth in response to the needs of certain specific and varying situations. Never has this struggle been more severe nor the contesting theories more diverse than at the present moment. To attempt to discover any single theory, any single thread of purpose which will explain the various phases through which labor organization has passed, is to attempt that undue simplification which is always a falsification of the facts.

If, then, we can look neither for any systematic philosophy nor for any one set or habit or attitude of thought, what can we expect to find in American labor? Has it had no ideals beyond the immediate aim of securing subsistence and avoiding starvation? Has it been inspired solely by the spirit of the leader who recently brushed away all consideration of the social consequences of strikes and of soaring prices with the succinct answer, "But we must somehow get enough to live on!"

We can, I think, answer with Hoxie: "If the history of unionism seems to admit of any positive generalizations, they are that unionists have been prone to act first and formulate theories afterward, and that they have acted habitually to meet the problems thrust upon them by immediate circumstances. Everywhere they have done the thing which under the particular circumstances has seemed most likely to produce results immediately desired. Modes of action which have failed, when measured by this standard, have been rejected and other means sought. Methods that have worked have been preserved and extended, the standards of judgment being always most largely the needs and experiences of the group concerned. So that, prevailingly, whatever theory unionists have possessed has been in the nature of group generalization, slowly developed on the basis of concrete experience."[1]

"The hopes and fears (of the wageworker) center primarily about such matters as employment, wages and hours, conditions of work, modes of remuneration—in short, the most vital concerns which immediately touch his present and future well-being—and the economic, ethical, and juridical conditions, standards, and forces that practically determine these

[1] Hoxie, *Trade Unionism in the United States*, p. 34.

matters; and his mind focusses on the problem of living as presented in these terms. In his attempt to comprehend and solve this problem he also develops some sort of social viewpoint—an interpretation of the social situation as viewed from the standpoint of his peculiar experiences and needs—and a set of beliefs concerning what should and can be done to better the situation, especially as it bears upon the conditions of living which he faces."[1]

Now, in so far as Hoxie implies that the social philosophy of the unions has grown up gradually and experimentally, and has ever remained a flexible instrument serving the purposes of those who have formulated it, he is undoubtedly right.   But he overlooks several important considerations.   In the first place, this process of gradual development occurs in the minds of the leaders, amongst that small group of men to whom American labor must look with gratitude for the progress it has made.   But for the mass of the workers there does not arise this interpretation of social forces and this program for action. The history of labor is the history of prophets, preachers of glad tidings— prophets who derive their importance indeed from the conditions which made their message acceptable, and the eagerness with which their appeals were met by their fellow workers—but prophets nevertheless, men like Skidmore and George Henry Evans, like Sylvis and Trevellick, like Stephens and Powderly, like Steward and Gunton, like Gompers and Haywood—men who had caught a certain vision of better things for the toilers and who went about the country gathering men around their standards.   The story of American labor is, in one sense, a story of organizers and of agitators, a story of small groups of men, inspired with an ideal, who were able to collect around them disciples and believers in the new gospel of organization.   And every preacher must have some definite ground on which to appeal, every prophet some inspiration from on high, some message of deliverance.   It was this necessity of finding something around which to rally, of justifying one's own notions in the light of constant criticism and hostility from without, that led the unions to the formulation of their platforms, as it led the early church to the definition of its creed.

Then again, the unions were driven to their theories by the necessity of defending themselves before the manifest hostility of the employers and of the courts of law.   Thus the early unionism emphasized the aim of securing to its members the opportunity to prepare themselves for the many duties of good citizenship, and the later, in its struggle for

[1] Hoxie, *Trade Unionism in the United States*, p. 56.

the eight-hour day, endeavored to prove the advantage such a change would bring to the employer himself. Nor is this apologetic development of social theory an altogether hypocritical piece of hoodwinking the unsophisticated. For, as will be seen, theories first developed in self-justification, and perhaps remaining mere camouflage for a number of unionists, have by the sheer force of their appeal become the means of inspiring their partisans with that very social vision whose lack they were developed to conceal. For this is but another phase of the response the unions have ever been ready to make to an honest appeal to their sense of social duty.

But the most important factor which Hoxie's view seems to neglect is the impossibility of isolating the unions from the society in which they are placed. After all, those men who developed the theories of unionism were Americans before they were unionists, and upon political and social matters they thought very much as did their compatriots. Schooled in the ideas and thoughts that found permanent form in the great documents left by the Fathers, accustomed to hear them expressed in every political campaign and on every occasion of patriotic festivity, to say nothing of the lessons they learned under whatever teachers they may have attended, the men of the last century who assisted at the birth of unionism were already imbued with a full-fledged political and social system long before they approached the particular problems awaiting them as craftsmen.

It was not a question with them, therefore, of gaining some sort of social viewpoint in their economic struggles; it was rather a question of the modification, slowly and painfully under the influence of bitter disillusionment, of those theories which they had come to regard as sacrosanct. Indeed, it is impossible to read the records of the early attempts at organization without feeling that, far from believing they were propounding new doctrines, the unionists believed rather that they alone were upholding the traditions of pure Americanism; and they called upon their compatriots to assist them in returning to the Constitution and the Declaration of Independence, whose message they felt had somehow been lost sight of.

The story of the development of the theories underlying labor organization, then, is not so much one of the first emergence of ideas about social questions as it is of the formation of a new sense of distinctness from the rest of the community and special solidarity, in theory at least, with a certain group. It is in the process of growing group consciousness that habits of mind and thought, group ways of looking at problems, became engrafted upon those conceptions which the entire community held, and built up, by gradual accretion rather than by any conscious rejection of the dominant philosophy and spirit, an individual and characteristic mental attitude peculiar to the group.

It is, indeed, this singularly American habit of the workers of regarding themselves as, individually, primarily citizens of the United States and only secondarily, in so far as their interests are concerned, as trade unionists or even as workingmen, that goes far to explain the contrast between the American and the British labor movements. In England society is stratified from top to bottom; every man, even though he be able to pass easily from class to class, is nevertheless always keenly conscious of to just what class he happens at any particular moment to belong. The workingman generally has a distinctive garb by which he can be recognized, even in places of public amusement; he is always aware of the gulf separating him from the "black-coated" clerk whose actual economic status may be below his own. He is not a British citizen who happens to be engaged in manual labor; he is first and foremost a British workingman. Moreover, his economic status and his trade organization had been practically developed before he was enfranchised and given to feel, in that vivid sense which only a feeling of personal responsibility can induce, that he was functioning as a citizen. He was an ardent unionist long before he was permitted to think, in the characteristically British expression, that he had "a stake in the country"; and when this latter favor was conferred upon him it was specifically as a class that he was enfranchised. He already had leaders whom he trusted and followed, and he could decide, with considerable assurance that his decision would become really effective, to throw his forces in with whatsoever party he chose, as a body. And when he became convinced that neither of the existing parties would achieve his ends, he was able to form a party for himself which easily attracted to it the organized workers. In a word, the British workingman, has from the beginning felt in politics as he has in industry, and has consistently shown himself class-conscious.

In America it has been very different. Until quite recently there existed very little social stratification in the United States. At its foundation the American republic recognized no separate classes or interests, and truly, as will be seen, there was in fact little social differentiation. The lowest member of an Eastern community was always aware that in a very few years he could if he would make his fortune in the West. He was enfranchised before the industrial revolution had even made its appearance, and had experienced all the vicissitudes of active political life long before he was called upon to organize as a craftsman. Indeed, labor organization generally took place just that he might retain the indispensable economic prerequisites to a proper fulfilling of his proud position as American citizen. While in England the ballot has always been a means for attaining the especial aims of organized labor, in America men have organized generally to preserve all those things which are symbolized by the ballot. Hence it has been that, despite the urgent appeals, time and again, on the part of their leaders, American workmen have never given up the proud position of being able to feel that they are in some real way arbiters of the nation's destiny on the important issues they see everywhere discussed in the press, for the more humble sense of being out to secure their own group interests. American politics, even when it has been most under the influence of moneyed interests, has always preserved a distinctly national character; divisions have generally been along lines of methods of achieving the general welfare of the whole country, not, as in Europe, on the basis of real conflicting interests. And labor leaders have never been able to deprive for long the unionist of his inalienable right to vote as an American citizen for one of the two great parties.

This determination to keep political and industrial matters separate does not imply any syndicalistic distrust of legislative action. The unionist has always been the first to turn to Congress and the state legislatures to secure a remedy for his ills; for him bourgeois parliaments hold no terrors. But it is always like any other citizen, through a lobby, or through the acceptance of a labor plank by one of the two major parties, that he has desired to gain his political ends. Not as labor, not as a special group with special interests antagonistic to other sections of the community, but as any other business enterprise whose prosperity directly affects the prosperity of the nation, the unionist has demanded that he be considered. The regulation and exclusion of immigration, for instance, has always been argued on the analogy of any tariff protection for infant industries. The Pennsylvania steel manufacturers ask that British steel be heavily taxed; just so do unionists demand the exclusion of the Chinese.

This separation of political and industrial interests has had two results. First, it has undoubtedly led to a strong sense of national feeling on the part of the individual, a national feeling which manifests itself in innumerable unexpected ways, perhaps strangest of all in the intolerance of dissenting minorities; and, secondly, and for our purposes more important, there has been a refusal to regard the political or national interest called forth in the exercise of the franchise as in any way extending also to economic life. English unions, organized in a political party, are coming to recognize the part they play in the national life, and the social duties incumbent upon them, just because they may at any moment be entrusted with the carrying-on of the government, of acting with the responsibility of the national well-being in view; and this political and social responsibility, being in nowise separated from their economic function, easily passes back into industrial life, so that they can consider political action as a means of obtaining their individual economic interests, or direct economic action as a means to a purely political and national end. But American unionists have felt that their responsibility to the community and to its well-being was entirely exhausted in their acts as individual voters, and conversely that trade union activities were not in the province of the government that persisted in unwarrantedly intermeddling with them.

For these reasons it is of the utmost importance to recognize the large part which the national political philosophy has played in all labor union theories; and to conceive the successive and simultaneous interpretations of social institutions and their corresponding suggestions for change, not as separate and isolated manifestations of group consciousness, but as so many variations upon the main body of American social theory. But in thus emphasizing the central core of agreement that has persisted thoughout American labor history, we must not blind our eyes to the fact that there always have existed very real differences between unionists and the rest of the community, and between the conflicting types of unionism itself, differences which from small beginnings with the increasing group spirit are accentuated until they may indeed work a transformation in the entire social theory of the group. These differences betray themselves in expressions, terms, concepts, in the habit of thought and attitude of mind they reveal. There are certain beliefs which to the average unionist appear axiomatic, which he meets constantly in the addresses of his officers and in the columns of his trade paper, and which would certainly be challenged by those outside union circles. These principles form the ultimate rules upon which he bases his actions; to prove to him that it is desirable to follow a certain course it is only necessary to show that it is based upon one of these deeply rooted principles. Most workers would be unable to explain the reasonings upon which they are based; but if pressed they would probably be able to give some kind of justification. And the more intelligent among the leaders would be sure to be ready with complete justification of all the group ways and habits, just such a plausible and convincing apologia as John Mitchel wrote in his admirable *Organized Labor*.

Moreover, the union furnishes an admirable forum for the intelligent workman to develop his ideas through discussion and argument. It is so rarely in the life of the laborer that there is an opportunity for him to display his intellectual powers that, if machine drudgery has not entirely quenched the rational spark and led him to seek diversion in the movies or the dance-halls, he welcomes his union as the one opportunity to find an intellectual outlet. He displays a sometimes really astonishing knowledge of economic and social theory, a knowledge which would put to shame most middle-class business men, and if young he is always prone to challenge the methods and aims of the older leaders. Hence there is wrought out in shop and in meeting a compromise between the theories of the radicals and the wisdom born of the long and hard experience of the leaders, whom responsibility and disillusionment with human nature have often transformed from men radical in their day to conservatives. There is always going on this intellectual struggle between the government and the opposition, and unless the government is able to justify itself in theory as in achievement it is apt to succumb to those who offer a new and hitherto untried but appealing remedy for the old evils. Moreover, the ranks of the leaders are constantly being recruited from these younger men; they are elected largely on the basis of what they can promise in theory and in new aim, and they are successful in proportion as their views prove sound in practice.

Thus it is that the actions of the leaders are nearly always based on considerations much more theoretical than those of the men in following them. On the basis of well thought out theories they devise slogans and rules of action which are taken over by the rank and file and become the principles guiding them in their everyday dealings with their employers. Sentiments are thus enunciated in convention and in the preambles to constitutions and programs of action which may never be understood by the majority of the unionists, and which yet are the real foundation of many of their methods and objectives. The reason for their insertion may even be entirely forgotten, and with the rise of new ways of thinking they may be expunged; yet when first they were inserted they truly represented vital currents in the workers' philosophy.

Take, for example, that assertion so common in all constitutions and programs which have come down practically unchanged from the eighties and nineties, that the interests of the workers are one with those of their employers. Few unionists today believe that; they have forgotten entirely the very real reasons which led the framers of those constitutions to insert that clause, and probably attribute it to a desire to mollify the employers. Their philosophy is now entirely different; yet during the eighties the philosophy of Ira Steward and George Gunton, whose very names would probably mean little to the present-day worker, and of which this is but one phase, played a tremendous part in molding those principles and axioms upon which trade unionism until very recently has entirely depended. No policy is so prominently identified with the American Federation of Labor as that of the eight-hour day; yet very few realize the fact that only by understanding Steward's theory can we understand the slogan which has gained thousands of recruits to the Federation standard:

> "Whether you work by the piece
>   Or work by the day,
> Decreasing the hours
>   Increases the pay."

In answering, then, our question, in what sense can we speak of a philosophy underlying American labor, we must endeavor to steer a middle course between those who see one simple set of theories as the all-explaining principle, and those who regard the movement as a mere impulsive and generally unintelligent response to certain inherent instincts, the action of men who obey their innate tendencies first and then later rationalize their impulses with a theoretical explanation. On either hypothesis an intelligent understanding of the spirit back of American labor is impossible; but if anything it makes matters the more unintelligible to treat unionism solely as the product of economic conditions reacting upon inherited instincts. Out of the ground supplied by such forces there have grown conscious aims and ideals, conscious attempts to penetrate the mysteries of social organization from the peculiar standpoint of the underdog; and these have in their turn given us that struggle of conflicting philosophies which marks the field of labor today. It is with these, then, that we are concerned: with these intellectual clarifications of purpose developed in the labor movement and controlling its activities and methods, with those theories, formulated by leaders, which have been seized upon by the rank and file and have become actually efficient in society, and, most of all, with those ideals which, however submerged and obscured in the exigencies of daily struggle, have nevertheless remained as the objectives for which the workers are striving.

If our view be correct, we have in this gradual evolution of social theories the record of the educative process to which labor has been disciplining itself; we have the growing consciousness by groups of their function in society and their responsibility for its performance. If this process seems disheartening, if the primacy of group interests over social interests appears at times too ingrained to promise aught of value or hope for the future, let us not forget that just so do individuals develop: the egotistic and self-centered adolescent is undergoing the necessary process of individuation preliminary to his later development of real moral character. Let us then regard these plans and programs, this union of selfish motives with generous ideals, in the same sympathetic spirit in which we would regard the self-education of a youth in the school of life; and let us endeavor to penetrate into those mysteries which are so often hidden from the man himself, into those underlying assumptions and conceptions which he is continually revising with added experience.

3. THE CHARACTERISTICS OF THE AMERICAN PHILOSOPHY OF DEMOCRACY

BEFORE we can intelligently consider those variations upon the fundamental core of social philosophy peculiar to early American theory, it is necessary to gain a clear notion of what that dominating philosophy was. At first blush it seems a comparatively easy task to discover those underlying attitudes and conceptions, those theories of the nature and purpose of social organization, which made up the national philosophy in the first days of the Republic. When asked what the United States then preëminently stood for, and what were its ideals and practices, there are few now, as there were few then, who could not confidently answer, "Why, the characteristic American ideal, the peculiar contribution of the United States to the social experience of the world, is Democracy"—and some, perhaps, focussing their attention on the contrast between early conditions and later developments, might be tempted to add, "pure democracy." Some, indeed, with social and economic as well as political facts in view, would probably hasten to add that the American spirit was primarily self-reliant and individualistic.

Now it is very well to answer "Democracy" or "Individualism," but such vague and indefinite terms hardly satisfy our purposes. Democracy is one of those comfortable concepts which, on being applied to a given set of conditions or a new proposal, while adding considerably to the aura of approbation surrounding it, scarcely furnishes much intellectual illumination and clarity. When, for instance, we are told in turn that France, drawing upon the period of her great Revolution, is inspired by the true principles of democracy; that only in England and the English tradition of representative government and liberty is democracy to be found; that democracy is so nearly identical with the capitalistic industrial system that no one can be true to the democratic constitution of America without giving capitalism hearty support; that the only democracy in the world is to be found in the Russia of Lenin; that to discover a democratic nation it is necessary to return to the happy days of the thirteenth century; and finally, that democracy exists at its best in China; it certainly seems that "Democracy" is more a term of laudation and praise than a definition of any principle with a discoverable extension and intention. Whether this be so or no, whether there be any "essence of democracy" or not, is hardly pertinent to the present investigation; but it is most clearly our duty to draw distinctions in this somewhat amorphous mass of material, to endeavor to delimit and describe the exact philosophy pertaining to American experience, and then, calling it, if we will, "Democracy," to pick out those elements which render it peculiar to the particular time and place under consideration. What did "Democracy" mean for those men who first started labor organizations in this country, and for their compatriots? Before we can hope to point out the especial and peculiar meaning it came to have for the workers we must answer this more general question.

Excluding all those conceptions of democracy which have developed out of dissatisfaction with the older notions, and all purely laudatory applications of the term to conditions quite innocent of the proud distinction placed upon them, it is possible to point to a certain body of opinions, a certain mass of doctrines and theories, which arose in Western European civilization toward the close of the eighteenth century. First in England, then in America, and finally in France men developed these principles into a theory of social organization and a social ideal which amongst Utopias has enjoyed the rather dubious distinction of having been more nearly realized than any other. It is within this comparatively limited field that we may confine ourselves, and endeavor to point out those particulars in which American democracy is differentiated from the contemporaneous philosophy of both England and France.

It was in England that this eighteenth century democracy was born, in the England primarily of the parliamentary revolutions of the preceding age; and it achieved its theoretical defense in the writings of John Locke. This English democracy was not, strictly speaking, a theory of social organization, although it did enshrine a social ideal; it was rather a practical expedient for getting along with a traditional and slightly faded but eminently respected organization of society. Its two principal features, liberty and representative government, had indeed both been developed primarily to check and render innocuous a self-seeking executive. No one thought seriously of changing that government; such a proposal would have been sacrilegious, and even such an iconoclast as Cromwell had hardly attempted it. His half-hearted efforts met with no success. The problem was rather how to keep it from interfering with the affairs of country gentlemen and city merchants; and the happy expedient of diverting its attention to the management of the uncivilized portions of the globe had hardly been put into effect. Therefore Englishmen were occupied mainly with building walls about themselves to prevent the king's men from coming too close; and this enforced fortification naturally kept off other intruders as well. The spirit of this English liberty is well contained in the old principle, "Every Englishman's home is his castle"; and once he has withdrawn into his private premises nor king nor peasant can enter against his will. The great documents securing British liberty, from Magna Charta down, have contained, not principles of government, but guarantees of good behavior and promises of forbearance from the government.

And the most effective of these guarantees was representative government. Get control of the king's purse and let him have an allowance only during good behavior, and you have cornered him. He can do no more harm; you can even pick out his officials for him, and they will be doubly powerless. It does not even matter who carries on the government; safe within your castle you can with equanimity watch the squabbles of those who have undertaken to keep the king in check, confident that while they will be strong enough to encounter the king's men they will still be weak enough through their constant quarrels to fear to attack your walls.

Such then were the democratic elements which England contributed: an insistence on the rights and liberties of every man to build a castle (if he could find the money), and a genial conspiracy on the part of the castle owners to keep the government from becoming too officious and interfering and to divert its attention to the other side of the world. They were scarcely counsels of perfection, nor yet the ideal way of getting along together; but they had the pragmatic advantage that they worked and kept the castle-owners so busy that they were content to let less fortunate individuals amass the requisites for starting buildings of their own; which after all was as much as could well be expected.

French democracy was entirely different. It was no expedient for getting along with tradition; it was rather an apocalyptic vision of the millennium, an assertion that all that is is illusion and wrong and that by concentration on the mystic signs it will vanish and leave in its place reality. And this concentration certainly did produce a startling change, rather to the surprise of its own advocates: for it blew off the top of society and released such an immense amount of energy that it spread its lava-streams on all sides. Just as the characteristic feature of British democracy was castle-building against encroachments of any sort, so that of the French was this hurried pushing up of men on all sides. Where the Briton withdrew within his shell, the Frenchman rushed out of his and endeavored to capture by *force majeure* the government itself. The Briton cared little who was on top so long as he was undisturbed; the

Frenchman wanted to be on top himself. The watchwords of the Revolution were "*Égalité*," "I'll be as good as you," and "*Fraternité*," "Come on, brothers, let us rise together." Liberty itself no longer retained its English meaning of "You keep off!" It became transmuted into the right of equal suffrage, something quite alien to the English mind. The Frenchman was happy to be thrown into prison if he were only sure that he had freely elected his gaoler. Perhaps the attitude toward the army forms as suggestive a contrast as any. The Briton had a democratic army if he were free to stay out of it; the Frenchman, if he and all his fellows were forced into it in one great brotherhood of equality.

American democracy bears little resemblance to either the French or the British doctrine. The fundamental difference is that whereas in Europe democracy was a philosophy of revolt, a Utopian cry for something better, the writing in universal terms of what was first and foremost an imperative, in America it was indigenous and of the soil. It was not a clarion call for a new social order, but rather the idealization of an existent situation. The doctrines of equality and liberty seized hold of the Frenchman's heart because all about him he saw inequality and oppression; they struck the American as eminently sane and reasonable because they coincided so closely with the society in which he lived. Or, to put the contrast in another way, the French developed their democracy as an instrument in the revolt against feudalism, while the Americans left the old feudalistic society to shift for itself, came to a virgin land, and developed their democracy as a justification for what they had already done. England invented the theory as a practical expedient; America was an enterprise founded on that theory, which necessarily gave birth to other elements in the erecting of a totally new social order; and France, gazing enviously upon England and America, tried to remake its ancient institutions on the new model.

In analyzing American democracy, it is convenient to adopt the French formula of Liberty, Equality, and Fraternity, which received its classic American statement in the words, "All men are created free and equal." In England this would have been received as a palpable untruth; in France, as a witty paradox needing metaphysical justification; but in America it seemed axiomatic. The two most striking features of American life *were* freedom and equality; never, perhaps, has a society existed in which there was a more equal distribution of both worldly and intellectual goods, nor in which the individual was by the necessities of his position as a pioneer in a new land thrown more upon his own resources. This equality was no political abstraction, no theory upon which a constitution might be based; it was a fact, a datum, with which all political organization and theorizing had to begin. Likewise, this liberty was no well thought out doctrine as to the social advantages of allowing every individual to follow his own self-interest; it was also a fact, a condition and a habit.

This approximate equality of social conditions in the United States was what struck all visitors to the country. De Tocqueville, so late as 1831, was so impressed that he began his great work, *Democracy in America*, with the words: "Amongst the novel objects that attracted my attention during my stay in the United States, nothing struck me more forcibly than the general equality of condition among the people. I readily discovered the prodigious influence which this primary fact exercises on the whole course of society; it gives a peculiar direction to public opinion, and a peculiar tenor to the laws; it imparts new maxims to the governing authorities, and peculiar habits to the governed.

"I soon perceived that the influence of this fact extends far beyond the political character and laws of the country, and that it has no less empire over civil society than over the government; it creates opinions, gives birth to new sentiments, founds novel customs, and modifies whatever it does not produce. The more I advanced in the study of American society, the more I perceived that this equality of condition is the fundamental fact from which all others seem to be derived, and the central point at which all my observations constantly terminated." [1]

De Tocqueville goes on to account for this equality of condition. America was first colonized by men who had no notion of superiority over each other. In New England the colonists were all of the same social class, and were bound together by the common tie of religious persecution. In the other colonies, the main incentives to emigration were poverty and misfortune, and these soon destroy all pretensions at superiority in rank. Moreover, whatever of social distinction was transported across the sea soon vanished amidst the necessary conditions of existence in the new country. There was in the New England colonies no room for men who lived upon the toil of others; the poverty of the soil demanded that every man who could should cultivate it in order to make a living for the community.

In those states where, as in New York, the land had formed the basis for a colonial aristocracy, the revision of the inheritance laws during the Revolutionary period and the abandonment of the English principle of primogeniture soon broke up the large holdings and prevented the con-

[1] De Tocqueville, *Democracy in America*, Century Co., p. 1.

tinued dominance of certain families; by the time of De Tocqueville only two of the patroons were left. But far more important even than the equal inheritance laws was the presence of constant supplies of new and unappropriated land to the westward, to which any one forced down in the struggle on the seaboard, or any younger son who did not receive the old farm or was not needed to till it, could always escape with the confidence of himself becoming independent in a very few years. America stood preëminently for equality of opportunity; there was no one who could not by his labors become the equal of any other in the community. There was no American lower class, no peasantry or proletariat; for all who in a European country would have been forced into such a class, had in this country the opportunity always crying out to them to go west and make their fortunes. This was the true influence of the frontier on American society; by affording an outlet to any surplus population it preserved the essential equality of condition.

The West was constantly in danger, however, of expropriation; throughout the nineteenth century it was a constant struggle to keep out speculators and land-grabbers who would speedily have made prevail in America the same conditions as in Australia, where the feudal estates of the ranchmen kept the population crowded into overgrown urban centers and reintroduced into a comparatively sparsely peopled land in an even more exaggerated form the problems of Europe. There is no labor program during the last century which does not include as an important feature of its aim the opening of the public lands of the West to all on equal terms and the rooting out of all special holders, be they speculators or railroads. The importance of this factor in the bringing about of the essential equality of American democracy can scarcely be overestimated.

Moreover, the equality of American life did not mean merely a general level of wealth and a common standard of living; it meant also a remarkable similarity of abilities and function. Equality does not in any sense necessarily imply identity or likeness; the employees of a great industry might well be equal in the sense of receiving equal wages and an equal participation in the control of the works while their peculiar functions remained most diverse and called for the most varying degree of skill. But in America there was not this differentiation and division of function. The colonists were overwhelmingly agriculturalists; they were all farmers who depended to a remarkable extent solely upon their own efforts for all the goods they needed. Every man did everything that had to be done for himself; from his dwelling to his clothing he made all that he required upon his own farm.   And every farmer developed a characteristic, hard-headed, Yankee shrewdness, an ability to meet all the exigencies of life himself, a knack at penetrating to the heart of any difficulty, no matter what the field.   Hence arose the general persuasion that any man was as good as any other for any job, a feeling quite natural and perhaps quite justified in those conditions when it was just that ability and jack-of-all-trades talent which was developed from birth, but a feeling quite alien to a society where ninety-nine per cent, for instance, can gaze with wonder upon the strange and alien skill displayed in swinging a pick-axe.

Never, perhaps, was intelligence and all around ability so equally developed; never was there such justification for believing that all men are born equal.

It must not, of course, be supposed that this general social equality brooked no exceptions.   There was always the South and its plantations to point to, and the moneyed interests, the merchants and bankers, of the towns.   It was, in fact, precisely upon these lines that in the early days of the Republic parties were formed; and the party representing those elements which were not participants in the general equality actually formulated the constitution and erected the national government.   But this party was always a minority; its prominence was due solely to its leaders, and when these disappeared from the scene the democratic elements swept triumphantly into power.   The complete collapse of the Federalists before the Jeffersonian Democracy and its heir of Jackson's day indicates the extent to which society was built upon this egalitarian basis.   And those principles which originally arose out of the conditions of New England and were kept ever warm by the frontier soon penetrated even into the different strata of the South.   But this scarcely concerns us, for it was in the North and West that labor organizations arose, and in the North and West society was fundamentally equal.   It required a war to break up the landed aristocracy of the South, but as the door of opportunity was kept wide open to every aspirant, the moneyed interests of the North were continually changing in personnel.

The theorists of the Jeffersonian Democracy recognized clearly this dependence of democratic institutions upon a real social equality.   Thus John Taylor, of Caroline County, Virginia, in his pamphlet *An Inquiry into the Principles and Tendencies of Certain Public Measures*, in 1794, assailed the pet scheme of the Federalists, the United States Bank, as subversive of the democratic principles upon which the government was founded.   "A democratic republic," he says, "is endangered by an immense disproportion in wealth.   In a state of nature, enormous strength possessed by one or several individuals would constitute a monarchy or aristocracy—in a state of civilization similar consequences will result from enormous wealth. . . . The acquisitions of honest industry can seldom become dangerous to public or private happiness whereas the accumulations of fraud and violence constantly diminish both." And Jefferson himself regarded with horror any increase of wealth in the hands of a few individuals or a single class.

Thus there was a very real equality of intellect and of possessions in the early republic; just as striking is the actual habit of liberty. The colonists had left England schooled in the British tradition of liberty, of curtailing the powers of the government and allowing it only a certain definite and circumscribed field in which to act. They had left largely out of a desire to get away from a government which was interfering too much with them. Their traditional theories of the function of government and the primary importance of guaranteeing their persons and property against its actions were only enhanced by the long struggles with the royal governors culminating in the Revolution, and the lapse into the executive weakness of the Articles of Confederation shows clearly the feelings of the majority upon the evils of too great governmental efficiency. The fact that their oppressors had been no alien monarch or foreign power, but Englishmen like themselves, only made them all the more distrustful of placing authority in any one's hands.

Joined to this general traditional predilection for liberty were the conditions under which they were living. The farmer is the man who comes least of all into contact with the agencies of organized society, and the Americans were not only nine-tenths of them farmers but for the most part actual pioneers, dwellers in lonely cabins where they could scarcely look to either governmental aid or restraint. Habits of independence and self-reliance, of following their own desires and impulses without interference, were bred in them by the experience of a lifetime. For them, doing what they pleased in so far as it did not encroach upon their neighbors' liberty was equivalent to almost unlimited control of their action; for there were few ways in which they could encroach upon the freedom of neighbors miles away. The government scarcely touched them at all; for the frequent meetings in which they came together to arrange all matters of common interest might be an association of men for an important purpose, but it certainly was not government in the traditional British sense. That, they were nearly always fighting: it meant unpleasant things like taxes for the king, and might, indeed, vanish entirely out of their lives without leaving any regret. To many it must have seemed as though the Revolution had been fought primarily to get rid of government.

This general feeling and attitude was the basis of American liberty. It was a conception far different from that reasoned liberalism of Victorian England that held that the most harmonious society was achieved through allowing every man to follow his own inclinations. This was a theory developed to justify the methods of rising capitalists; the former was a temper of mind which needed not to justify itself. It was a temper transmuted into theory through the conception of "natural rights": that, in the doing of which men instinctively felt they should be free from meddling, became endowed with the quasi-legal quality of inalienable "right." That which men had always done, it became *ipso facto* their "right" to do; having long lived pretty much without interference they insensibly came to feel that such was their natural "right." Thus in its origin the conception of a "right" is intensely conservative, an appeal to traditional custom. To become revolutionary it must first become reactionary. It must go back of present custom to an assumed past custom now fallen into desuetude. That is precisely why some conception of a primitive "state of nature" is necessary as the traditional time in which men were allowed to do what they now desire to do. "Natural," in the phrase "natural rights," in France meant "rational," but in America, to a far greater extent than one might suppose, it preserved its characteristically English sense of "habitual." Right dwelt in that middle region between custom and recognized law; partaking somewhat of the nature of both, it stretched so far back into the past that it quite easily came to be felt that "rights" were not only customs crowned with the halo of immemorial antiquity, but had even existed for men before there had been any organized society at all. This interpretation had in its favor precisely those elements which made the Roman *jus gentium* or natural law so attractive. It provided a methodology for introducing ethical criticism of legal institutions which, in common law especially, were assumed to be impervious to change. By seizing upon recognized "rights" it became possible to deduce therefrom further privileges which should be granted to the individual that he might exercise those rights, and this process could go on until the conflict of rights resulted in a deadlock.

Thus those habits of liberty and independence which the primitive and undeveloped state of the country had instilled into the minds of the American farmer and pioneer were transmuted first into rights legally recognized and finally were hypostasized as eternal and inalienable possessions of the individuals. Once raised above the level of custom they became sacrosanct, and could be appealed to as final authority by any man who found it to his interest so to do.

One of the most firmly established of these rights was that of private property, for here custom and tradition had been strongest. In the words of Samuel Adams, "The security of right and property is the great end of government. Such measures as tend to render right and property precarious tend to destroy both property and government." [1] In a society where property depended upon the personal exertions of individuals in clearing and cultivating land, and was always associated with the actual labor of the owner; in a society where any one could acquire it for the work it involved, and consequently where everyone did own property, the right of property was erected upon the firmest of bases. As De Tocqueville says, "In America, the most democratic of nations, those complaints against property in general, which are so frequent in Europe, are never heard, because in America there are no paupers. As every one has property of his own to defend, every one recognizes the principle upon which he holds it." [2] And in another passage, obviously based directly on American observation, he practically identifies democracy with the equal and general distribution of private property. "I am aware that, amongst a great democratic people, there will always be some members of the community in great poverty, and others in great opulence; but the poor, instead of forming the immense majority of the nation, as is always the case in aristocratic communities, are comparatively few in number, and the laws do not bind them together by ties of irremediable and hereditary penury. . . .

"Between these two extremes of democratic communities stand an innumerable multitude of men almost alike, who, without being exactly either rich or poor, are possessed of sufficient property to desire the maintenance of order, yet not enough to excite envy. Such men are the natural enemies of violent commotions; their stillness keeps all beneath them and above them still, and secures the balances of the fabric of society.

"Not, indeed, that even these men are contented with what they have got, or that they feel a natural abhorrence for a revolution in which they might share the spoil without sharing the calamity; on the contrary, they desire with unexampled ardor to get rich, but the difficulty is to know from whom riches can be taken. The same state of society

[1] Merriam, *History of American Political Theories*, p. 62.
[2] De Tocqueville, I, p. 312.

which constantly prompts desires, restrains these desires within necessary limits; it gives men more liberty of changing and less interest in
change." [1]

This widespread distribution of property in America and the consequent general belief in the right of property contrast strongly with modern English democracy.   When the working classes were about to be
enfranchised in 1867, Lord Shaftesbury warned the Conservative party
who were letting down the bars that the English worker did not believe
in the sacred right of private property and would not respect it.   Experience has fully justified his warning.   British workers, never having
possessed any property to speak of, allow those who do to retain their
possessions only on tolerance; hence while nationalization and other
schemes of expropriation of the landed and moneyed interests of Great
Britain appeal very naturally to British Labor, they are still entirely
alien to the ways of thought of Americans brought up in the tradition
of small individual holdings.   Nothing can be more important in study-
ing American labor organizations than to recognize that their conservatism is the product of the very traditional equal distribution of property which they exist to restore.

Thus those habits of independence and liberty naturally engendered
in the primitive society of the colonies, fortified by the long struggle
against governmental authority, received their legal sanction in the
various bills of rights attached to the Federal and State constitutions
shortly after the Revolution, and took their place in the social philosophy of democracy.   Based on deep instincts and sentiments rather
than on theoretical deductions from experience, this American liberty
was able to resist the changed conditions of industrialism much longer
than the more rational liberalism of England simply because it was so
irrational; and Bryce could say in 1880, "So far as there can be said to
be any theory on the subject, in a land which gets on without theories,
laisser aller is the orthodox and accepted doctrine in the sphere of both
Federal and State legislation." [2]

We have thus analyzed the American conceptions of equality and of
liberty; it remains to consider whether we find any exemplification of
the third traditional ingredient of democracy, fraternity.   What this
meant to the Frenchman is clear.   It was that brotherhood of arms, of
soldiers battling side by side to defend their newly erected institutions,
that flaming spirit of nationalism which, called into being by the tocsin

[1] De Tocqueville, II, p. 421.
[2] Bryce, *American Commonwealth*, II, p. 421.

of alarm at foreign invasion, carried French grenadiers to every corner of Europe, and took the new gospel to the sands of Egypt, the plateaus of Spain, and the steppes of Russia. Compounded of idealistic humanitarianism and the French yearning for *la gloire militaire*, it overthrew the complacent cosmopolitanism of the Enlightenment, and proved one of the most potent forces in the nineteenth century.

There was no such nationalistic spirit in America. Even the patriotism of the Revolution was purely defensive, and the jingoes of 1812 were unable to awaken general response. Historians have, in fact, been prone to regard fraternity as an element totally lacking in American life, and have based their criticism of our democracy largely upon this assumed failing. But the mere fact that in America fraternity did not take the form of European nationalism by no means proves that this, the one solidifying and cohesive force in democracy, found no exemplification in American life and theory. On the contrary, fraternity in our country led to a type of social cohesion which, if less spectacular and awe-inspiring, was certainly more productive of immediate good—it caused the formation of voluntary associations.

"Americans of all ages, all conditions, and all dispositions," says De Tocqueville, "constantly form associations. They have not only commercial and manufacturing companies, in which all take part, but associations of a thousand other kinds,—religious, moral, serious, futile, general or restricted, enormous or diminutive. The Americans make associations to give entertainments, to found seminaries, to build inns, to construct churches, to diffuse books, to send missionaries to the antipodes; they found in this manner hospitals, prisons, schools. If it be proposed to inculcate some truth, or to foster some feeling, by the encouragement of a great example, they form a society. Wherever, at the head of some new undertaking, you see the government in France, or a man of rank in England, in the United States you will be sure to find an association. . . . Thus the most democratic country on the face of the earth is that in which men have, in our time, carried to the highest perfection the art of pursuing in common the objects of their common desires, and have applied this new science to the greatest number of purposes."[1]

This ready resort to voluntary associations is the direct outgrowth of the practical liberty men enjoyed. Schooled from birth to rely upon their own exertions, and to regard the encroachments of the government with a suspicious and a hostile eye, when they desired to effect special

[1] De Tocqueville, II, pp. 129-130.

purposes men naturally turned to voluntary group action. The very equality of conditions made them incapable singly and individually of accomplishing any large ends, and forced them to unite with others of like minds in order to make their individual efforts efficacious. There were few figures of outstanding power and influence to whom could be entrusted any considerable undertaking. Moreover, there was another condition which powerfully promoted the growth of associations and habituated men to employ them as a means to achieving social purposes, that fear which impressed nearly every disinterested observer—the tyranny of the majority.

We have seen how the American habit of liberty was a traditional and irrational feeling, not a carefully elaborated theory of politics or economics. Hence, while for all ordinary purposes it sufficed to keep the acts of government within certain definite limits, whenever men were deeply stirred in the more emotional parts of their nature, whenever a question presented itself, not as one of mere political expediency, but as a great moral issue, they realized that they did possess a most powerful weapon for attaining their tremendously vital aims in the political power of the majority. They were not bound by a theory, but they acted from a habit; and thus, paradoxical as it may seem, that very liberty and independence which individually led them to fight against any restriction of their attempts to enforce their own wills, led them collectively to enforce upon a minority their collective will. Their liberty consisted in having their own way; why should not they as a majority have their own way with their fellows? In this respect American liberty takes after the French rather than the English conception; the latter nation, long trained in opposition to a hostile government, has preserved such a wholesome fear for the invasion of the magic circle every individual drew around himself that it still hesitates to operate socially through political means.

The fact that the restraint placed upon the action of the majority in this country is rather customary than legal and rational, coupled with the fact that the American form of government provides for no responsible executive and no recognized opposition, has necessitated the organization of all minorities that they may most effectively provide against such attacks. The political decentralization of the country and the great emphasis placed upon local self-government have been the most effective legal methods of opposing the tyranny of the majority; thus the Southern states have been able to nullify the Fifteenth Amendment in a way that would have been impossible in centralized France. But these constitutional provisions have naturally been supplemented by innumerable associations for resisting and if possible changing through persuasion the will of the majority; and this habit of organizing to protect one's habitual rights against the government has naturally fortified the other strong motive toward the formation of groups for particular purposes.

Moreover, in all of the newly settled portions of the country the government itself was largely entrusted to just such private associations; the early days in California, the vigilante committees, and even more significant, the practical formulation of an entire code of mining laws and rights through voluntary coöperation, bear witness to the ease with which Americans accustomed to a large amount of practical liberty combine to further common purposes. The town-meeting differed very little from the church meeting or the political club; and for the American it was quite natural to regard government as merely that association in which he united with his fellows for certain definite and particular ends. It was but one of the many groups to which he belonged. Each of these groups had some definite purpose and restricted its operations to the attainment of this purpose; government performed some peculiar functions, but there was nothing to lead one to think that it either ought or was able to perform any others than those it had always done.

What was this peculiar purpose of government? The early Americans quite clearly recognized that it was to take care of those interests which all the members of the community had in common. The constitution of Vermont, for instance, urged "that the common benefit, protection, and security of the people, nation, or community, and not the particular emolument or advantage of any single man, family, or set of men who are a part only of that community," is the proper aim of government. The constitution of Massachusetts carefully contrasted the function of the government as the guardian of the general interest with the special privilege idea, and declared its aim to be the common good and happiness of the entire people,—"not for the profit, honor, or private interest of any one man, family, or class of men." [1] Any interest less general than that of the entire community was wholly beyond the sphere of the particular association of government. For all such purposes men must form other groups and help themselves. And for the Fathers there was only one interest which the nation did possess in common. John Hancock phrased it: "Security to the persons and property of the governed is so obviously the design and end of civil government, that to attempt a

---

[1] Merriam, pp. 61, 75.

logical proof of it would be like burning tapers at noonday to assist the sun in enlightening the world." [1] The purpose of government was, not to interfere with the rights of the citizens and to keep every one from interfering with those of his neighbor while guaranteeing his own; only in time of dire calamity would a man think of calling upon it for positive aid. Indeed, the Fathers were much clearer and more definite in their ideas of the powers that government had wrongfully usurped than they were of those which it ought to exercise; and the dominance of the commercial Federalists at the outset of the republic's history, while it gave a strong government to the nation, only served to confirm the mass of the people in their conviction of the wrongness of allowing the political power to serve the private interests of any particular class or group of the community. Jeffersonian democracy stood for the closest restriction of executive and legislative power to those interests which were beyond peradventure of doubt common and general; and it necessarily gave a strong impetus toward the formation of other associations that should attain group aims not including the entire community.

Fraternity thus found expression in American democracy as the tendency of free and equal citizens to unite together for the promotion of the interests that appealed to the group; instead of as in France being the coöperation of all the members of the nation in a common political or military enterprise, it was the voluntary coöperation of certain groups to serve their own private interests. It was the inevitable result of an individualistic society; the social interests and impulses constantly brought about the formation of larger and larger individuals. The importance of such a habit and attitude of approaching social problems when men are brought into contact with the changed conditions of an industrial age are apparent; labor organizations sprang up to express the interests of the laborers in just the same way as political or religious organizations or purely benevolent associations might have come into being.

Having completed our examination of the three elements making up American democracy, equality or the independent Yankee-farmer ideal, liberty or the habit of self-reliance and having one's own way without interference, and fraternity or the tendency to unite with one's fellows in the pursuit of group interests, and having contrasted them with the similar conceptions in English and French democracy, we have arrived at the point where we can sketch the social ideal of the early American republic. Nothing is so illuminating in trying to discover the

[1] Merriam, p. 62.

theories and conceptions actuating the past as to find out what were its ideals, what was its Utopia: for a clue to the society men wished to attain, even though they actually fell far short of realizing it, is an insight into their inmost thoughts and motives. There was developed, in the period between the downfall of the Federalists and the beginning of the slavery contest, in the era of the democracy of Jefferson and of his successor and heir Jackson, a social ideal which has remained until very recently, amidst all the changes of industrial expansion, the goal at the bottom of all forms of labor organization, and the goal even now inspiring the majority of the American Federation of Labor.

The ideal of democracy, that which to later generations of workers seemed a truly golden age, was the ideal of the simple, frugal agricultural community as it was known in New England. It was that of a society of farmers, each owning and tilling his own land, each working largely upon his own initiative, yet coming together with his fellows upon a basis of equality in town meeting and contributing his share of the shrewd wisdom born of a lifetime of sturdy independence. Educated in the common school, equally intelligent and fully able to hold their own in argument with the parson, possessing not very much more and not very much less than their neighbors, they would live their lives in this new world untroubled by the inequalities and injustices of the feudal estates and the industrial centers of Europe, happy and contented in their rural community. It was in a society approximately realizing such an ideal that democracy was born in America; it was only in such a society that democratic institutions could hope to flourish. The history of the labor movement of the century is the history of the attempts of men to struggle against the inevitable, to retain, under rapidly transforming conditions, that same status which they had enjoyed as equal members of a free society of farmers.

This specific nature of the democratic community was recognized by some of the most penetrating men of the time. Thus in the great controversy between the Republicans and the Federalists, John Taylor declared that "land was the real basis of democracy." [1] J. T. Mercer made the same claim in a speech in Congress declaring that the democracy of the Republican opponents of Hamilton was the democracy of the farmer. The opponents of the Republicans recognized the same fact. John Adams declared the conflict to be between the rich and the poor, the seaboard merchants and the farmers. Marcellus, author of

[1] John Taylor, *Inquiry into the Principles and Policy of the Government of the United States.*

Letters from the Virginia Gazette, declared specifically that what democracy really meant was that society of New England founded on free labor and small land holdings.[1]

But it is to Jefferson himself that we must go to see this most clearly. He hated cities and the conditions which industry brought about; although he appealed to city laborers for support he hoped to keep their number as low as possible. As Beard says, "His very democracy was founded on an economic system of small land-owning farmers,—upon that wide distribution of property that was possible only where land was cheap and plentiful. It did not embrace a working class, as that term is conceived in modern life. The incompatibility of an immense proletariat and an equalitarian political democracy he clearly realized, but he never attempted to solve the problem which it presented. In fact, he apparently believed that the problem was insoluble and the only hope of American democracy was to escape from it, by preventing its appearance in the society of the United States." [2] In his *Notes on Virginia* he bids manufacturers keep away from America. "Those who labor on the earth," he says, "are the chosen people of God, if ever he had a chosen people, whose breasts he has made his peculiar deposit for substantial and genuine virtue. It is the focus in which he keeps alive that sacred fire, which otherwise might escape from the face of the earth. Corruption of morals in the mass of the cultivators is a phenomenon of which no age nor nation has furnished an example. . . . Dependence begets subservience and venality, suffocates the germ of virtue, and prepares fit tools for the designs of ambition." [3]   And Beard concludes, "Jeffersonian Democracy simply meant the possession of the federal government by the agrarian masses led by an aristocracy of slaveholding planters, and the theoretical repudiation of the right to use the government for the benefit of any capitalistic group, fiscal, banking, or manufacturing." [4]   And Jacksonian Democracy, in substituting farmer for planter leadership, simply removed the Jefferson aristocracy in favor of a purer form of the agricultural community.

This was the ideal, this was the meaning of American democracy during that period when it is acknowledged to have persisted in its purest form; and a recognition of this fact will throw a great light on the meaning which has been given to "democracy" by American labor.

[1] Beard, *Jeffersonian Democracy,* p. 237 ff.
[2] Beard, *op. cit.,* p. 422.
[3] Jefferson, Washington ed., v. 8, p. 405 ff.
[4] Beard, *op. cit.,* p. 467.

Just so soon as the program of a trade union has risen above mere self-defense it has endeavored in some way to cope with the problem of creating in an industrial society so much of the old agricultural ideal as can possibly be recovered:—primarily, the equality of condition which existed in that golden age, and, perhaps just as important, those habits of independence, of self-reliance and self-respect and general position in the community, which made the life of the American farmer worth living. It is an ideal which persisted as long as the frontier was there to keep it green; and it is an ideal at the very basis of the notions of those who yearn after "industrial democracy." Thus Mr. Graham Wallas recently declared that the essential requisite of any truly democratic society was a practical equality amongst its members—and he pointed, as those countries where the democratic spirit was today most in evidence, to Norway, to Switzerland, and to New Zealand—and what are they but those lands where the old agricultural civilization, having rid itself of feudalism, has not yet succumbed to the industrial revolution?

There were, however, certain other elements introduced into American democracy which, though in reality but the logical development of the ideas of Jefferson's period, nevertheless did add new and characteristically American notions that played a great part in the development of the labor movement. It was in the period of Jackson that the theory received its elaboration, and it was in the period of Jackson that we first find labor organizations springing into existence. What, then, were these new ideas?

They were the product of two new conditions—first and foremost, the growth of the frontier and pioneering element, secondly, the rise of an urban and quasi-industrial population. During the period immediately succeeding the Revolution America had been occupied mainly with consolidating those portions of her land that had already been staked out, with developing rural and farming lands where the pioneer had already blazed the trail. Jefferson was the spokesman of these older agricultural interests. But beginning about 1800 there was a tremendous emigration over the Appalachians into the Northwest and into Louisiana. By 1830 nine new states had been added to the union, seven of them from beyond the mountains; by 1850, sixteen. Jackson of Tennessee and his followers represented this new and more primitive society, this society in which those elements of equality and liberty we have found characteristic of the Revolutionary period were even more accentuated. And simultaneous with this growth of the west was the rise of handicrafts in the cities of the East, and the consequent increase of the poorer classes. During the decade 1820–1830 these propertyless men were nearly all enfranchised: the states revised their old constitutions, New York in 1821, Massachusetts in 1820, Virginia in 1829–30.   For the first time they were an important political factor; and we shall see how they made use of their new ballot.

The most important modification these new elements made in the Jeffersonian democracy was to sweep away the old landed leaders of the South.   The previous era had been one of power to the legislatures, who were left to govern the country, not according to its will, but as they themselves thought best.   These aristocratic bodies had served the interests of the planters in the South and the merchants in the North, no matter how devoted they might also have been in a benevolent way to the sturdy farmer.   The plain people of the west and of the cities now sought to break down this legislative aristocracy and to curb it through a strong executive.   Jackson was elected as the tribune of the people against the patrician legislators, and the blows he so doughtily dealt at the moneyed and slave interests were inspired by a sense of his public trust.   The governors of the states also received an immense accretion of power; as Merriam says, "One pronounced feature of the democratic movement in the first half of the century was the elevation of the executive and the degradation of the legislative power.   The early distrust of the executive, which once took the form of a fear that monarchy might return, had disappeared, and also the early confidence in the legislature. Popular suspicion seemed to be directed, not so much against a tyrannical monarchy, as against ' encroaching aristocracy.'" [1]   Together with this increased responsibility of the executive went the abandonment of the old theory that the people's representatives were to legislate as they thought best.   The electoral college lost its meaning; legislators came to bind themselves to their constituents; their terms were shortened, and property qualifications, with the aim of securing the cultured gentleman, were abandoned.   Rotation in office, on the theory (a by-product, as we have seen, of the Yankee-farmer age) that one man was as good as another for any position, and that too long tenure of office made one unresponsive to popular needs, took the place of permanent appointments.   Everything tended toward a democracy in which one strong, responsible head was chosen by all the people and was held accountable to them for his act.

This ideal of the strong but responsible executive has become a very important part of American democracy.   Other countries—Russia, for

[1] Merriam, *op. cit.*, p. 186.

instance,—have developed a form of consultative, deliberative, and coöperative action, on the model of the village mir. Such has been the general tendency in most European lands—witness the supremacy of the legislature in France, of Parliament in England. A cabinet jointly responsible for its actions, where policies are worked out in collaboration, indicates just such a conception of coöperative democracy. In America the pioneering, liberty-loving habit has proved too strong; our ideal is the business ideal, the ideal of the board of directors who give their manager carte blanche but require him to "produce the goods." General Goethal's erection of the Panama Canal illustrates admirably this notion of the responsible executive. It has been our habit to idealize strong leaders, like Roosevelt, and then when they no longer please us to throw them into the discard. We abolish city councils and install commissions of a few men; we advocate the short ballot and its implied increase of executive powers. But we also demand the recall. We require that our officials be red-blooded men, but we desire to keep an eye on them. The effects of this policy are today apparent in our political life, when we have failed to discover any leaders; we are driven to the entire abandonment of legislative action in favor of direct enactment through the initiative and the referendum.

This characteristic is markedly apparent when we come to consider labor organizations. There has undoubtedly been a tendency to leave everything to the leader, and to "fire him if he doesn't produce the goods." This has led to much of the complaints against labor leaders; fearful of losing their prestige, they have been continuously exposed to the insidious dangers confronting the Bonapartist. Confident that if they could only "put it across" their men would not inquire too closely into methods, they have at times both precipitated unnecessary strikes, and they have resorted to means which have only discredited their organization in the public eye. For there has been likewise a loyalty to every successful but persecuted leader, no matter what he has done; witness the persistence of the Bridge Workers in reëlecting the officers who have been convicted of dynamiting. But this habit of mind and action is also responsible for the difficulty with which American labor has been persuaded to adopt any of the forms of "industrial democracy" which appeal to their European brothers; the very idea of "works-councils," of collective participation in the management of industry, which to the Russian is perfectly natural and strikes the Englishman with no shock, involves a totally new orientation for the American worker. He has been for so long trained to let his employer do the directing while he has been content to glean the harvest that it is only in recent years that he has begun to outgrow this product of old American conditions.

We have now completed our sketch of the dominant social philosophy of the Jeffersonian and Jacksonian periods, the truly formative era in American history. It was an idealization of existent conditions, not a philosophy of revolt—save in so far as those very conditions were in themselves the products of revolution against feudal and aristocratic Europe. It offered an ideal which for a brief interval seemed fairly attained, and then gradually and imperceptibly slipped away into the background, and ascended to the heavens, whence it might cast its cheering beacon, but whither man could scarcely hope to follow it. It held out the ideal of the peaceful, virtuous, idyllic rural community,—sufficiently elevated above the state of nature to have attained the civilization of thought and art, but sufficiently remote from the iniquities of the city to preserve itself from the contaminating influences of urban life. A society of free and independent farmers, self-reliant and intelligent, uniting freely for the furtherance of their common purposes, be they religious, educational, benevolent, or political; a society which utilized national politics rather as a fascinating intellectual diversion than as a serious part of daily life, and which consequently preferred a single responsible representative who could be counted upon to do the acting while he left the discussing to the home circle,—such was the ideal democratic community of the first half of the last century. It never actually existed anywhere, of course; but in the villages of New England it was closely approximated, and the plain living and high thinking of a Concord, was the inspiration and hope of many a mind that would otherwise have given up in despair the struggle for a more complete democracy. Here was democracy: here at least every man had a fair chance to show what was in him; and in the succeeding years, as men in the rising factory towns looked back upon the age of the country village, it was this ideal which led them to combine, it was this vision which inspired them with a desire to recreate it anew.

4. THE MECHANICS' MOVEMENT OF THE TWENTIES AND THE THIRTIES

WE have seen the very definite ideal which permeated the American society of the first half of the last century, and which represented, especially to those who had not quite attained it, a state of affairs that could in no wise be improved upon. But no sooner had the new republic been established upon these political and social principles than certain members of the community found themselves in a position quite different from the equality laid down in the Declaration of Independence. And as time went on, particularly during the industrial depression following the close of the Napoleonic wars, this class of men found themselves dropping lower and lower in the social scale, losing their status in the farmer community. The men who thus saw their ideal slipping away from them, and regarded it all the more tenderly because it represented a something that had obtained in the "good old days" but seemed gradually to have receded, were the "mechanics" of the towns of the eastern seaboard, the handicraftsmen and skilled artisans who manufactured those products that in increasing numbers were no longer made upon the farm or in the home. Their status in society was being lost; their standard of living, which had placed them on an approximate level with the other members of the agricultural community, was being forced down. There were those who feared the emergence of conditions resembling the old-world squalor and poverty; and the men who thus found themselves sinking turned to the only philosophy of which they knew and phrased their grievances in the ideology of natural rights, of equality and freedom.

Thus arose what, if we except what fragments of guilds had ever been imported from English life, were the first labor organizations in America; and they arose in response to the very definite questions, "How can we retain our old status? how can we maintain ourselves in a condition wherein we shall be truly free and equal? how, in the face of these adverse circumstances, can we gain the rights which, as members of a democratic community that has once and for all recognized that all men are created free and equal, are assuredly ours?" In answering these questions, inspired as they were by the typically American ideal of democracy, and confident as they felt themselves to be in merely calling the nation back to her former state, the mechanics of the cities really contributed much to the modification and further development of that ideal.

The first general movement in which laborers can be said to have formed themselves into groups as a distinct class took its rise in the rather ephemeral associations and sporadic strikes that are revealed in the records as having existed between 1792 and 1827, but it only assumed importance with an individual aim and a generally accepted theory in the decade between 1827 and 1837. It ended abruptly in the panic of the latter year, and did not really begin again until the fifties; and it is thus a fairly isolated development with a definite beginning and a clearly marked growth of aim and philosophy. Its importance for our purposes, apart from the fact that it represents the first emergence of a distinctive philosophy of American labor, lies in the interesting fact that in its brief course it reveals nearly all of those characteristic tendencies and ways of thinking that we shall find on a much greater scale in the larger movement springing directly out of the industrial revolution; and upon this small stage it will be possible for us to pick out with some ease threads of purpose, bits of attitude and character, tendencies of theory and bents of philosophy, that will serve us in very good stead when we come to trace our way through the far more complex drama of conflicting ideals that emerges after the Civil War. It will be our aim, then, in the present chapter to deal with the motives and theories, the purposes and ideals revealed in this first American labor movement, and in the next, using the material herein discovered as a basis, to form generalizations and hypotheses which we can later verify in the strictly industrial movement.

It is important at the outset to bear clearly in mind that this movement of the thirties was in no sense an industrial movement, nor did it concern the few factory operatives even then in existence. Unlike the formation of labor organizations in England, their formation in this country was not called forth by conditions arising out of the industrial revolution, and the growth of the factory system. It was not till the period just preceding the Civil War that America was appreciably influenced by the rise of factories, and it was only during that struggle itself that they assumed great importance. "Labor organization and the 'class-struggle' of wage-earners in America preceded by many years the factory system which finally separated the worker from the ownership of the tools," says Saposs.[1] It was not till the Trades' Union of

---

[1] Commons and Associates, *History of Labour in the United States*, I, 26.

Pennsylvania was organized in the autumn of 1833 that we find factory operatives playing any considerable part in labor organizations; and it was in the same movement that extended warnings against the dangers of the factory system as developed in England were first seriously made a part of an American program.   Even the New England Association, which had its stronghold in that part of the country where factories were most numerous, found in 1833 that it could not count upon the operatives for much support.   "The absence of delegates from the factory villages," it found in its 1833 convention, "gives reason to fear that the operatives in the factories are already subdued to the bidding of the employers—that they are already sold to the oppressor, that they have felt the chains riveted upon themselves and their children, and despair of redemption.   The Farmers and Mechanics, then, are the last hope of the American people."[1]   And in the convention of the National Trades' Union in the next year the delegates could only look with dread upon the fearsome spectre of English conditions and commiserate the fate of the Lowell women operatives as a problem analogous to their own but nevertheless not touching them directly.[2]

No, this early movement was preëminently a movement of the skilled mechanics and handicraftsmen, of printers and shoemakers, carpenters, tailors, and the like.   These were just the men most able to set up in business for themselves.   The unskilled workers were not interested, largely because they found their wages were rising; and it was to the body of unskilled labor that the factory appealed.   Thus the wages of common laborers had risen from less than $4 a week in 1784 to $7 or $8 in 1810, while those of the skilled had remained stationary and had in real wages considerably declined.[3]   It was against this falling standard of life, this growing inequality in a society whose ideal it was to preserve an approximate equality, that the skilled artisans protested.   The movement of the twenties and thirties was primarily a movement of men who felt, "I am as good as you are; I am your equal"; and it was a protest against a capitalistic system, though not against one erected on an industrial foundation.   The fall in the status of the mechanic was primarily due to the enlargement of the market brought about by the improved means of transportation, to the consequent intensifying and widening of the field of competition, and the growth of a class of so-called "merchant capitalists" or wholesale investors to cope with the

---

[1] Carey's *Select Excerpta*, IV, 435.
[2] Commons, *A Documentary History of American Industrial Society*, VI, 216 ff.
[3] Commons, I, 105.

credit situation. Steamboat transportation and the frenzied building of canals were probably the immediate physical causes of the grip the merchant capitalists were able to get upon the artisans in all the large cities.[1]

But the detailed economic reasons for the lowering of the condition of the artisan, the inevitability of sweating conditions with the growth of a handicraft system upon an individualistic premise, were not known to the mechanic himself. He felt his old assured position in society, economic, social, even political, with the growth of party machinery and bossism, unaccountably slipping away from him, and he clutched at the means nearest at hand and most natural: he formed an association with his fellows to regain his lost status. Thus the preamble of the Mechanics' Union states that the object of the organization is "for the purpose of affording to each other mutual protection from oppression," and continues, "We, the Journeyman Mechanics of the City and County of Philadelphia, conscious that our condition in Society is lower than justice demands it should be, and feeling our inability, individually, to ward off from ourselves and families those numerous evils which result from an unequal and very excessive accumulation of wealth and power into the hands of a few, are desirous of forming an association which shall avert as much as possible those evils with which poverty and incessant toil have already inflicted, and which threaten ultimately to overwhelm and destroy us. . . . Are we, who confer almost every blessing on society, never to be treated as freemen and equals and never be accounted worthy of an equivalent in return for the products of our industry?"[2] Again, the platform of the New England Association asserts, "that we are determined by all fair and honorable means to exalt the character and promote the cause of those who by their productive industry add riches to the state and strength to our political institutions . . . that we regard all attempts to degrade the working classes as so many blows aimed at the destruction of popular virtue—without which no human government can long subsist."[3] The call issued for the formation of the General Trades' Union of New York and Vicinity announces, "The time has now arrived for the mechanics of our city to arise in their strength and determine that they will no longer submit to the thralldom which they have patiently borne for many years, nor suffer employers to appropriate an undue share of the avails

[1] Commons, I, 105.

[2] *Mechanics' Free Press*, October 25, 1828.

[3] *Boston Courier*, August 28, 1830.

of the laborer to his disadvantage. . . . They have now become alive to the necessity of combined efforts for the purposes of self-protection." [1]

This motive of self-protection was partly economic; it found expression as a desire for security of wage and continuity of employment. Thus the striking carpenters of Philadelphia in 1827 declared that the real objection of their masters to the ten-hour day was "because they are aware that if this alteration takes place, it will deprive them of the power they have hitherto had of employing a man during the summer, in the long days, and either discharging him in the winter or reducing his wages, as it will make a journeyman of nearly as much value in the winter as in the summer." [2] But it was also something far more than merely economic security that the men desired: it was the restoration of that position in the community, that social status, so imponderable yet so profound in its effect, which as honest artisans they had once possessed. The chief grievance of the New England Association was "the low estimation in which useful labor is held by many whose station in society enable (sic) them to give the tone to public opinion. . . . All who can do so resort to some means of living without hard work, the learned professions are crowded, and combinations are formed by that portion of society who have money and leisure, or who live by their wits, to increase and maintain their own relative importance, whilst the more industrious and useful portion of the country, who are too intent upon their daily occupation to form combinations for mutual advantage, or to guard against the devices of their better informed or more enterprising neighbors, are reduced to constant toil, stripped of the better share of their earnings, holding a subordinate if not degraded situation in society, and frequently despised by the very men and women and children who live at ease upon the fruits of their labor. There is no consideration more discouraging, and at the same time more destitute of foundation, than a prevailing opinion that the industrious and unlearned portion of the community cannot govern themselves." [3]

The general ideal of the movement as it finally emerged in the thirties with its humanitarian interests rudely shattered, is that of the Philadelphia Trades' Union: "There is an institution now forming for the maintenance of a fair price for labor. . . . Each individual would

---

[1] Finch, *Rise and Progress of the General Trades' Union of the City of New York and Its Vicinity.*

[2] *Democratic Press*, June 20, 1827.

[3] *To the Workingmen of New England*, pamphlet, Boston, 1832.

then receive a compensation that would enable him with economy to provide a comfortable subsistence for his family; to give his children an education that would enable them to become useful and respectable members of the community—to provide against dull seasons and sickness, and lay by a fund that would support him when the infirmities of age should render him unable to work." [1]   In a word, the men who engaged upon this new movement desired that same security from want, that same assured and recognized position in society, which fell to the lot of the hardworking in any farming community.   It was the old ideal of democracy that was inspiring them; and thus the writer in the Mechanics' Free Press was right when he offered hope after the set-back of the election of 1830.   "Meetings have already taken place and committees have been appointed to carry into effect our principles, and we look forward, from the zeal manifested by our friends thus early, that the principles of *practical democracy*, and those of the revered Jefferson, will assuredly triumph at the next election." [2]

This, then, was the motive inspiring the entire handicrafts movement of the twenties and thirties; but the methods which were employed, and the immediate objectives, as well as the general theoretical justification for such action, naturally changed and varied.   The first and longest period, beginning in fact in the nineties of the previous century, was one of simple self-defense against the encroachments on the position of the workers.   It was marked almost exclusively by sporadic "turn-outs" or strikes, concerted attempts at preserving their economic status carried on by men with no previous organization, and followed by speedy dissolution of whatever associations had sprung up at the conclusion, successful or unsuccessful, of the turn-out.   Indeed, it was in only two trades, the shoemakers and the printers, that any organization at all was kept up between strikes, until 1818. [3]   The Philadelphia shoemakers formed a society in 1792, which soon disappeared; they formed again as the Journeyman Cordwainers two years later, and existed until the conspiracy trials of 1806. They conducted in 1799 a ten weeks' strike, the first "organized" strike on record.   A Typographical Society was formed in New York in 1794, and persisted with interruptions. [4]   Various other bodies are recorded which limited themselves strictly to endeavoring to preserve wages and shorten hours.   The weapon was always the

---

[1] *Pennsylvanian*, Jan. 9, 1834.
[2] Commons, *op. cit.*, I, 214.
[3] *Ibid.*, I, 109.
[4] *Ibid.*, I, 109.

turn-out; the immediate aim was to prevent a reduction of wages, to protest at an invasion of customary and therefore "right" standards. The workers would be notified that a reduction in wages would take place, and the immediate response would be an indignation meeting, usually culminating in a disorderly quitting of work and a refusal to come back save at the old wages. There was no reasoned theory as to why the men should receive what they had always been receiving; there was merely a feeling of outrage that time-honored customs were being violated by the new masters, with perhaps a connecting of the phenomena with the "monopolists" and the holders of United States Bank bonds, whom political agitation and election campaigns had taught them were a new aristocracy seeking to corrupt the purity of American democracy and introduce aristocratic elements into the country. There was not even much comprehension of the position of the master workman at the mercy of the rising merchant capitalists: and there was not, of course, the remotest notion that anything was wrong with the prevailing economic system. Since every journeyman still hoped to become a master, assuredly no organization of journeymen would advocate any measure tending to make the position they hoped eventually to obtain any less desirable; but nevertheless it was not "right," with all of the unreasoning obstinacy and clinging to traditions which the word implies, for the masters to interfere with established rates of wages.

This attitude on the part of the journeymen is further evidenced by the other method which, when unsuccessful by turning out to force the masters to continue their old wages, they employed in this early period. This alternative was coöperation; but it was not undertaken, as in the forties, with any idea of remodeling the social structure. It simply meant that journeymen who felt that to continue at their low wages was impossible and who had not the means to set up immediately for themselves as masters would band together to make up the necessary capital between them and thus enable each other to enter the group of masters. And when they had entered the latter group they announced that they would show the public how it was possible to earn profits and at the same time to preserve the old scale of wages; they would thus prove that the masters had been guilty of unfairness, and that the old system if carried on by just men was entirely just. Thus in 1791 the Philadelphia carpenters, after a strike, proposed to undertake building operations at 25% less than the current rate, as a rebuke to the master carpenters; and in 1806, when the outcome of the cordwainers' conspiracy trial made combinations to better their conditions illegal, the shoe-makers of Philadelphia announced that they themselves would open a shoe warehouse. "They have been compelled to resort to this undertaking as the only expedient left them to maintain themselves and families from the most abject dependence. They have had no other alternative but adopting this course or submitting to employers who could take away or lessen their wages whenever their caprice or avarice might prompt them. . . . The wages, which they claimed themselves, and for asking which they were punished, they intend to give to those who may be employed by them. They have therefore engaged the best workmen in the city, and will spare no means to give satisfaction to such as will favor them with their custom. Their work shall be made of the very best materials and sold at the most moderate prices." [1]

There was thus in all these early sporadic strikes and abortive attempts at organization no feeling that those who engaged in them were in any way modifying the dominant theory of society or the tenets of American democracy. They were concerned solely with hours and wages, with conditions so traditional as to have become of the nature of rights, and the journeymen had no idea that the public were in anywise implicated or needed to be considered in this private altercation between them and their treacherous masters. True, there were certain moneyed interests in the country who themselves were striving to destroy American ideals, and to fight these men they would at the polls vote the Jeffersonian ticket; it was these men and the creatures they had placed upon the bench who were responsible for the conspiracy trials and the obvious unfairness of the court in those episodes. It was only when the early strikers thus came into direct conflict with the courts that they felt the necessity of any theoretical defense of their position, which to them seemed so obviously a case of simple justice. Here the Jeffersonian party some to their rescue with its powerful organs, like the Philadelphia *Aurora*,[2] and made of their grievances part of the general outcry against the commercial Federalists. This support by the great political democracy both won the workers all the more closely to the Jeffersonian ideals and precluded any independent development of social or political policy.

These early efforts at maintaining their position in society collapsed with the close of the Napoleonic wars; English merchants dumped upon the American markets great quantities of goods they had been storing

[1] Commons, I, 129.
[2] *Ibid*, I, 142.

up, and well-nigh destroyed the American manufacturers whose business war conditions had fostered. Unemployment was the order of the day; crafts employing 9672 workmen in 1816 in Philadelphia three years later had discharged all but some 2000. In 1819, according to Niles' Register, there were some 20,000 unemployed in Philadelphia, 20,000 in New York, and almost 10,000 in Baltimore.[1] Those trades in which organization had survived, the printers and the cordwainers, were too busy endeavoring to find places for their menbers to bother about the conditions under which they worked or their social position. The printers had established benefit funds, and by this means managed to keep above water; the cordwainers, whose power had depended solely on strikes, were forced to disband.

But this depression had by 1820 reached its lowest point; from that time on there was a rapid improvement in conditions. But the merchant capitalists had taken the advantage of the breakdown of all opposition on the part of the laborers to extend their influence over the whole country; and in this they were aided by the great public improvements in transportation. The Erie canal was built in 1825, and was speedily followed by many others; steamboat transportation had extended to the vast network of rivers in the Mississippi Valley. All these extensions of the market opened the way for the merchant with a plentiful supply of credit and capital, while they at the same time led to a much keener competition than had hitherto obtained; for the merchant capitalist not only had to compete with the English markets and goods, but was exposed to the attacks of all those within the widened transportation area. In the absence of strong opposition, his labor cost was that item of his expenditures most easy to cut down. He turned eagerly to the employment of convicts and cheap labor, and he so dominated the market that he gradually came to force over to his side the small manufacturers, the master workmen, who were more and more clearly differentiated from the journeymen or laborers.

These prosperous times, moreover, naturally caused a rise in prices, and the workmen soon were once more forced to organize to protect their position; this time they demanded higher wages, but what they were in reality doing was to prevent inroads upon their real wages. Hence the early twenties display once more on a more extended scale the same characteristics of unorganized strikes giving place to more permanent organizations: this time other trades enter the lists, such as the weavers, painters, hatters, stone-cutters, nailers, in addition to the

[1] Commons, I, 135.

older printers, shoemakers, carpenters, and tailors. By 1825 this general prosperity and the consequent success of the labor movement had reached its height;[1] men, feeling that there was some prospect of hope for the alleviation of their conditions, began to think in terms larger than their individual grievances; those who stood at the top of the industrial scale, the skilled mechanics, came to have a feeling of social interest in advancing the interests of the less fortunate workers. The industrial class had largely grown, for this was the period in which our cities were making their most remarkable advances. Those laborers who had been somewhat successful in organizing were led to reflect upon the why and the wherefore of their existence, and thus there arose in the late twenties the first attempts at what could be called specifically workers' theories or conceptions of society and of their place in it.

It was the extension of the franchise in the twenties that gave the impetus to the new attitude. Men were just beginning to realize that the old Jeffersonian party had hardly kept true to its original ideals. Success in 1800 had proved disastrous to it, and had led, not directly to the Jeffersonian ideal of the agricultural community, but rather to the substitution of a planting for a commercial aristocracy. Moreover, the merchants had by this time had opportunity to leave the old Federalist party and win the new Republicans over to their own side. All things considered, the time was ripe for another recrudescence of the democratic urge, and another temporary setback to the forces of inequality. This, in fact, was the especial mission of Jacksonian democracy; and it was but natural that this new revolt on the part of the dominant small farmers should find peculiar and individual expression amongst the laboring classes of the seaboard cities. Fully alive at last to the economic inequalities that the new order had forced upon them, they were finally aroused, partly by the responsibilities of full citizenship, partly by the new feeling of solidarity with their fellows, to the failure of the old parties to bring about actual social equality. Hence in the years 1827–1831 we notice a sudden broadening of interest and scope, on the part of laboring men everywhere, the formation of central unions in the large cities, and the rapid passing over of these unions into politics. Everywhere there is the claim of the labor organization, no longer to be merely fighting for its own individual rights, but to stand for the true interests of America and the American democracy. Against the merchant capitalists and the new factory owners, the bankers and money interests of the cities, the new movement poses as the champion

[1] Commons, I, 157.

of the older ideal of complete equality, and it carries that ideal to further limits than had before been necessary. It feels that something must be wrong with American institutions if they can be so perverted from the ideals of the Declaration of Independence. And it eagerly sets to work to destroy the most obvious abuses which in its opinion can be remedied by legislation. Throughout this period of four years, we must not forget, the mechanics were busy in their separate trade groups maintaining their economic rights; consequently the motives and aims which appear in the federations and the political parties do not supplant, but merely supplement the old method of the turn-out. And when the object of the workers is achieved, when they have engrafted their demands upon the platforms of the regular parties, and the Jacksonians have arisen to combine the small minority of the cities with the immense group of the farmers and backwoodsmen, they return once more to the pursuit of their economic ends confident in the substantial achievement of the demands they have made, yet somehow having failed to secure that reversion to primitive equality they felt would of necessity follow.

The characteristic note of this second stage of the mechanics' labor movement is the demand it makes, not so much for economic equality and security—this had inspired the first stage, and this was to dominate the last—but for social and political equality. It was not a protest of the wage worker against the employer, but rather of the producer against the capitalist, of the poor against the rich; it was the last attempt to realize the ideal of Jefferson by a direct appeal to the principles of the Revolution, to destroy the power of that sinister force of capitalism which had been the bane of the Democrats from Washington's day down. When we next behold a labor movement, we find industry accepted and the doctrine of natural rights supplanted by other and more efficacious theoretical considerations.

The second and broadly social phase of the mechanics' movement arose almost simultaneously in New York and Philadelphia,—in the latter city during the summer of 1827. Springing out of an unsuccessful attempt of the carpenters to establish a ten-hour day with more regular employment, it created first a central union of trade societies, and then, as the demand of leisure, the first requisite of equal citizenship, called up its second, popular education, it passed into a workingman's party. The economic demand was the ten-hour day, the political, free schools. It is significant of the spirit of this Philadelphia movement that it was ushered in by a pamphlet on education, and that its most enduring monument has been the Mechanics' Library. "It is true," said the pamphlet, "in this favored nation we enjoy the inestimable blessing of 'universal suffrage,' and constituting as we everywhere do, a very great majority, we *have the power* to choose our own legislators, but . . . this blessing . . . can be of no further benefit to us than as we possess sufficient *knowledge* to make a proper use of it." [1] And later it was claimed that "real liberty and equality have no foundation but in universal and equal instruction." [2] "When the committee contemplate their own condition, and that of the great mass of their fellow-laborers; when they look around on the glaring inequality of society, they are constrained to believe that until the means of equal instruction shall be equally secured to all, liberty is but an unmeaning word, whose substance, to be realized, must first be planted by an equal education and a proper training in the minds, in the habits, in the manners, and in the feelings of the community." [3] And it can hardly be maintained that a movement in any sense failed that resulted directly in the establishment of our system of popular schools.

In June the carpenters turned out for the ten-hour day. "We believe," they announced, "that a man of common constitution is unable to perform more than ten hours' faithful labor in one day, and that men in the habit of laboring from sunrise until dark are generally subject to nervous and other complaints arising from continued hard labor, and (we) believe that all men have a just right, derived from their Creator, to have sufficient time in each day for the cultivation of their mind and for self-improvement; therefore, resolved, that we think ten hours industriously employed are sufficient for a day's labor." [4] The masters had been in the habit of having all their work done in the long summer days, and leaving the journeymen idle in winter; and the strike was in part caused by the desire to force the masters to employ them all the year round. Thus early the characteristic desire of the worker for continuity of employment makes its appearance. The carpenters received the support and sympathy of the house-painters, the bricklayers, and other trade societies, and it was soon determined to unite in one body for mutual aid and protection. Thus was born in the autumn of 1827 the first union of crafts— the Mechanics' Union of Trade Societies—as a protest against the degradation of the worker.

[1] *Mechanics' Free Press*, June 21, 1828.
[2] *Ibid.*, Jan. 21, 1829.
[3] *Working Man's Advocate*, March 6, 1830.
[4] *Democratic Press*, June 14, 1827.

The mechanics felt that in uniting with other trades they were transcending the limits of individual interest and were acting as trustees for the common welfare. "Believing that whatever is conducive to the real prosperity of the greatest numbers must in the nature of things conduce to the happiness of all, we cannot desire to injure, nor take the smallest unjust advantage, either of that class of the community called employers or of any other portion. . . . If as members of the community they (the capitalists) are desirous to prosper, in vain will they expect to succeed, unless the great body of the community is kept in a healthy, vigorous, and prosperous condition. . . . The real object, therefore, of this association is, . . . to promote, equally, the happiness, prosperity, and welfare of the whole community—to aid in conferring a due and full proportion of that invaluable promoter of happiness, leisure, upon all its useful members; and to assist, in conjunction with such other institutions of this nature as shall hereafter be formed throughout the union, in establishing a just balance of power, both mental, moral, political, and scientific, between all the various classes and individuals which constitute society at large." [1]   There hovered before the workingmen the spectre of European conditions, fondly believed to be forever banished by the Declaration of Independence, and they undertook the task of preserving the old America of liberty and equality. "We are fast approaching those extremes of wealth and extravagance on the one hand," they declared, "and ignorance, poverty, and wretchedness on the other, which will eventually terminate in those oppressive and unnatural distinctions which exist in the corrupt governments of the old world." [2]

And quite naturally, in view of the social and political aims of the movement, it turned to political action. The broadly social nature of its program, in fact, was the source both of its strength and its weakness; for it enabled the Jacksonian Democrats to take up its measures and incorporate them into their platform, and thus they soon passed into the common heritage of American institutions. The workmen thus gained their immediate demands, but only at the expense of their own organization and of their most vital economic interests. After electing a number of candidates who had also been endorsed by other parties in four-cornered fights in 1828 and 1829, the Working Men's Party disintegrated after its defeat in 1820. But the ends it sought were soon achieved; and the importance of the movement lies in the light it throws on the nature of the ideals of the mechanics. Rather than wonder at the generally

[1] *Mechanics' Free Press*, Oct. 25, 1828.
[2] *Ibid*, May 1, 1830.

interested actions of trade unions when performing their functions as business organizations, the observer should rather marvel at the apparently unquenchable zeal of the worker to act on occasion directly against his own immediate advantage in following now one, now another, scheme for reforming society at large.

The chief aim of the Working Men's Party, and the one upon which the campaign of 1829 and 1830 was based, was the establishment of free schools for all. But in addition they protested against the banking monopolies and the issuance of banknotes, the lottery system, compulsory service in the militia, and other blemishes upon the purity of American democracy. All these were measures which appealed to the poorer portions of the community, indeed, but they had little direct connection with trade union activities. These latter were steadily progressing; and when the political party collapsed, carrying with it the Mechanics' Union, the trade societies were left to pursue their economic policies and to unite again on another basis.

The political phase of the mechanics' movement in New York was marked by much dissension between the various radical leaders who placed themselves at its head and gave it the appearance, at any rate, of supporting "agrarianism" or the equal redistribution of land. It sprang, like the Philadelphia movement, out of a ten-hour agitation, this time against the lengthening of a day already won, and at bottom, despite surface differences, it was dominated by the same motives of protection, equality, and education for citizenship. On April 23, 1829, a meeting of mechanics, called to protest against encroachment on the ten-hour day, was induced by Thomas Skidmore, a machinist and an earnest follower of Tom Paine, and somewhat of a philosophical radical, to adopt resolutions questioning the right of private property. They are by no means representative of popular ideas in their conclusions, but in their mode of reasoning they show the easy connection between the national philosophy of the social contract and the Declaration of Independence and the "rights" of the workers. "Resolved, that all men hold their property by the consent of the great mass of the community, and by no other title; that a great portion of the latter hold no property at all; that in society they have given up what in a state of nature they would have equal right to with others; and that in lieu thereof, they have the right to an equal participation with others, through the means of their labor, of the enjoyments of a comfortable subsistence. Therefore, resolved, that if those in whose power it is to give employment withhold such employment, or will give it only in such a manner as to exact excessive toil, and at a price which does not give a just return, such persons contravene the first law of society, and subject themselves to the displeasure of a just community." [1]

Five days later a large meeting was held which appointed a Committee of Fifty to consult and adopted resolutions against the eleven-hour day, among them one as follows: "Resolved, that in the first formation of government, no man gives up to others his original right of soil, and becomes a weaver, a builder, or other mechanic or laborer, without receiving a guarantee that reasonable toil shall enable him to live as comfortable as others." [2] In reality, Skidmore only went a little further than the majority of democrats in developing the theory of agricultural equality, and in just the same direction. On Oct. 19 the Committee of Fifty submitted a report that advocated the abolition of debts and the division of all property. This report was hurriedly adopted, and served as the basis of a new party which had considerable success in the ensuing election. But on December 29, another large meeting dissolved the Committee of Fifty, which had become involved in political quarrels, and rejecting its report resolved that it had "no desire or intention of disturbing the rights of property in individuals or in the public." [3] The mechanics, in fact, so soon as they fully comprehended them showed violent antipathy to Skidmore's agrarian views, and they substituted for them demands for general education and the abolition of the lien and militia laws, much in the spirit of the Philadelphia movement. Skidmore's book, *The Rights of Man to Property*, had meanwhile appeared, and on second thought his communism appeared incompatible with the American ideals for which the mechanics above all stood. He himself accordingly withdrew from the party with some followers and started another of his own.

The attention of the Working Men's Party was now turned to education, and soon a new source of friction was there discovered. Robert Dale Owen, son of the famous English socialist, desired to establish "State Guardianship" schools, in which the children would be fed and clothed as well as educated at public expense; he believed social regeneration was possible only when the children were caught while still very young. "Public education," said the advocates of this plan, "will regenerate America in one generation. It will make but one class out of the many that now envy and despise each other. It will make American citizens what they once declared themselves, 'Free and Equal.'" [4] The

---

[1] New York *Morning Courier*, April 25, 1827.
[2] *Morning Courier*, April 30, 1829.
[3] *Working Man's Advocate*, Jan. 16, 1830.
[4] *Ibid.*, June 19, 1830.

party split again on this issue, and there thus being three factions in 1830 it of course lost. Thereafter the movement, as in Philadelphia, was absorbed into the regular political parties, and the workers, their social and legal reforms either accomplished or well on the way toward accomplishment, turned their attention once more to their purely economic grievances and their trade society activities. The nineteenth century faith in universal education, to solve every problem of political democracy, burned strong within them; this achieved, they waited confidently the restoration of the older colonial equality.

The Working Men's Parties in Philadelphia and in New York were only the outstanding examples in a movement that spread everywhere throughout the eastern and northern parts of the country. The aims were fundamentally the same: the establishment of free and popular education, and the removal of those political restrictions that bore heavily upon the lower portions of the community. The strike had little place; when employed it was to secure or maintain the ten-hour day. And the argument for universal popular education was nearly always the civic one: popular sovereignty demanded popular knowledge, together with the natural rights theory; an equal education would of necessity secure equal ability. It was the orthodox liberal theory of democracy; the workers merely insisted on removing it from the realms of theory and actually putting it into practice, and giving a trial to the panacea which the official philosophers were everywhere proposing.

In New England the movement took the interesting and peculiar form of a general labor association with political and social aims—a form destined to be revived fifty years later by the Knights of Labor. It was neither an industrial or a trade society; it was not even limited to wage-earners, but included all those who would naturally be opposed to "privilege and monopoly," farmers, mechanics, small tradesmen, and the new class of factory workers. Like the other movements it started in a ten-hour strike, which led to the calling of a convention and the formation of the New England Association of Farmers, Mechanics, and Other Workingmen, in 1832. Its chief aim was the establishment of universal education as the means of raising and restoring the social status of these lower sections of the community; the rising factories of New England are reflected in the great emphasis laid upon child labor and the education of factory children. "Children should not be allowed to labor in the factories," it was resolved, "from morning till night, without any time for healthy recreation and mental culture; as it not only endangers their own well-being and health, but ensures to the country the existence of a population, in the approaching generation, unfitted to enjoy the privileges and to exercise the duties of freemen and citizens." [1] The New England Association naturally turned to politics, waging campaigns in 1832, 1833, and 1834, and as naturally was absorbed by the Jacksonians. Its appeal was too general to gather much strength, and the factories were not yet organized sufficiently to make them good field for labor developments.

The second phase of the mechanics' movement lasted in general some two or three years; but even before it had entirely died out there was a sharp reaction away from the political and social point of view to strictly economic associations—to what later came to be known as "pure and simple trade unionism." The third and final stage saw the great increase in strength and number of the craft societies, and the successive federation of these strong units into city and finally into a national trades' union. The workers had at last discovered where their immediate advantage lay; they organized, not on some theory of education, but on sound business principles. They had sought to bring back the old colonial society of the farmer and the settler, and to transplant to the city the intelligent and self-respecting farmer of the Revolution. When they found that both merchants and farmers were too much interested in their own advancement to care anything about restoring this happy state of affairs, they fell back upon the methods they had never forgotten nor allowed to fall wholly into disuse, and set about improving their immediate condition with little thought for anything else. National politics, too, were just entering upon their most exciting period, and industrialization had not yet advanced sufficiently to make any workingmens' question a national issue.

The turn of the tide is shown in the changed character of the oldest trade societies. The New York Typographical Society, since its foundation in 1809 largely a benevolent society, was in 1831 supplanted by the New York Typographical Association, whose new purpose was "to elevate the character and advance the interests of the profession, by maintaining a just and uniform scale of prices for their labor." [2] The Philadelphia society, founded in 1802, was also superseded in 1833. Other societies, like the Pennsylvania Society of Journeymen Cabinet-Makers in 1829 and the New York Benevolent Society of Journeymen Tailors in 1833, revised their constitutions and took up strictly trade union activities. The merchant capitalist was, with the increased markets both for goods and for labor opened up by the transportation projects

[1] Carey's *Select Excerpta*, IV, 435.

[2] Stewart, *Documentary Hist. of the Early Organizations of Printers.*

of the twenties and thirties, constantly driven into keener and keener competition, and constantly seeking to reduce his labor expenses by applying to women, young apprentices, and convicts as a source of cheap work. Moreover, the years from 1834 to 1837 were marked by wild speculation, inflated currency, and a consequent rise in the prices of all commodities. Flour went up from five to twelve dollars a barrel from 1834 to 1837; pork, from thirteen to thirty dollars; rents were enormously increased. As a consequence of all these conditions, the workers' real wages, even when there were no general wages reductions, were continually being lowered. The standard of living was rapidly sinking; there was no longer time to trust to the beneficent effects of universal education or to the remote results of legislative action. Trade societies and turn-outs would alone be able to meet the crisis. From 1833 to 1836 the number of such societies in Philadelphia alone increased from 21 to 53, from 29 to 52 in New York, and in other cities in proportion.[1] In 1834, it is estimated there were some 26,000 organized workmen in the country; by 1836, almost 300,000.[2] Almost every skilled craft was represented.

It was natural that the various crafts in a single city should unite for mutual support and protection, and thus grew up the "trades' unions" so characteristic of the time. The first was formed in New York in August, 1833; Baltimore, Philadelphia, and Washington followed the same year. Boston formed one in 1834, and by 1836 there were at least thirteen trades' unions, as far west as Louisville. [3] These new unions fell over one another to repudiate all connection with the earlier working men's parties, and with the various suspicions of agrarianism, atheism, and men's polygamy which the leaders had drawn down upon them, particularly in New York. In Philadelphia the union declared in its constitution that "no party, political, or religious questions shall at any time be agitated in, or acted upon, by this union."[4] Time and again the various unions were forced to repudiate political meetings called in their name by ambitious politicians. They remained, however, save in Baltimore, steadfast in their resolution not to turn to "panaceas or crack-brained schemes," and to devote all their energies to questions of wages and hours.

The New York Trades' Union originated in the combined support

---

[1] *National Laborer*, Nov. 12, 1836; Commons, 351, 352, I.
[2] *Ibid.*, June 4, 1836.
[3] Commons, I, 360.
[4] *Doc. Hist.*, V, 347.

some fifteen trades gave to a strike of carpenters for higher wages in 1833. The printers took the initiative, and the first president, Ely Moore, belonged to that craft. The records of the meetings reveal little discussion save over the difficulties and turn-outs the various members were engaged in. The suppression of convict labor, in which the president took an especial interest, marks the only other issue brought up. It was not that the workers had lost all interest in the larger schemes of the preceding years, but rather that they had learned not to intrude them into union matters. Their restraint was crowned by distinguished success in raising wages until they became involved in a conspiracy case.

The Trades' Union of Pennsylvania was formed in the summer of 1833 of factory workers around Philadelphia, as a protest against a 20 per cent wage reduction. This is the first example of factory operatives organizing, and also the first direct attack upon the factory system and warning against English conditions; but it proved abortive, as did all attempts at organizing these early factory workers. It was succeeded by the Trades Union of the City and County of Philadelphia, on the New York model. At first made up exclusively of mechanics, it later took in factory hands and unskilled labor. It was exceedingly successful, having by 1836, under its able president, John Ferral, some 48 trade societies.[1] More than half of these had struck and won their demands in the last six months; and the union was chiefly concerned with the support of various authorized strikes.

These numerous strikes were from 1833 to 1835 largely directed at the ten-hour day, demanded on the familiar grounds of citizenship. This generally achieved, the workers turned to wage increases. The old basis of a natural right to social equality, the traditional ideology of the Declaration of Independence, still formed the basis of their justification. The spirit lying back of this movement nowhere finds better expression than in this statement of the Philadelphia cordwainers, in 1835:

"The Declaration of Independence 'holds these truths to be self-evident, that all men are created free and equal,' how can we be free when we have no control over the prices of the only commodity we have to dispose of—our labor?. . . True, we assemble on the Fourth of July and mingle our shouts of approbation as we hear the invaluable Declaration of Independence read,—we may join the multitude in paying fulsome adulation to some popular orator as he descants on the blessings we enjoy in the land of Liberty, and flatter ourselves for the

---

[1] *Pennsylvanian*, Feb. 4, 1836.

time, that what he says is true, that we do enjoy to the fullest extent the liberties the blood of our Revolutionary fathers bequeathed to us: but when we leave the festive board, and return to our humble homes; when the thrilling accents of eloquence have ceased to vibrate on the ear, and sober reason resumes her sway—then, fellow-mechanics, do we awaken to the sad reality of our condition—then is the flimsy veil which blinded us to our true interest, drawn aside, and we behold ourselves in our real characters, humble, dependent, and miserable—we behold ourselves, perhaps, the slaves of some haughty tyrant, who to augment his already overflowing coffers, is perhaps at that very moment, framing some pretext for reducing our scanty wages; and secretly rejoicing, that the dollar we have spent on our country's natal day, enables him the better to accomplish his object. Let us then set about making ourselves free indeed—before we boast of our freedom—let us take measures to enjoy, and secure the freedom after it is obtained." [1]

In less eloquent but no less indignant words, the Boston carpenters make the same complaint. "If our employers had used us like men and had not been so overbearing, we should not have spent so much time in having our grievances redressed. We were all born free and equal, and we do not ask to have our grievances redressed as a favor, but we demand it as a right." [2] Something is wrong with American society, but the workman is not quite sure what it is. The good old days were never like this.

From the organization of city trades' unions it was but a step to a national Trades' Union. The New York union accordingly called in March, 1834, for delegates from every union to assemble " to advance the moral and intellectual dignity of the laboring classes, sustain their pecuniary interests, succor the oppressed, and by all just means maintain the honor and the respectability of the merchanical profession." [3] When they gathered from six unions under Ely Moore, they declared their aim to be " to prevent a reduction of wages and secure a proper number of hours for labor." There ensued a vigorous debate on the question of political action, finally decided in the negative; and the union contented itself with advisory and educational powers. It discussed the factory system, the conditions of the Lowell women operatives, and other similar matters, and resolved to attempt the organization of the factory workers. During the four years of its existence it did valuable propaganda

[1] *Pennsylvanian*, April 4, 1835.
[2] *Independent Chronicle and Boston Patriot*, May 23, 1832.
[3] *The Man*, May 3, 1834.

work, but was not strong enough to extend its activities to anything further then discussion and agitation.

More important than the National Trades' Union were the craft unions which at this time were organized on a national basis,—the cordwainers, the printers, the comb makers, the carpenters and the hand loom weavers. Transportation had brought different cities into competition, and it was becoming necessary to act together. In 1836 the cordwainers called a convention " to endeavor to equalize the wages as nearly as possible—to create that concert of action necessary to insure a steady and sufficient price for our labor." [1] This union desplayed all the earmarks of the strictly business union. It declared for shorter hours in order to "make work," limited apprentices, asked for the organization of women to prevent ruinous competition, asked the prohibition of foreign imports, and provided for a strong protective fund. Its statement in regard to the ten-hour day is particularly interesting in the light it throws on the various citizenship arguments commonly advanced in behalf of shorter hours. "Whereas, a surplus of the products of labor is calculated in almost all cases to reduce the wages of labor; and whereas the evils of excessive competition among the journeymen bears particularly heavy on those of our own trade; and whereas a reduction in the hours of labor has been productive of beneficial results in the character and condition of other mechanics; with a view to enable the Journeymen Cordwainers of all branches to enjoy the advantages pecuniarily, intellectually, and physically resulting from a reduction in the number of the hours of labor—be it resolved, that it is seriously recommended to the journeymen comprising the various Societies represented on this Convention, to reduce the number of their working hours so as to conform as near as practicable to the rules adopted by outdoor mechanics, believing that by so doing they will be better enabled to obtain a proper compensation for their labor." [2] This theory of "making work" probably represented a good deal of the unexpressed reasons for the enthusiasm with which the ten-hour day movement was received.

Perhaps the statement of the aims of the National Typographical Society best sums up all the threads that entered into this final phase of the mechanics' movement. "Our Association, as societies, is not to oppress others but for self-defense. To secure a living compensation for our labor, and to sustain the generous, liberal employer who is willing

[1] *National Trades' Union*, Feb. 6, 1836.
[2] *Ibid.*

to allow such compensation. To defend ourselves from undermining and base-spirited journeymen, and thereby protect our friends among employers from those of their number who would take advantage of their liberality—who would underwork masters' prices, by dispensing a beggarly pittance to their journeymen. We have still another and higher motive—it is benevolence." [1]

In 1837 came the panic and the end of prosperous times. In the face of unemployment the trades unions crumbled away; a few of the stronger turned to coöperation, but for the most part unionism disappeared. It was not for twenty years that the workers were again able to organize a really strong movement; and then it was the factory workers of the industrial era and not the mechanics and skilled artisans of the thirties who led the way.

[1] *National Trades' Union*, October 17, 1835.

5. THE DOUBLE STRAIN IN THE AMERICAN LABOR MOVEMENT

SHARPLY defined as it was, the mechanics' movement offers an excellent opportunity for the analysis of the motives and tendencies of labor activities. Although it appeared and ran its course before America had advanced far on the road to industrialism, it nevertheless contained within itself all of the basic features that have since marked the American labor movement. The problems confronting the worker, however much social environment may necessitate varying technique in the attempt to solve them, remain, like the fundamental problems of existence in which they play so basic a part, throughout the years essentially the same; and the manifold complexity with which the state of the industrial arts and the organization of the social and economic and political superstructure compel the toiler to approach his problem serves only to set off in bold relief the essential simplicity of his ultimate aim. The merchant capitalist has given way to the huge corporation, the tool of the skilled artisan to the machine of the specialized factory hand; but the questions that arose a hundred years ago differ only in degree from those that rise today, and the leader of the thirties could take his place in a modern union debate and find the issues changed only in intensity.

The fundamental aim of labor, revealed as the motive back of the mechanics' movement and equally potent today, is the desire for a secure and equal position in society—a position of freedom from the fear of want and unemployment, and an enjoyment of the goods of life not markedly disproportionate to that of one's neighbor. In certain conditions,—slavery or serfdom, for instance,—the worker is willing to give up one of these aims for the sake of attaining the other; but both are in the long run essential, and both have played their part in the American labor movement. Equality of status is perhaps the more fundamental; it is, as we have seen, the essential component of the American ideal of democracy, and it hearkens back to the day of the settler and the frontiersman. It motivated the outcry against the monopolist and banker of a century ago, and it lies at the bottom of the present indignation against the profiteer and the "capitalist." It is significant that in the early days the unionists were called by their enemies "levelers"; though since what they wanted was so obviously a leveling up they could never understand the accusations of wishing to level down. By the common man this equality has never been considered, unless under the influence of some Tom Paine, as a metaphysical and mathematically equal state of affairs; even the agrarians who wished to divide up the land did not feel the force of the argument that new inequality would speedily ensue. For the common man has always recognized differences in ability, and concurred in their reward; some have a knack of getting along, others are naturally shiftless, and the good workman has always despised his lazy brother. Of course some will be better off than others; but that some should be better off because they are privileged to use their power in spoiling the chances of honest workers, that, labor has never admitted, and it is just that fact which lies at the bottom of American democracy.

But if equality is the basic aim, security always accompanies it and often becomes of far greater pressing immediacy. The greatest fear that haunts the modern worker is the fear of losing his job. There is a custom in the coal-fields of Pennsylvania that aptly symbolizes the advance modern progress has made over medieval superstition. Every evening at sunset as the workers emerge from their underground burrows a bell is rung; and just as of old the peasant was wont to look forward to the vesper bell of his parish church, to cross himself as he heard its tones and to pray for the safety of his soul, so the present-day worker anxiously awaits this modern angelus. When its first stroke rings out a breathless hush falls on all the grimy mining town, and men and women everywhere pause to count its peals. For by their number they are told whether or no there will be work for the morrow, whether or no there will be another day's pay in the weekly envelope. Thus has the fear that men used to have lest they lose their souls been by modern progress transmuted into the fear lest they lose their work; for in our modern up-to-date methods of mining there is little bothering about men's souls.

It is this haunting fear of unemployment and destitution, the poignancy no description can bring home, that has led to most of the actions of labor condemned off-hand by the superficial observer. The worker has ever been prone to seize upon any course of action that promised to "make work," however loath at times he may be to admit it; and hence follows, as the very natural result of the desire to escape starvation, the opposition to machinery, the shortening of hours, the curtailment of production, and the various other sins that cause the editor of the metropolitan daily, secure in the possession of a generous and assured salary, to hold up his hands in editorial horror. Thus in what is probably the most advanced of all unions today, the Amalgamated Clothing Workers, the proposal to secure the 44-hour week was carried by the plea of a delegate that the many refugees of Europe would soon be with their friends seeking work. A dreadful act, no doubt; yet unfortunately men do not come into the world in accordance with the law of supply and demand, and some of them obstinately prefer to increase the cost of clothing rather than to starve to death.

An equal and secure position in society—this was the aim of the mechanics of a hundred years ago. To obtain it they employed two distinct methods. They organized trade societies, they turned out, and they demanded higher wages and shorter hours for themselves. But they also pursued another course; haltingly, perhaps, and with no such measure of success, but nevertheless they pursued it. They endeavored, by forming a general class organization, and by using their newly acquired political power, to secure their aim, not primarily as an individual right, but rather as a social condition. They sought to restore the America of their Fathers. What mattered it that that America had, strictly speaking, never existed? In their characteristic Anglo-Saxon fashion they were trying to reform society through idealizing the past. They demanded education for fulfilling the duties of citizenship. They demanded leisure to pursue that education. In exercising the rights of citizens they thought as citizens about the society in which they found themselves.

Corresponding to these two methods of securing the aim of labor, and determining their employment, are two distinct motives. The first is self-interest, individual economic advantage; the second, in that it is relatively objective and apart from immediate gain, can best be described as social idealism, as a desire for a better organization of society in all its parts. Neither, of course, existed exclusively, in either the political or the economic stages of the movement; there was probably no single individual in whom the two motives were not hopelessly mixed. Yet nevertheless it is apparent that in strictly trade society activities the motive of economic interest predominated, while in the political campaigns for education social idealism played a very conspicuous rôle.

These two motives will be found to run jointly throughout the labor movement. Both are prominent at the present day, and both will undoubtedly continue as the springs of social action. They stand as the two limits between which the labor movement vibrates. The character of any particular organization depends primarily upon the relative emphasis placed upon each. Both are always present: no labor movement is ever disinterested, though its leaders often are, and even the most self-centered has always a justifying philosophy that its actions result in the general welfare of society. There is, indeed, far from being any necessary antagonism between the two motives, the closest possible relation; and the problem of social organization is just that of securing a harmonious blend of social and individual interests. And it must not be forgotten that the fundamental postulate of nineteenth century economic theory and the society erected upon it has been that social welfare is best secured through every individual's seeking his own interest. Men have but lately come to question this theory, and to realize that it implies as actual a state of affairs that in reality is but a hope and a goal for the future; that it is far too optimistic to fit the present state of mankind. This theory holds still well-nigh absolute sway in the world of industry: it is, in fact, only to labor activities that it ever occurs to men to apply any other standard than that of prosperity and business success.

It is, then, all things considered, quite remarkable the extent to which the labor movement has at times pursued a course which when the two were at variance followed social rather than individual interests, and has persisted in seeking the larger aim when the lesser would clearly have redounded more to its advantage. It indicates that the analysis that economic liberalism made of the springs of human action was far from exhaustive, and suggests the point of view toward which social psychology is painfully struggling. For nothing is more clear to the observer of the development of the American labor movement than the struggle, the persistence, the successive emergence of now, one, now the other, as the dominating motive of the workers' efforts. The rivalry appears in the mechanics' movement; it will be apparent throughout its successors.

These two motives, individual interest and social interest, produced two distinct types of general aim. The former is conservative: it accepts things as they are, it is "realistic," it is "practical," it despises "theories". It takes the social situation in which it finds itself for granted, and bends its efforts toward making the most of what it has to start with. In the measure in which it succeeds it rejects change; for it too has become a vested interest. It acquires the attitudes and the reactions of the common business man. It is playing the game as it finds it, and playing it well; far too well, indeed, for many of the other participants. And, just like the business man, in its indifference to any larger considerations than its own individual advantage it often happens that its activities become definitely anti-social. When circumstances give it the power to hold up the community to fill its own pocket, it is apt to use that power; just as the broker on the corn-exchange or the monopolizer of some necessity like sugar might raise his price and cause a nation to starve. The motive of individual interest is indeed found at its purest in the criminal, who is at once the most conservative and the most anti-social force in society.

The other motive tends to produce a quite different type of aim. It is necessarily more revolutionary; it does not accept conditions as they are. It questions the social situation in which it finds itself; it imagines others in which those things it dislikes have no place. It seeks to change conditions rather than to make the best of them. It does not adapt itself to its environment, it tries to make that environment conform to what it considers right. At times it elaborates imposing edifices of theory and hypothesis to guide it and to justify its cravings for change. It does not play the game. It refuses, so it seems, even to "play fair," because it questions the justice of the rules. And it often happens that to those who have become skillful players under the old rules the new seem abhorrent; for at the first they certainly are confusing. It is thus definitely subversive of the old order, but it is never what the other type of aim readily becomes, anti-social. Ignorant, "impractical," yes, dangerous, oftentimes, yet inspired with a noble aim and of priceless worth withal, it seeks to bring about conditions that shall make anti-social action impossible.

Both of these motives may naturally employ either political or economic means to achieve their respective ends. In politics individual interest seeks no fundamental changes, but rather works for "reforms; desiring only to achieve certain definite legislative measures, it does not bother to form and manipulate a political party. That would necessarily involve it in considerations of social policy for which it has no stomach. Instead it endeavors to utilize for its purposes existing parties. It tries to hold the balance of power between the two, and by threats of "rewarding its friends" and "punishing its enemies" to secure the recognition that politicians accord to well-organized blocks of voters. It employs large and powerful lobbies at the seats of legislative dispensation. It favors log-rolling and all of those highly intricate and ingenious methods whereby modern law-makers transform bills into laws. Its political method is opportunistic, to adopt the most efficient means of getting its measures through.

In the economic field it strikes for higher wages, for shorter hours (primarily to make work) and for better conditions. It prefers, however, the peaceful path of collective bargaining, of wage-scales and agreements with employers; its strikes are strategic incidents in its campaign for more and more bargaining power. In accordance with its desire to observe the rules of the business game it makes contracts and religiously abides by them. It deprecates sympathetic strikes; as in the case of the United Garment Workers and the Amalgamated Clothing Workers, if it is to its own advantage it is willing to scab on another union. It jealously preserves its craft lines, and engages in jurisdictional disputes with other crafts for members. Its representatives are fittingly called business agents—they tend to be of the politician type, they are kept in power so long as they are successful, and they occupy the place of go-betweens between their constitutents and their employers. They could hardly be called leaders, for they are rather professional men retained to look after the union's interests. Yet they are often inspired by an intense devotion to their clients, and their vision is on the whole more broadly social than that of the average unionist.

Social idealism as a motive tends to emphasize the political method. Thinking in terms of social reconstruction, it naturally turns to the political means whereby alone such reforms can be peaceably effected. It favors a labor party and independent action; it disdains opportunistic tactics and piece-meal reforms, and seeks rather the power to reconstitute society. Incidentally it creates as many parties and as many planks as there are differing visions of a better community. Often intransigeant, it is apt to succumb to trained and unscrupulous politicians.

In the economic field its strikes always have a further import than their immediate objects. They are often used as political weapons; even when their chance of success is slight they are favored as creating solidarity among the workers. They are employed not so much to increase effective bargaining power as to serve as incidents in a larger campaign for social ends. Social interest is apt to lead to strikes in sympathy with other trades; it rather overlooks the nice points of the customs of contracts. It seeks inclusiveness rather than exclusiveness. Its leaders are apt to be real leaders, followed perhaps with a blind devotion when they are wrong as when they are right.

Robert F. Hoxie has made a most suggestive attempt to classify the labor organizations that appear in American history on the basis of their aims and methods; he has discovered four general functional types, two of which have subdivisions. He recognizes first, business unionism, the type we have seen approached in the later development of the mechanics' movement; second, friendly or uplift unionism, emphasizing mutual benefits; third, revolutionary unionism, which may be either socialistic or syndicalistic according as it emphasizes the political or the economic method; and fourth, predatory unionism, which may be either guerilla or hold-up, sincere or corrupt, in its activity. Hoxie inclines to consider these types as ultimate, the product of certain distinctive situations; and undoubtedly their historical genesis is so to be explained. But it is apparent that these four types can be regarded as resultants of the varying combinations of the two fundamental motives or strains, individual and social interests. According as the one or the other becomes dominant or as the relative emphasis which certain conditions cause to be placed on now one and now the other shifts, the organization will tend to conform more or less closely to one of Hoxie's four types. By going back of the four functional forms to the more ultimate motives inspiring them it is possible not only to arrive at a bond of union, but also to explain how a single organization, in the course of its history and as the result of varying conditions and leaders, may pass rapidly from one type to another, and even run the entire gamut from extremely conservative business unionism to extreme revolutionary unionism. It shows how it is possible at a single bound for the Railroad Brotherhoods, for instance, to throw the Plumb Plan enthusiastically into the midst of an amazed world. For it is the very essence of the double strain that both strains are always present, that it is fundamentally double—that the passage from one to the other involves only a very slight alteration of emphasis—the shifting of a few votes in convention, the election of a new leader, the necessity of meeting a specific situation.

Thus Hoxie's four types might well be arranged in a square as follows:

```
        Business Unionism_____ Uplift Unionism
Indi-              |                           |          So-
vid-               |                           |          cial
ual In-  Predatory Unionism         Revolutionary Unionism  In-
terest   Hold-up _____Guerilla_____ Syndicalistic _____Socialistic  terest
```

The scale from left to right would indicate the amount of emphasis given the social motive, that from top to bottom the relative conservatism. The diagram is not, of course, accurate, but it reveals some interesting relationships. It will be seen that the business and the predatory union possess in common the emphasis on the individual interest and the disregard of social consequences; and this makes the passage from one to the other easy. Likewise the predatory and the revolutionary union are bound together by their similarity of methods, which makes it clear how an organization like the I. W. W. really can exemplify in its personnel and tactics both types. It is well, however, to insist with Hoxie that these are but ideal types, never found in their purity in any union and but rarely in any individual.

But not only does a study of the American labor movement reveal the presence of this double strain—it also seems to show a somewhat recurrent cycle of emphasis, a career of progress from a period when one is in the ascendant to the other and then back again. Like all attempts to trace any regularity in the immensely pluralistic fabric of human affairs as they are spread out through time, this cycle at once fails when too closely pressed; if there be indeed any laws which obtain in history, they are far too complex for statement in any simple formula. Yet the attempt to draw the parallel between different periods of labor history is as illuminating in the differences it reveals as in the similarities. It is clarifying to observe the way in which history, superficially at least, appears at times to repeat itself.

It has already been noted that the mechanics' movement was an isolated event that had a definite career of three stages. It is possible to observe these three stages in the far more important movement that began with the Civil War and reached its maturity in the nineties; and it is even possible to observe the beginnings of a third cycle with the unskilled. This cyclical movement starts as a crude protest against intolerable conditions; at its outset it has little ultimate aim beyond the immediate one of making life a little more bearable, and even less of theory and philosophy. But it rapidly becomes critical of its aims and methods; the original motive of self-interest persists and grows stronger, but there springs up in addition the desire to reach more fundamental causes, to alter underlying conditions. The scope broadens rapidly and becomes more and more social; the unionists develop a theory of society, they appeal to their fellow-citizens to join them in a movement of mutual advantage. Thinking in terms of society as a whole, they are apt to adopt political means to alter the structure of the state. They call on the majority to unite with them to vindicate American democracy. But the majority repels their advances; it is not willing to risk its own varied

interests in attempting any social reconstruction. Rebuffed and defeated the workers accept the philosophy of the majority and seek once
more the most effective means of maintaining their own status. They
take their place in the business life of the nation to engage in the competitive struggle that has thus far marked the industrial age.

Thus the mechanics' movement started as a protest and a revolt against
the violation of the status of the artisan in the early American democracy.
At the outset it emphasized individual rights, seeking to arouse the workers to an assertion of their power against individual men whom it imag-
ined had willfully taken from them what was their rightful due. Spontaneous turn-outs directed against specific reductions in wages or excessive
hours marked this stage.

Then the movement became more reflective and critical. It passed
over into a protest, not against the individual primarily, but against those
features of the social system which permitted his acts. Where before it
had emphasized *rights* it now turned to *justice*—justice being, in one
aspect, "rights" viewed from the standpoint of the community as a
whole. It became political in its methods and broadly social in its aims,
attacking monopolies, debt-laws, currency systems, and privilege in
general. Education and its prerequisite leisure, for the sake of citizenship
and the general welfare, tended to supplant higher wages as the primary
demand; and even the economic desire for an improved social status was
advocated for its effect upon the nation at large. The workers at least
thought in terms of social values—political duties, citizens' responsibilities, intellectual development.

Its immediate aims largely achieved, it was left without a distinctive
program, and it as yet represented too small a portion of the community
to appeal successfully for a more thoroughgoing revision of the social
structure. The special interests it was combatting were strong and
unscrupulous. The agricultural population, still wedded to the frontiersman's love of independence and hatred of social interference, were
definitely unsympathetic. Nowhere meeting any response to its appeal
for the purging of democracy of the corruption that had crept into it, it is
little wonder that it turned to less exalted but more practical policies.
America of the thirties and forties was indeed full of "reformers"; it was
the golden age of utopian schemes for the complete regeneration of
society. But the estimable gentlemen who flocked to the numerous
communities and phalanges that dotted the western prairies, who responded to the visions of Fourier eloquently put forward by Albert
Brisbane, had no desire to engage upon the laborious modification of

existing institutions. They wished to journey into the primeval forest and build from the very bottom up an entirely new society; for them civilization was already hopelessly corrupt. And it is entirely possible that the pilgrims of Brook Farm preferred not to jeopardize their secure incomes while they were experimenting with new forms of social existence. So long as there was an untold wealth of land lying idle to the west the best minds were loath to put forward the sustained intelligence necessary for a real grappling with social problems. Not until the western lands were all gone was the situation acute enough to call for really drastic measures.

But be the cause what it may, there came in the thirties a rapid reaction to strict business unionism. The social idealism that had secured universal education did not at once evaporate; the workers sought a social justification for their efforts at collective bargaining, and secured a recognized place in society. But they soon adopted the prevailing ideology of competition, and were absorbed into the general business life of the nation as units. The fundamental aim of the movement—the achievement of a definite and secure status in society—was, they thought, in some measure obtained. Their position was indeed far from equal, and security was rather precarious, as 1837 proved, but in the steady growth of their bargaining power there opened before them a vista of further advance. The labor movement had reached a condition of relative stability which only some radical change in social conditions could upset. That change did not come until the twentieth century, and then only with the slow growth of industrialism.

When the labor movement sprang into being once more in the late fifties the same cycle was repeated with slight variations. At first there grew up organizations of individual protest and revolt whose aim was self-protection, organizations which improved transportation made national and which previous experience rendered in a measure less spontaneous and unguided. Then the purely individual motive was once more supplemented by social idealism, the workers made another appeal to the community to engage in serious social control. Once more attempts were made at a humanitarian and class-conscious organization opposed to the "interests" and in behalf of the "common people." Economic advantage was supplemented by social aims. First the National Labor Union, then the Knights of Labor, arose and drifted into political activity; and at the outset they too were relatively successful. But the same influences that had swamped the working men's parties fifty years previously destroyed them: the hostility of the employers and the apathy of the public. Once again immediate interest conquered; strict business unionism again proved its advantages from the economic standpoint, and the American Federation of Labor waxed while the Knights of Labor waned. They had their philosophy of social justification at first, the theory of Ira Steward, which by dint of much educational work in the early nineties had become ingrained in the older unions; but that philosophy has been forgotten now, and survives only among the older members and in the underlying presuppositions upon which the leaders act. Once again the labor movement had reached a state of relative stability.

But by this time industrialism had progressed sufficiently to change the situation. As will be seen later, under modern conditions there has grown up a great number of unskilled workers who have little with which to bargain except their manual labor. Their monopoly of skilled craftsmanship has been stolen by the machine. Among them there arose the familiar revolts and protests, revolts which have been in some instances incorporated by organizations such as the I. W. W. Amongst western lumbermen and miners, and the textile workers of the east, these revolts have partaken of the same lack of aim, the same spontaneous character as those occurring at the beginning of each of the two former cycles. And these unskilled have likewise developed social aims and theories that have found fruit in a new kind of unionism, perhaps best represented by the industrialism of the clothing workers. Because of the persistence of the craftsman's business union, the development is not clear; for it has taken place as much within the older organizations as without them. What will be the further course, it is impossible to say; it is with a consideration of probable and possible developments that this book attempts to deal. It is entirely within the bounds of possibility that the hostility of public and employer will cause the cycle to pursue its wonted course, and that the so-called "new unionism" of the unskilled will merge into a new form of business unionism in which the motive of individual advantage has overcome that of social idealism—into something between the business and the predatory union. But many considerations which will be developed later make it at least doubtful whether the conditions that favored this type before have not radically changed, and whether it will not be likely that this time the appeal to men to alter their social structure will meet with a more favorable response. It is at least significant that this newer, more socially-minded movement is at present appearing rapidly in the very heart of the older business unionism. This important question, however, must be postponed for later consideration.

There is thus evident this alternation between emphasis upon the individual and upon the larger social interest permeating the history of American labor. But lest it appear that the two strains are opposed, that one must overcome or supersede the other; lest it seem necessary to choose between the two, let us approach the matter from another angle. Hitherto we have contrasted the two, and remarked upon their successive rise and fall. Now let us examine the history of labor with a view to the remarkable simultaneous persistence and permanence of both. For every action of labor, every decisive step it has advocated, has been supported by both these motives together. There has been to an extraordinary degree a blending and interaction between these two strains. Measures advocated by far-seeing leaders because of their beneficial social consequences have secured support from the rank and file because of the immediate interests to which they also appealed. And as those measures were put into force, those same workers have come to see the social side of their activities and to advocate further measures in which the immediate individual gain is not so apparent. The labor movement has thus proved of immense educative value to the workers in developing social-mindedness, as will be seen later.

Let us examine some of the leading features of unionism. Consider first the outstanding fact of the coöperation of the workers to secure a common end, the actual bond of union between them. The great right of free contract is undoubtedly in certain situations a privilege to be battled for and loyally guarded; it is indeed, as we have so often been told, a great moral principle. Nevertheless trade unionists are cold to it; they build their societies on the basic principle of each one giving up his individual freedom of contract and submitting rather to collective agreement. What leads men thus to give up their liberty of action?

At first and at bottom, of course, it is because in so doing they gain a larger freedom. Economic conditions have placed the individual worker at the mercy of the employer in bargaining power; since a free contract necessarily implies an agreement between equals, it is essential for the worker to combine with his fellows to place his collective bargaining power upon a basis of approximate equality with that of the employer. This is the very essence of labor unionism; it is the cornerstone upon which the whole structure of trade union activities is builded. The worker eventually gains more through surrendering an individual privilege; hence for reasons of his private advantage he unites with his fellows.

But that association into which he enters itself imposes upon him a very definite social viewpoint and attitude. Suppose he has joined solely in order to gain the benefit of the higher wages in a certain union shop. In working with his fellow-unionists, in meeting and in shop, he perhaps unconsciously comes to absorb their point of view. He grows loyal to his fellows, and to the association which means so much to them. He comes to feel their abhorrence for the scab, the man who puts his individual advantage first, the upholder of the great principle of the freedom of contract. Perhaps he is tested in the fire of a strike; he feels the spirit of determination to win for his union. He uses his savings to aid the families of his less fortunate fellows. And when the test comes, he will refuse to accept a job at high wages if to do so he must forsake his union; he will engage in a sympathetic strike which to him can mean only loss of money, he will even make large contributions to fellow-strikers elsewhere upon which he knows he can get no possible return. Anyone who knows aught of trade unions knows of the remarkable spirit of loyalty to the group and of personal responsibility for its success or failure that permeates every member and makes immediate personal advantage a secondary consideration. It is the spirit of the crusader; in our modern civilization it replaces that disinterested devotion that has characterized religious bodies in the past. It is in many respects even more remarkable; for the martyr went to his death in the full confidence that he was about to be received into the communion of the saints.

In this cardinal instance it is clear that both strains, both the motive of individual advantage and that of social idealism, are inextricably united in the labor movement, that policies begun instinctively in self-preservation have broadened into means for the attainment of a social purpose. It is no less apparent in other phases of labor activity. Closely allied to the coöperation that unionism develops is the equalization of the general standard of living toward which it tends. In the business life of the community the theory upon which men operate is that of "plenty of room at the top." Every man seeks to raise himself above his fellows in the economic scale in the simple confidence that there is a position of eminence awaiting him. So there is—just as the presidency awaits every boy. Unfortunately there can be only a small number of presidents in each generation. This truth has impressed itself upon the workers, and their aim is thus to raise all, the great mass of the community, to a higher status, rather than take their chances on individual preëminence. Hence the creation of maximum standards, the dislike of the piece-system and its consequent pace-setter, the discouragement of too great "individual initiative" when it results in forcing down the standards of the less skilled. In countless ways labor has gradually learned that in the long run it is to the advantage of all its members taken as a whole to reduce the difference between the best paid and the worst paid worker. The "aristocrats of labor," the skilled crafts-men, have as machinery replaced handiwork seen their skill grow less and less valuable; they have beheld the constant approach of the lower grades of labor to their own standard as organization of the less skilled has proceeded. In a time of rising prices it is the lowest paid who, if strongly organized, gain the greatest increase in wages. Each broaden-ing of the craft basis has brought a greater proportional advantage to the lower grades.

This tendency toward equalization has been directly inspired by the individual advantage it brings to the unionists, once they have given up the notion of "plenty of room at the top." Its wisdom is apparent in the greatly increased bargaining power of the union. Yet here too what began for personal advantage has been expanded into a very real ideal for the working class. The same group loyalty that grows up within the craft union has overleaped its bounds and tends to include ever larger units. The workers are the best friends of the lowest paid laborers; they are the bitterest opponents of sweating, they lead the way in or-ganizing other trades. Where others are content to commiserate, they are prepared to go on a sympathetic strike, to contribute money, to help in that best of ways, through organizing activity. When the Amalgamated Clothing Workers contributed to the fund of the steel strike in the fall of 1919 one hundred thousand dollars, they merely symbolized in a spectacular fashion the solidarity which is binding all classes of labor together in a social ideal of approximate equality—that ideal which the mechanics of the thirties saw as the older Jeffersonian democracy.

Or take the allied question of the inclusion of various groups within a given labor organization, women, foreigners, negroes, et cetera. The impulse has been at first to exclude them; keep them if possible from engaging in the trade, that the group already organized may not meet their competition. Women have been told to retire to their proper sphere of activity, the home; negroes have been kept in the commonest class of labor. But it soon becomes apparent that it is to the true in-terests of the union, not to exclude, but to include them, not to attempt to drive them from the industry, but to eliminate their competition through securing for them the same wages, and admitting them on a basis of equality. From the enemies of these oppressed groups the unions have become their strongest supporters—at first largely to secure their own gain. But here once more the motive of individual advantage is speedily supplemented by that of social interest, and the same men who first voted to admit women to their union to secure their own wages are the very ones who later insist on organizing and helping them for their own sakes. Such a policy, originating in a desire to increase bargaining power, soon grows into a social ideal advocated and fought for on its own account.

Voluntary arbitration is another policy that has secured the support of both motives of the double strain. It is usually the weaker side to an industrial dispute that proposes arbitration by an impartial third party; that side which trusts to its own strength complains of unwarranted interference in its affairs. Labor seizes upon arbitration when it is weak; yet it also has come to embody an impartial settlement of disputes in its ideal as a social measure. It is the same with that other instrument of orderly progress, the collective agreement. Self-interest advises the keeping of contracts; without a guarantee of fulfillment collective bargaining becomes obviously impossible. Yet all but the most revolutionary unions jealousy regard their reputation for honesty in abiding by their contracts. If they feel that the employer is attempting to worm out of his agreement, they have no compunction in breaking theirs; it is the spirit and not the letter that claims their allegiance. But if they feel that they are being treated fairly they will play square even to their own loss. Contrary to the popular and carefully educated public opinion, in the vast majority of cases it is the employer and not the union at all which first violates a collective contract.

Or consider the question of industrial rather than craft unionism—of organizing all the workers in an entire industry into one large union rather than breaking them up into numerous small craft groups on the basis of the particular tool they use. With the growth of the subdivision of labor in the machine process and the consequent reduction of the task of every hand to a relatively simple performance, so that strike-breaking is very easy, and with the growth of large combinations of capital controlling entire industries, there is a great bargaining advantage in being able to mobilize every plant as a unit. From the standpoint of bargaining-power industrial unionism is the most effective type of organization. It has developed as a fighting weapon, as it alone can control a great mass of relatively unskilled workers. But even more clear in this case than in the others is the emergence of the social motive: industrial unionism is the best type of union for fighting, but it is at the same time the only type suitable for purposes of production and participation in the control and management of the industry. Only when organized as an industry can the workers learn to think of their union activities as a part of that industry, and to regard themselves as in any sense responsible for furnishing society with the product. It is significant that amongst far-seeing workers it is this consideration even more than that of increased bargaining power that is leading to the rapid spread of industrial unionism.

These instances are sufficient to indicate the interplay between the two motives; they make plain how actions originating spontaneously for private advantage come to possess social significance and are consciously advocated in its behalf. To nearly every policy of the unions both motives have applied. Some men, indeed, have been and will remain actuated almost wholly by the first alone; others place great emphasis on the second. The relative intensity of the two at different times of American history has depended to a large extent upon social conditions. When the workers have met the active hostility of the employers aided and abetted by the apathy and indifference of the general public, if not its actual enmity, they have naturally tended to fight for their status and to disregard, unless impelled by some magnetic leader, the larger social consequences of their acts. When public interest has proved more favorable, when strength of organization or weakness of capital has left them a brief respite in their fight for existence, they have uniformly developed an interest in the better functioning of society and a regard for far-reaching plans of social modification and control that lends much color to the contention that the labor movement needs but half a chance to become the most forward-looking element of the community, and to surprise even omniscient editors with the breadth of its sympathies.

The significance of this interpretation for our main problem is obvious. It means, in short, that to secure that general feeling of social responsibility, that habit of response, not to pecuniary gain at the expense, tacit or conscious, of the rest of the community, but to the requirements of society; to develop an attitude that will make functional service to the community the primary motive in economic life, it is not necessary to attempt the impossible task of creating in the workers' minds something which at present has no existence. Were that the case, were man in no sense a social animal, the future would indeed be as gloomy as we have painted it. The task that actually remains is surely hard enough. It is to foster what has always been, to a greater or less extent, present in the life of labor groups; it is to endeavor to create conditions favorable to the emergence of the second or socially-visioned strain that has always beein in evidence in the labor movement, to the end that it may take its proper place beside the first in our economic life. It is only when the two are entirely merged into one, when there is no longer any question of choice between private advantage and public weal, that man can be said to have reached the ideal set for him by the theorists of nineteenth-century economics. That state is hardly even within sight at present; yet the persistence of the social motive throughout the history of American labor, and especially its vigor at the present moment, give adequate ground for at least setting forth on the difficult road of social readjustment.

6. THE EFFECTS OF THE INDUSTRIAL REVOLUTION

THROUGHOUT the mechanics' movement there was evident beneath the surface, rising now and again to a brief moment of prominence and then sinking back once more to its wonted quiet, the swell of a new factor in industry. It appears in the speeches of delegates to conventions as something ominous in the distance, something which their methods failed to touch; and one has the feeling, as one listens to impassioned demands for the restoration of the good old times of the Declaration of Independence, that the more thoughtful workers pause now and again to glance over their shoulders into the misty future, only to hasten to their work lest it be accomplished too late—lest this strange new peril arrives before the mechanics have strengthened the bulwarks of democracy. For it seemed as though Jefferson's prescience were in danger of verification; in the outlying towns of New England, in the districts about Philadelphia, there was appearing the advance guard of an enemy far stronger and far more deadly than any the workers or their cherished agricultural democracy had yet encountered, an enemy whose ravages in England caused the American laborer to shudder and pray that by the grace of God he be spared its visitations—the factory system.

No organization existed among the early factory workers; what labor difficulties arose were in the nature of sponteanous turn-outs against some reduction in wages or other interference with wonted custom. Labor was too abundant and skill too little required to give the few employers who were operating mills much trouble. Moreover, the industrial revolution made no very real headway in American life until the fifties, and large scale production did not become general until the Civil War and the industrial era succeeding it. Our internal struggle, which settled the political questions that for so long had been occupying the attention of the nation, marked the real turning point in our economic development; thereafter business enterprise and manufacturing initiative became the order of the day. Jefferson's vision of a nation of contented farmers immune from the cities and mill towns of Europe had definitely and irrevocably vanished. Industry had come to stay; if democracy in the older sense were also to remain, it must find some means of reconciling itself with the machine.

The romantic tale of the industrial revolution has been often recounted; the grim facts lying behind man's triumphant march of conquest over the secrets and the treasure-houses of Nature are also known to those who care for such unpleasant details. With them we are not concerned. Our task is rather to examine the changes that were effected in the social situation in which the workers found themselves, changes that made their earlier theories and methods largely irrelevant. We have seen how the mechanics' movement was fought through on a social philosophy that had originated in the mid-eighteenth century; we have seen how it reached before its demise a form that promised to remain stable until some profound change produced an entire realignment of the forces of society. That change came in the industrial revolution; and it is with that realignment that we must now deal.

The fundamental effect of the industrial revolution was to take the great mass of the people, comparatively undifferentiated and homogeneous, predominantly agricultural, which in the eighteenth century comprised the overwhelming bulk of the world's population, and to introduce within that mass a differentiation of function and a division of labor that made irrelevant the remnants of special classes that hung over from an earlier civilization. In a word, within a body of men which existed with very few relations between its members, which consisted of innumerable small units set down in villages and upon farms throughout the world, all capable of self-support without the aid of their fellows from other units, the industrial revolution effected upon a nation-wide and even a world-wide scale a complete social integration and organization. The important effect, socially speaking, of the invention of the machine was not the automobile, the telephone, airplane—those features of modern civilization which bulk so largely in our imaginations. It was the division of labor and the consequent organization of society into a single unit—a unit infinitely larger and infinitely more complex than that ideal of ancient times, the Greek city state.

But the industrial revolution produced not one, but two entirely different bases of differentiation. First, it subdivided the community into a number of industrial groups or vocations on the basis of their function in production; and secondly, it produced a marked stratification into classes on the ground of their relation to the market. The one division runs on lines of industrial technique; it is determined by the machine, by those physical processes necessary to turn raw materials into finished products. The other runs on lines of economic and legal control; it is determined by the laws of property. The one is fixed by man's knowledge of nature, the other, by his social conventions, his experience of human nature. The one is responsive to the trained technical expert; the other, to the collective social will of mankind.

The first basis of differentiation, the industrial organization and interdependence of society, we have already considered. Industrial society is rapidly approaching the stage when it will become, if indeed it is not already, a single machine in which no part can live isolated from the rest. The elements are functionally differentiated, and therefore are all integral parts of the whole. Certain elements are indeed more fundamental than others: a man can live without arms or legs, but not without a head. Yet such a piece of living flesh is hardly a man; and a society restricted entirely to its so-called "essential industries" for any length of time would resemble a bee-hive rather than a human community. The loss of any single part is a direct loss to the whole; the loss of many parts makes the life of the whole impossible.

There thus exist exceedingly powerful common interests in favor of the harmonious functioning of all parts of society; otherwise the entire machine disintegrates. Were this the only type of division that existed in society, the vision of perfect and harmonious coöperation that hovered before the eyes of the early political economists and their liberal followers might long ago have been achieved.

But in striking contrast to the industrial technique that demands unity of purpose and coöperation is the economic system that reflects the most divergent of opposing and conflicting interests. This cuts squarely across the other division lines and creates great classes of men upon the basis of the relative distribution of the spoils of man's campaign against nature. These classes are three in number: the employers, or "capital"; the wageworkers, or "labor"; and that much misunderstood group, the "public." As members of the community organized as a machine for the production of the necessities of civilization, all these classes of course have the great common interest of aiding and forwarding the coöperation of all that the social machine may function efficiently; but as members of their respective classes, their interests are at times diametrically opposed. Let us examine these conflicts of interest in some detail.

The interests of the employers are at bottom to sell their products in the market at such a price as to make the largest possible profit. The profit depends upon the difference between the cost of the article and the price at which it can be sold. Hence it is their interest to reduce costs to the minimum and to raise prices to the maximum possible.

In a competitive market this margin of profit tends to become as slight as will induce men to engage in the industry, and they aim to increase their gain by producing more articles upon which to make this small profit. But there is a practical limit to the amount of any commodity which any community can, under given conditions, absorb; and this limit is in practice soon approached. The employer then finds it to his interest to increase his price; and to do so he must either agree with or combine with his competitors to secure a price that will give them a "fair profit." This combination, whether it takes the form of a monopoly or not, by relieving the individual manufacturer from competition at the same time makes it possible for him to increase his price to what he thinks "the traffic will bear." That this course of action is pursued, and pursued to the marked gain of the employer and the expense of every-one else, needs no proof in these post-war days of the profiteers. All that must be pointed out is the exceeding difficulty of deciding when a "fair price" becomes "profiteering."

So long as the market is a strongly competitive one, the interests of the employer are pretty much one with those of the consumer in pro-ducing excellent goods at the lowest profits and prices. But no one thrives on "cut-rates" and "price-wars"; some effective form of agree-ment is bound to result, and in the measure that it does the interest of the employer diverges from that of the public. "It is a fundamental law that production is always a question of profit," authoritatively announces the president of the United States Steel Corporation, and he ought to know.[1] It is carried on first, last, and all the time, not for the needs of the community, but for the market. Profit is primary, service secondary. The higher the price, the greater the profit to an industry that has eliminated competition if its product be a necessity. And since by a well-known principle of economics prices can be raised either by increasing the demand or by reducing the supply, the capitalist does not hesitate to employ both methods indiscriminately. Hence modern advertising; and hence the interesting device of curtailing production, shutting down the plant, in order to "steady the market" and keep prices up.

The interests of the employer, who produces for the market, are thus often if not fundamentally opposed to those of the public of consumers. They lie in increasing prices; whereas the latter's lie in reducing them. It is needless to add, also, the inefficiency and waste, from the stand-point of production, entailed by a system which takes no account of the

[1] J. A. Farrell, quoted in Gleason, *What the Workers Want*, 9.

varied needs of consumers, but throws upon the market products which bring good profits rather than products which are required. Thus, for instance, farmers everywhere are flocking into automobile factories while the cost of food rises higher and higher. This lack of intelligent adaptation of means to end is another instance of the disparity of interests between employer and public.

But the interests of the capitalist were twofold: not only to increase prices, but also to reduce costs. It is of the essence of the present industrial system that it regards labor as an element in the costs rather than in the profits. Consequently it is the employers' interest to pay their employees the lowest possible wage consonant with the maximum of productivity; to get the most for the least cost, the greatest return for the smallest wage. In general, it has been found that higher wages give the more efficient results, though this is by no means fully conceded and in many industries is not true. Slavery, for instance, insures a supply of cheap labor, but that labor is not efficient and requires expenses for upkeep when it is not needed as well as when it is. Production for the market necessitates periods of full operation and periods of small output, good times followed by periodic depressions. It is therefore to the interests of the employer to have a very flexible supply of labor to which he can turn at once when he needs help but which shall be no expense to him when he does not. The free man has the advantage over the slave of not requiring any upkeep unless he is actually employed, besides being more productive when he is working (if not made lazy with too high pay). Hence the employer wants a labor market plentifully supplied with men willing to work at the wages offered; and this inevitably entails a mass of unemployed when business is not at its peak. The hordes of migratory laborers in the west who drift from mine to farm and from farm to lumber camp are only an extreme example of a situation to gladden the heart of any employer.

But great an improvement as the free laborer is over the slave, and valuable as is his advantage over the machine of not tieing up capital when he is not being used, he does have certain disadvantages. He is prone to hearken to agitators, to become restless and cause annoying difficulties; a machine is always docile and dependable. Hence of late it has seemed worth while to take measures to keep the workers contented; it does seem extravagant, of course, but in the long run it increases efficiency and reduces costs. After all, men require as great care and attention as machines; and so the most up-to-date employers have installed labor managers to cultivate the human machine, and through scientifically managing their workers seek to produce contented and dependable machine-tenders,—an enterprise perhaps most extensively carried on at Gary, Indiana.

In general, then, the interests of the employer as against those of his employees are to obtain at the lowest prices consonant with efficiency reliable machines that will not tie up capital when not working but can be secured in a well-stocked market at the desired low cost.

The second class that has resulted from the industrial revolution is that of the wage-workers. Dependent upon the wage-system for their existence, living from hand to mouth, at the employer's mercy in bargaining for a wage since they know that if they reject the wages he offers someone else will snap up the opportunity, they are always on the brink of unemployment, always fearful lest they lose their jobs and face starvation. They have very little reserve to fall back upon; when wages stop they are at the employer's mercy as soon as their week's credit runs out. In April, 1920, the average weekly wage for factory workers in New York State was $28.45, which, even were unemployment absolutely eliminated, and work continuous, which it never is, would amount to but $1491.40 a year—and the minimum amount necessary to support a family in decency in that month was calculated as $2250, a year.[1] The labor turn-over, besides, is immense, in some plants as high as two and three hundred per cent a year, which means that a job lasts no longer than a few months.

No longer is the bulk of the working class made up of the skilled artisan. The subdivision of function and the increasing application of machinery has not yet eliminated all skill from the worker's life, but its result has been to create a mass of machine tenders—men and women whose sole duty is to stand by a whirring machine hour after hour and with monotonous regularity make a few simple motions over and over again. Highly specialized and differentiated, with perhaps hundreds of distinct operations necessary to produce the finished product, the workers are yet coming to be all equally unskilled—and every day a new machine is installed to eliminate some process requiring intellectual effort and "save labor," which means to save wages.

Moreover the industrial revolution has in America called forth a flood of cheap alien labor, in part imported to keep the labor market well supplied, in part attracted by promises of the golden age. These aliens have commonly lacked the old American native spirit of social equality; they have brought with them a habit of class consciousness and

[1] Bureau of Statistics, State Industrial Commission, *N. Y. Times*, July 3, 1920.

solidarity within the class which is weighty with both good and ill for the future. They have brought foreign philosophies, foreign reactions, foreign ways of thinking. All of these things are profoundly important when we remember that in our basic industries some 60% of the workers are foreign-born.

The interests of this great class do not, it is true, in the long run clash with those of the public; they themselves form too large a portion of the public to permit that. But at times and in groups they seem to oppose them—the public at least feels itself immediately attacked. They demand first of all a living wage, a wage that may increase the price of the product for the consumer; and though it ought to be obvious that it is to the advantage of society to produce its commodities at a sufficient remuneration to the workers to preserve their social well-being, it seldom strikes the public in this light. An increase in wages does generally mean an increase in prices; this the public cannot forgive.

Moreover, it is the interest of the wage-earner to raise his standard of living; and more leisure may mean lessened production, scarcity, and perhaps famine prices. The solution is of course to divert more men into that industry; but the inefficient system of social control and the interconnection of this with other problems seems at times to preclude such a course. An eight-hour day rather than a twelve in the steel industry, just when the public finds its immediate interest in reducing the cost of motor cars and structural steel for building houses, just when the world so urgently needs steel—the public has little sympathy with the steel-workers' desire to raise their standards.

But the sharpest clash comes over the means and not over the end. The weapon of labor is the strike—war, industrial dislocation, the curtailment of production and the consequent inconveniencing of the public. It may be to the ultimate advantage of the consumer to raise the workers' standards; it is never to his advantage to suffer from a strike. The public at best only tolerates strikes; if they touch it in any vital spot, it at once becomes more hostile than the employers. It will force a settlement in the quickest manner possible. The workers strike, knowing that the public will force a settlement and believing it will be easier to coerce the employers than themselves.

But the fundamental opposition is that between wage-earners and employers. In the modern economic organization it is easy to prove that the employer can under no circumstances get along without the worker, that the interests of capital and labor are one to the extent that it is capital's interest to give the worker what he wants and get his profit from the consumer. But it is far more difficult to show how the capitalist is necessary to the worker. Capital, indeed, is as necessary as labor, capital as the machine and the raw material, the physical side of industry, capital as the knowledge of the technique of organization and production. But the capitalist as the one and only source of the necessary capital—that involves a long and laborious justification in intricate economic theory, and even then it fails to appeal with the sense of a priori necessity.

If it is to the employer's advantages to pay his workers as small a wage as possible with high efficiency, it is to the workers' to receive as much as possible. The issue is direct. There are limits, of course; just as it seems unwise to reduce wages to a point where no men will accept work, so it is foolish, under our modern system, to raise them to a point where no men will furnish capital. But within limits the two interests are mutually exclusive; and there is the further disquieting thought that while the capitalist may be the best source of capital, he is by no means the only one. There appears, indeed, no theoretical reason why one man or one group of men should not combine in their persons the function of both workers and capitalists, and thereby add to the wages of the laborer the profit of the capitalist. In the measure that this theoretical possibility becomes practicable, the very existence of the capitalist grows inimical to the interest of labor.

Labor thus seeks an ever larger share of the product of industry, an ever rising standard of living. It also demands permanency and security of employment, thus conflicting with another of capital's interests, a very elastic labor supply. So long as production is carried on for the market, with its periodic fluctuations, its surpluses and its depressions, the demand for security will oppose the desire to lay off workers in slack season, to reduce wages, and to force overtime at the peak.

There is a third point of conflict: capital requires complete docility and obedience. The more closely a laborer can be made to resemble a machine, the greater the consequent profit. Hence the recent vogue of "scientific management," the reduction of the few remaining elements of skill and personal initiative that machine tending has left the worker to a routine-like monotony of repetition. The elimination of the unreliable human factor just so far as possible—this is the ideal of the modern factory and its owner. To this the worker flatly opposes a demand for the opportunity of self-expression, a refusal to become mechanized and to be made the slave of any system. A recent advertisement urges the installation of water-coolers throughout offices so as to do away with the wasteful habit of conversation and relaxation in a trip to the washroom.

If this spirit typifies even our office procedure, how much more do we seek to destroy in our factories this inefficient failing of the human being to attain the perfection of iron and steel! The worker is willing to sacrifice great financial gain to preserve some remnant of his personality; the employer has little interest but his profit.

The third class to which we have referred was not, strictly speaking, a direct product of the industrial revolution. The best definition of that elusive entity, "the public," is that it consists of those who are left over when capitalist and laborer have been subtracted. In any specific sense it comprises, first, the farmers, then the professional and salaried classes, the artists, writers, and "intellectuals," and a portion of the business and commercial classes—the clerks, the tradesmen, and other miscellaneous categories coming under what the French call *la petite bourgeoisie*. In general, "the public" consists of all those varied elements of society not yet caught up directly in the industrial machine, including most of those engaged in our manifold machinery of distribution. It is the "middle class" between the employer and the wage-earner. By definition, with the advance of the industrial revolution it is constantly decreasing, as tenant farming or the application of capitalism to agriculture grows, as industrial unionism with its constant inclusion of hitherto unattached classes gains power. As this process continues "the public" ceases to be composed of distinct individuals, and tends more and more to give place to the community considered in the light of one of its interests, consumption. Even today the term "the public" as commonly used implies "the consumer"; its individual members are usually allied indirectly in interest and directly in sympathy with either capital or labor.

The interest of "the public" or the community as consumer is simple: the uninterrupted production of the greatest possible number of commodities at the cheapest possible prices. Since in a competitive market, this interest merges into that of the capitalist, the public favors "trust busting" and the "good old days." But in agreeing with the capitalist it clashes violently with labor; and since labor is increasingly becoming identical with the public, a conflict of class interest tends to merge into a conflict of motives within the individual. And in so far as the public is composed of a distinct class, its interests are opposed to both high prices and high wages, and irrevocably to strikes.

We have now completed our survey of the conflicts of interest between the three classes produced by the industrial revolution. But while such an analysis of interests is most suggestive, it by no means follows that these interests play the only or even the main part in social life. The one fact that the nineteenth century taught the eighteenth in social theory, and that our modern social psychology seems to be establishing upon a firm basis, is that men's actions rarely proceed from a rational consideration of their interests; that they often, in fact, run directly counter to their personal advantage. Interest, it is true, does play a most important part, but only as it forms the foundation for what men believe their interests to be; here as so often in man's life the belief is practically far more significant than the actual fact. Moreover there are a thousand considerations that enter into the humanistic logic of the industrial situation to modify or even to nullify some of the considerations already alleged; and hence it will be necessary to examine once again these three classes, this time with a view, not to what the objective facts of the situation are, but to what the very human individuals concerned imagine them to be and how they react to them. Let us consider the psychological effects of the industrial revolution upon the three economic classes it produced. And here again we cannot do more than represent typical states of mind, which in their entirety probably find exemplification in no single individual.

The employer has, in general, preserved both the method and the accompanying state of mind of the early American pioneer. When the frontiersman could look around his clearing in the forest and reflect upon the riches that his individual strength and skill had been able to wring from the reluctant grasp of Nature, he assuredly had that strongest of all psychological bases for affirming the divine right of property, the consciousness of wealth entirely the product of work well done. What wonder that a Jim Hill, surveying the empire of the Northwest, should feel that even though the capital he started in with was considerably less than nothing, he had well earned the right to consider most of the Northwest as his property, morally as well as legally? And the history of American industry was in the last century largely just such a story of huge raids upon nature conducted by men of "masterful personality." That type of industrial enterprise has today largely disappeared, but the attitude of mind that went with it is still the dominant attitude of Jim Hill's successors.

The strongest factor in the employer's mind is his profound sense of property rights. "This is my own business," he feels, "I have created it and built it up, and it belongs to me to do with as I will. Ask me humbly for what you want, and I may give it to you if I feel like it; demand anything of mine as a right, and I'll show you who has the law on his side when it comes to rights!" He resents any interference on the part of the public and its politicians. "Think of crack-brained theorists coming around to tell me how to run my own business! Let the public keep off!" And even more incensed is he at similar attempts on the part of "his men." "What right have my men got to interfere with the conduct of my business? They owe their support to the wages I give them, and then they dare prescribe to me how I shall run my plant!" There is no single worker he needs; they all need him. "If you don't like the pay, get out! There are plenty of other jobs for you." But of course not in that industry; "undesirables" are well provided against. What angers him more than anything else, however, is to be told whom he shall and whom he shall not employ. The right of discharge, the right of "hiring and firing," is, with reason, the most precious of all to him: for he has by it absolute power over the income of his employees. It is to him what the right to strike is to the worker, except that it is immensely stronger.

It is true that in these days of great corporations, of boards of directors and of "public service," few employers care to give vent publicly to such sentiments. Nowadays it is not the rights of the business man that are aired; industry has become instead one great charitable enterprise wholeheartedly devoted to the support of indigent widows and orphans. Though it break their hearts the men at the head of modern corporations are unable to grant the demands of their men and of the public; they have a great sacred trust to think always of the wolf at the door of the lone widow. And probably a large part of their solicitude is quite genuine; though one wishes it were more in evidence during transactions in high finance upon the stock-market. But in the case of the men at the head of industries the position of trustee has not altered their basic sense of personal proprietorship. The determining motives lying back of their actions are fundamentally those more candidly expressed a generation ago.

Second only to this sense of ownership is the desire to secure the maximum of production, both in hours and by the piece, at the minimum cost. This translates itself into a feeling of the sanctity of conditions established at an earlier period. It is not "right" for men to want to stop work when the machines are willing to go on turning out salable products. It is not "right" for them to want more time off for lunch, and as for the five-day week—such blasphemy against the moral laws of the universe is stupefying. Every minute taken from possible work is a minute robbed from the employer's profits.

Nor is it right for a wage-earner to receive more than a certain amount a week. That men who work with their hands should be able to afford diamonds, to dress as well as their employers, to enjoy the luxury of an auto—such a state of affairs is utterly subversive of the moral order. Workingmen have always been accustomed to a certain standard; if a rise in prices necessitates a rise in wages to preserve a standard, that, while foolish and to be opposed, is nevertheless understandable. But that a common workingman should desire to improve his standard, to live better than he is living,—that is far too revolutionary for any employing mind to grasp. Not that the owner of the mill would deny to any man the right to rise in the world, to reach the stupendous success of million-airedom; that is the goal still freely offered to all Americans. But the rise to luxury must be by way of the approved "up from the masses" path; the worker must himself become an employer. That he should achieve a measure of luxury and still remain a worker is not to be tolerated; that the masses themselves should rise is unthinkable.

Firm as is the conviction of the ultimate rightness of "reasonable wages" and "honest work" to keep the cosmos in order, the obvious facts of the increase of efficiency that comes with a higher standard have finally managed to penetrate most minds. Overwork, under-nourish-ment, and ill-health are qualities that men can be taught to regard as undesirable in employees as in other cattle. The striking success of ventures like Robert Owen's and Henry Ford's aids a latent sense of humanitarianism, although there exists the lurking suspicion that it is not "right" to treat mere laborers so well: it is sooner or later bound to "spoil" them. There is indeed much experience to fortify such a con-clusion. "Welfare work" and high wages rarely succeed in keeping men "contented." They tend rather to provoke thought and to lead to new demands; hence, thinks the employer, a compromise had best be struck somewhere between sweatshop methods and lavish paternalism.

This eternal rightness of the established distinctions rests upon a generally frank and candid acceptance of an aristocratic absolutism as the only method for governing industry. No employer can understand the charge that he is seeking to "oppress" his men, to keep them down and deprive them of opportunities for advancement. He knows he is always eagerly searching for "good men," for men who have in them the stuff of employers like himself. The employer is on the lookout for "strong men," executives, bosses, foreman, managers, and other capable exponents of his ideas and masterful lieutenants for his purposes. These he is willing to aid by promoting them to his own class; and in the past the men perhaps most able to direct and guide the forces of labor, sometimes unconsciously, sometimes with conscious purpose, have been drawn off in just such a manner.

But together with the willingness to recognize native ability wherever found is coupled the equally firm conviction that the great mass of workers are distinctly inferior men, capable only of being led and directed. Immigration has added racial to economic prejudice; the workers are foreigners, hunkies, dagoes, hardly human beings. Americans and able men in general are alone able to carry on industry; without this leaven in the mass the country would crumble to ruins. What use is it to talk about other "systems" of economic life? No system could alter the fact that the many must toil and suffer while the few control, direct, and reap the advantage. The city states of ancient times had no firmer supporter of the theory of natural aristocracy than the magnates of the industrial age. The best are on top; the rest owe them implicit obedience.

But this faith in aristocracy has not yet become attached to a hereditary institution. It is tempered by a strong belief in the efficacy of natural selection. Let things work out for themselves; provided no one interferes, the good will be bound to rise to the surface. The honest and capable workman will succeed; at least, the workman possessed of the energy and personal initiative requisite to be a leader in the modern age. "I succeeded. Why not other good men?" There is a sincere belief in the moral duty of *laisser-faire* and of competition to weed out the unfit. Yet at the same time the sancity of private property is firmly upheld, and men are ever ready to resort to the courts and to the government when a too generous policy of *laisser-faire* seems to be going against them. For the widows and orphans, of course, require careful protection.

And lastly there is a sense of benevolent paternalism which every employer feels to some extent towards his employees. It is to him as though somehow he is conducting a great philanthropic enterprise for the sake of his mill-hands. "I am giving (sic) them work; they ought to be profoundly grateful to me for it. Where would they be if I had not taken them in, clothed them and fed them? And now they show no gratitude at all—they want more! With all I'm doing for them, with my new rest-room and the sanitary wash-room, they must be thoroughly contented!" And although in his heart he knows he would never have provided better working conditions had not his expert proved how greatly they would increase his output, he regards every outlay made on the health and well-being of his employees as somehow a direct gift to them. In the face of the most direct testimony he cannot conceive that his men are discontented. "They have absolutely no grievance; I am

doing everything for them." All labor unrest is due to malicious interference from the outside: self-seeking labor agitators, walking-delegates,
foreign gold, alien spies—there is nothing too extreme or too fantastic
for him to assign as the cause of the otherwise quite unaccountable
unrest among his men. Perhaps he is seeking to salve his own conscience
and arguing as much to convince himself as anyone else. For the sake
of his workers themselves and their own interests, which he alone knows
best, he seeks, like the coal companies of West Viriginia or like the Steel
Corporation to build a wall around his plant and keep the men pure
and undefiled. Keep off the agitator, and he will be glad to improve the
lot of his men in any way than will not affect his profits.

Such is the portrait of the type "employer," repeated with variations
in countless factories, and happily already disappearing in many. Essentially a product of the industrial revolution, he is confronted by
another product, the worker. In the life of the worker the fundamental
fact is insecurity—insecurity and instability. From a society founded
on status, said Maine, we have progressed to one founded on contract.
This progress means for the worker that no longer can he count, as once
he did, upon nature to furnish her crops with approximate regularity.
He must always have a job; when he has none he must get one, when he
has got one he must keep it. Any moment he may fall from the ranks
of the wage-earners and join the want of the unemployed. Fear is his
dominant motive—fear of losing his job. It is little wonder the motive
to "make work"—to produce less than he otherwise might so as to
stretch out his job—is very strong; mistaken as it may be, it is the
workers' form of thrift and providing for the morrow. The future hangs
over him threateningly like a dark cloud—not the future of old age, or
even of next year, but the future of next month, of next week, of tomorrow.
Everything must give way to the course of immediate advantage. Only
as he gains a more settled position is he able to take a longer and more
comprehensive view. Hence his readiness to snatch at any stabilizing
factor offered him. Benefits, workman's insurance, pensions—if only
they be immediate enough he eagerly grasps them. Old-age pensions,
being more remote, make less appeal.

The worker fears nothing so much as losing his job; he hates nothing
so much as working on it. His loathing for the machine and for the daily
task of tending it becomes at time unbearable. Fortunately stern
necessity usually soon dulls his sensibilities. No one who has not worked
nine or ten hours in a modern factory, with its ceaseless whirring of
machinery, its unending noise, its atmosphere of monotonous repetition,

above all the impression it gives of never ceasing or altering its pace for a single minute; no one who does not know what it is to feel that you cannot stop, cannot slow down, cannot spurt a little and then rest, that you must become another creature of tireless iron limbs like your pacemaker, can realize the horror with which men come to regard the factory. The moment the worker enters the door his personality departs and his individuality, whatever remnants he is able to preserve outside, oozes away, leaving him worse than a machine—a machine's slave. Most workers manage to achieve a patient endurance; with the years their first rebellion is deadened. But many can never adapt themselves to it; their natures demand some change and excitement, they remain on one job for a new months, then drift away to another. Hence in part our tremendous labor turn-over. Hatred of machine-tending can overcome even fear of losing one's job.

Modern civilization has yet to meet the human problem of the machine. The worker can think only in terms of shorter hours, more lesiure for relaxation; how to get away from the machine as long as possible. His individual initiative and responsibility are slowly crushed and atrophied; they are not required to watch machines. He develops oftentimes a dull stolid sense of despair; of the utter futility of attempting to think ahead to the morrow. The machines will go on—on—on—, and he will go on—on—on—with them until he is no longer wanted. What can a man do against those iron masters? It is useless to attempt to change the "system"; it is irrevocably fixed by a malignant destiny. It will go on and on until—and it is just in this attitude of mind that the Marxian sweep of history finds its strongest support among the workers—until something happens. The machines finally break; will not the Great Machine break too, with a resounding crash? Until then we must push, pull, screw,—push, pull, screw,—push, pull, screw,—

This is the usual result among the older men and women; with the young folks nature is stronger. A day's life must be crowded into a few hours of evening; when work is at last over flesh and blood rebounds all the more strongly. Excitement, artificial pleasure, the movie, the dance-hall—these are the only available outlets. What wonder that *carpe diem* reigns as the philosophy of most young workers—that improvidence and extravagance are the dominant strain in their lives? It is at least better than the dull despair of their elders.

One determination is left—not to allow any decrease in their standard of life if it can possibly be avoided, not to sink any lower into the pit.

And coupled with this is an intense yearning for improvement, a dim hope of eventually rising above their squalid surroundings. As despair of ever lifting themselves out alone takes possession of them, their hopes and desires pass over into a great passion for social change. The father will toil and save "that my children may not have to go through what I have gone through"; but when he fails he turns, and even more his children turn, to rising not above but with their fellows. Apocalyptic visions of a future life on earth appeal to the young; they at least furnish an outlet for the pent-up emotions and the suppressed desires crushed by the machine. Utopias arise again and again as a way of relief and a dream of consolidation. Some men prefer the romance of Marx to the romance of the movies. It is indeed strange how much of patient thought is left over for devotion to practicable schemes for action.

Gradually the hatred of the machine crystallizes into a hatred of the entire system; it comes to be symbolized in hatred of the "capitalist," regarded as the devilish fiend who invented and applied the system rather than as the entirely unintentional profiter by it. The impersonal economic conflict becomes personalized; it is treated in terms of love and hate, of will and purpose, when both sides are largely irresponsible for their actions. Against the "capitalist" the worker unites in mind if not in fact. The group loyalty that arises within a small body of workers, with its deep hatred of the crime of scabbing or treason and its substitution of coöperation for competition, gradually spreads to larger and larger groups, while at the same time the forces of social loyalty and patriotism seem to shrink to the same compass, and the two unite in devotion to class. As society comes to be regarded as a battle-field, and life a struggle against the capitalists, more and more stress is laid on the virtues of combat: treachery, treason, failure to coöperate, become the supreme crimes, and loyalty and self-sacrifice the supreme virtues. The solidarity of labor increases; class consciousness comes to dominate its actions. Within the group, individual aims are subordinated to group aims; outside, the latter are supreme. And they are a desire for security and for improved and eventually equal status.

In describing the attitude of "the public" the peculiar indefiniteness surrounding that body makes generalizing difficult. If it be regarded as the entire community taken as consumer, its mind is obviously profoundly modified by its other interests. Perhaps the largest single item going to make up the attitude of "the public" is the oracular voice of the metropolitan editor; for those whose business does not lead them to take sides directly it is the molding force. It has taught them that they have paramount interests that are apt to coincide with those of the capitalists.

But in so far as "the public" represents an independent attitude, it is in general one of absolute indifference to industrial struggles. Especially is this true of the farmer, who in economic disputes does not usually suffer any inconvenience. But at times the public gives an impulsive, unreasoning, and usually not very long sustained approbation to the efforts of the "oppressed" to obtain "justice"—to the desire of the classes worst off to rise to the level of their fellow-workers. Its humanitarian motives are easily aroused and as easily extinguished; and it is of course the aim of both employer and employee to manipulate this impulse to his own advantage. For while capital can win a strike against public opinion, such an achievement is very difficult indeed for labor. And while the public will support labor so long as it thinks it is trying to approximate the standards of the better-paid workers, when any attempt is made to raise those standards themselves the public at once ceases to sympathize and regards the union as a monopoly bent on raising prices. It is this fact that in a strike forms the basis of the propaganda campaigns on both sides; if the workers can make it appear that they have been markedly worse off than most of their fellows, the sympathy of the public is assured.

But when once the interests or the convenience of the public themselves are touched, which with the growing industrialization and organization of society is bound to become increasingly frequent, the public is aroused to a self-interest far surpassing that of the capitalist himself, a self-interest all the stronger in its supreme and unintelligent shortsightedness. It demands cheapness and low prices for the present, no matter what the ultimate results; the treatment of government employees is a significant case in point. The postal clerks, the federal employees, the school-teachers, are all woefully underpaid, and the future of the country is jeopardized to save a cent or two on the tax-rate. That its passion for cheapness is not partial, but falls alike on the employer and the laborer, is shown by its attitude toward street-car fares. It is willing to disrupt service and drive companies into bankruptcy and suspension before it will consent to a rise in fares.

The supreme disregard the public displays of other interests has a most important bearing on the state-ownership plans of the socialists. President Gompers was right in the Montreal convention of the A. F. L. in calling attention to the danger that confronts workers under this type of government ownership. It may not be so conclusive as he imagines, but it should at least give pause to too eager reformers.

But where the public is most concerned is in the industrial disputes growing out of the use of labor's weapon, the strike. As strikes become more and more inconveniencing, as all industries increasingly take on the nature of public service utilities, the public's wrath is aroused. It demands unconditional peace, peace at any price. "Settle the strike at once, and let none ever happen again," is its immediate verdict, untainted by any knowledge of actual conditions. Of all the vast and intricate problems of economic adjustment that makes strikes at times the lesser of two evils, it knows not a whit and cares less. Of the justice or injustice of the contentions of the two disputants, it is quite oblivious; it is equally willing to pass Adamson laws or enjoin coal-miners, if it can only preserve the peace.

This powerful engine will serve those who are able to manipulate it. The strategy is to make it appear that it is the other side that is preventing a settlement, or that is the easier to bludgeon into quietude. So far the employers have generally been able to utilize this desire for peace at all costs in their own interests, but it is equally possible for labor, as it increases in strength, to compel an outraged public to force the acceptance of its demands. The difficulty of coercing a functional group will make it easier and easier to compel the employers to give way for the public weal. For the public is ever crying, "Peace! Peace! Peace at any price!"

This, then, has been the most important social consequence of the industrial revolution: this stratification of society into great classes whose interests are far from identical and whose frequent clashes frequently upset the delicate workings of that other great organization, the industrial machine. Without a knowledge of these classes and their attitudes it is impossible to understand the modern labor movement or its aims. But before proceding to the activities which men facing these conditions have been led to engage in, let us pause to ask what the effect has been on the traditional American social ideal. An agricultural democracy was what our country first aimed to be; an agricultural democracy was the goal of the mechanics' movement. How has that ideal been modified? What is left of the old farmer equality?

Assuredly the Yankee farmer type has almost disappeared; industry demands specialization, differentiation, the antithesis of the all-around jack-of-all-trades. And between the classes, between different capitalists and between the various members of "the public" there are chasms so wide that it seems sheer folly even to mention equality. The goods of life were probably never so unevenly distributed as today. Yet nevertheless we have seen how within the laboring class this approximate equality is steadily growing—equality no longer of similarity but equality of the parts of an organic whole. And as an ideal it is more potent than ever, because it has been stripped of the elements of sameness and identity of function to become one of equality of value and of worth. And already the gap formerly existing between the "public" as a whole and the worker has been closed in; doctors and bricklayers enjoy not dissimilar incomes.

Liberty, essentially a relation between equals, has suffered more seriously from the disparity between the classes. It has tended to relapse into the older "liberty" of the *bellum omnium contra omnes;* economic aristocracy has played havoc with the pioneer's freedom. The liberty of doing as one likes has disappeared with industrial organization, and as yet little of the liberty of free coöperation has taken its place. The older "rights", notably the "freedom of contract", have been kept alive largely in the interests of the stronger party; they are otherwise paid a lip-homage, but have been gradually deprived of their reality. The old freedom has indeed suffered a decline, while the new has hardly yet been born.

Fraternity as a general social cohesive, binding all citizens together, has probably lessened, though in great crises, like the war, it has shown remarkable vitality. But as a tendency to act in concert, to coöperate rather than to go it alone, as a really strong group motive, fraternity has vastly increased. Seldom have men been so closely bound together as they are in their union groups; even the employers have found countless associations for joint activity. And within the classes an increasing class-consciousness is welding men into a single purpose. Between classes, however, there is little but bitterness and strife. It almost seems as though the increase within groups had been made at the expense of the larger social solidarity.

Yet, in spite of these modifications, there has been a marked persistence, albeit in an altered form, of the old American ideal of Democracy. The workers in increasing numbers are demanding a more equal status in society, a more secure position. The farming ideal has been translated into industrial terms. Liberty has remained as an ideal of group rather than of individual activity, of free coöperation within and between groups. And fraternity, as group and class solidarity, as a longed-for social aim, has never ceased to inspire the workers.

The industrial revolution has both united society in inextricable bonds and split it far asunder. The great social problem is how to bridge the chasm between the *industrial organization* and the *economic stratification* of modern civilization. What has labor succeeded in doing to solve it?

7. THE CONFLICT OF THEORIES AND THE TRIUMPH OF BUSINESS UNIONISM

THE panic of 1837, so disastrous to the mechanics' movement, inaugurated a period of hard times that did not end until about 1850, when the gold of California revived trade. During this interval the constant fear of unemployment, scarcely removed by the growing influx of Irish laborers, kept the workers' organizations weak and concentrated their efforts on retaining any job they might have. Until the brief period of prosperity from 1851 to 1855 they kept their own counsel, seeking as best they could to remain above water. In industrial questions unions were superseded by a great number of enthusiastic and rather visionary middle-class "reformers" who with the confidence of the utopian offered their various panaceas for social ills. These plans of social regeneration made quite a stir in the advanced press and in the drawing-rooms of Boston and New York. But they failed to arouse either enthusiasm or emulation amongst the wage-earners. Amidst all the welter of theories and philosophies, when every congress called together proceeded duly to discuss at least a dozen entirely different theories of building society anew, there can hardly be said to have been any real labor movement. The worker was an abstract entity to be saved and reformed; as to what he himself might want, he was never consulted. Horace Greeley, the shepherd of the whole flock, was strongly opposed to the strike and to trade unions in general. Hence the "windy forties" hardly concern us here. The following quotation reveals the general attitude of the associationist follower of Owen or Fourier toward the "miserable compromise of the Working Men's Movements": "We wish however that we could impress upon this country the degrading littleness and insufficiency of this attempt at a compromise of their rights, for it is neither more nor less than a demeaning compromise and dastardly sacrifice of their rights for them to make terms which only modifies the condition but does not change the terms of dependence upon masters. In wretched England, where the laborer is indeed a poor degraded helpless being it is well that any amelioration can be obtained; but here, where the laboring classes are intelligent and generally possess the ability to do full justice to themselves, it does appear to us to be excessively weak and trifling, for them to talk about a reform which at the most can relieve them temporarily of a few hours' oppressive toil—can convert them from 12 and 14 to 10-hour slaves—but cannot elevate them to the dignity of true independence! What a force is boasted American freedom, if free men are reduced to such beggarly shifts? Do they not see that they exhibit the badge of slavery in the very effort to mitigate its oppression? Free men would not talk about terms which involve only a question of time of subjection to the authority and will of another—they would consult and act for their own good in all things without let or hindrance!" [1]

Occasionally, indeed, a few mechanics, like the Cincinnati iron-molders or like several of the German trades, would seek in coöperative enterprises to imitate the associationists, but with little success and with less permanence. Only two movements, in fact, in this period really concern the workers themselves: the movement for the ten-hour day by legislation among the factory workers of New England, and the movement for land reform.

The ten-hour movement was really a hangover from the earlier period. President Van Buren had established it for federal employees in 1840; it was now sought from state legislatures. But at most of the conventions called to agitate the question, in Fall River in 1844, in the New England Working Men's Association, in Lowell among the factory workers, in Lynn, the reformers and associationists gained control and passed resolutions in favor of their plans; and it is little wonder that the workers took small interest in such efforts. New Hampshire passed a ten-hour law in 1847, Pennsylvania in 1848; but not being compulsory these had little effect.

Land reform was a much more important issue. We have already seen how the question of keeping the public lands open so that any man, defeated in the economic contest in the East, could go West and realize at once the agricultural ideal, at the same time relieving the pressure in the East, was of primary importance for the American labor movement. The workers' success was of great advantage to them individually, but it also retarded their organization. The land reform movement of the forties grew out of the agrarian agitation of the previous decade, but its real roots were in the old agricultural ideal of Jeffersonian democracy. George Henry Evans secured support for his "new agrarianism" because he founded it firmly in the traditional philosophy of natural rights. In 1830 he had advocated a division of private property as a consequence of the social contract theory; now he

[1] *Phalanx*, May 18, 1844.

turned his attention to public land, and sought to give every man his equal share of it. The National Reform Association which he founded sought freedom of the public lands, together with homestead exemption from debt laws, and a limitation of the amount of land one man could own. These latter aims, and the elaborate deductions of the whole theory from the natural rights premises, found little acceptance among the workers themselves, but the belief that there were enough public lands to last at least a thousand years made Evans's impassioned appeals to "Vote yourself a farm" quite alluring.[1] The National Industrial Congresses which met annually from 1845 to 1856 carried on considerable land reform agitation, which finally bore lasting fruit in the Homestead Law of 1862. The kinship between this land reform movement and the early agricultural ideal—the desire, as it were, to seize the last chance offered to man by Nature's bounty in this western hemisphere—is revealed in a resolution of the New York Industrial Congress in 1850: "That all men are created equal—that they are endowed by their Creator with certain inalienable rights, among which are the right to life and liberty, to the fruits of their labor, to the use of such a portion of the earth and the other elements as shall suffice to provide them with the means of subsistence and comfort, to education and paternal protection from society." [2]

But with the revival of prosperity following the discovery of gold in California the workers themselves began to take heart, and, forsaking the many well-intentioned but quite irrelevant schemes of those who came to them as with authority, started to reconstruct some semblance of the organization they had enjoyed prior to 1837. When it was proposed to create in New York a city industrial congress, after the model of the national congress of the land reformers, there were a number of locals that received the call with hopes of a city federation. Some fifty groups took part in the meeting and adopted a preamble resolving to use "all available means to promote their moral, intellectual, and social elevation." [3] But the control was in the hands of reformers of all shades of opinion; many unions, distrustful from the first, had not joined, and when it became evident that a general trades' union was not to result, most of the others withdrew in disgust. The workers were unwilling to forsake the tried and intelligible method of the strike for vaster schemes.

[1] *True Workingman*, Jan. 24, 1846.
[2] *New York Tribune*, July 3, 1850.
[3] *Ibid.*, July 3, 1850.

In the brief period of prosperity before the depression of 1855, which culminated in the panic of 1857, set in, the craftsmen who had so distrusted the plans of the reformers adhered religiously to their "pure and simple" business unionism; strikes, not of the trade but of the single shop, efforts at collective bargaining, and the establishment of minimum wages with employers were its distinguishing features. In 1853 and 1854, when the movement was at its height, there occurred some 400 strikes. The older societies like the printers and the cordwainers, reorganized upon a strictly "protective" basis. But all in all the unionism of the early fifties was but a belated revival of the earlier mechanics' movement: it was in the hands of the skilled artisans, it was local, and it pursued the same policies that had proved successful in 1835 and 1836, and had persisted under the surface ever since. Even the attempts at nationalization, in emulation of the printers, who had formed a national union in 1852, are carried on by the local mechanics; they are neither the results of the advancing industrial revolution nor are they the unions which are later to take the initiative.

The very first real national unions of the new era were in the iron trades, symbolic of the industrial age; in 1859 were organized the Molders International Union and the National Union of Mechanics and Blacksmiths. Both originated, in characteristic union fashion, as efforts of self-protection against the attempts of the employers to force down wages and standards. William H. Sylvis, the great leader of the molders, tells how the competition induced by the consolidation of the east and west trunk lines in the fifties forced the employers in Pennsylvania to make determined efforts. They reduced their prices and their margin of profits to the minimum; they then started reducing wages, required the men to furnish their own tools, introduced division of labor and boys as "helpers." "Thus this system went on until it became customary for each man to have one to five boys; and . . . prices became so low that men were obliged to increase the hours of labor, and work much harder; and then could scarcely obtain the plainest necessaries of life."[1] Similar conditions obtained among the machinists. "Unfair dealing on the part of the employers had long been a grievance with the men. The baneful system of paying in orders was common. The taking on of as many apprentices as could possibly be worked was considered the indubitable right of every employer. . . . As the business came to be more fully developed, it was found that more capital must be employed and the authority and supervision of the owner or owners must be delegated

[1] *Fincher's Trades' Review*, July 18, 1863.

to superintendents and under-foreman. In this manner men and masters became estranged and the gulf could only be bridged by a strike, when, perhaps, the representatives of the workingmen might be admitted to the office and allowed to state their case. It was to resist this combination of capital, which had so changed the character of the employers, that led to the formation of the union." [1]

In both these cases it is the industrial revolution that through changing conditions has made organization in self-protection inevitable; 1859 was not a year of prosperity and good prices; the workers demanded a livelihood, not an increased standard. It was a spontaneous protest that effected national organization, and neither a vision of social improvement nor a far-sighted attempt to improve status. Hence the aims which it set itself were purely protective, that fundamental strain of self-interest dominating the workers' minds. In the next decade the other strain came to the front again with success. Powderly, looking back from 1889, said: "The organization of labor means far more in 1889 than it even shadowed in 1859; then the supplication was: 'Give us an advance in wages and shorter hours of toil, and we will be content with our stay on earth.' Today the demand is: 'Give us the earth and all that it can produce, for to no man, or set of men, belongs the right to monopolize it or its products." [2] Elsewhere he states that despite the wider ideas of their leaders, the men at this time were interested in but two things, wages and the regulation of the number of the apprentices. [3] These were the immediate problems; the workers were still suspicious of the extravagant theories of the forties.

The machinists thus stated their aims: "Whereas, in the present organization of society, capital and labor being, as a matter of necessity, united in all kinds of productive industry (and, as is generally the case, represented by differing parties), it has come to pass: That, in consequence of the smallness of the number representing capital, their comparative independence and power, their ample leisure to study their own interests, their prompt coöperation, together with aid of legislation, and last, but not least, the culpable negligence of the working classes themselves; that notwithstanding their joint production is amply sufficient to furnish both parties the necessaries, comforts, and luxuries of life, yet the fact is indisputable that while the former enjoy more than their share, the latter are correspondingly depressed . . . " resolved,

---

[1] *Machinists' and Blacksmiths' International Journal*, Feb. and March, 1872.
[2] Powderly, *Thirty Years of Labor*, 5.
[3] *Ibid.*, 42.

that we hereby form our union.[1] "And we hereby proclaim to the
world, that so far from encouraging a spirit of hostility to employers,
all properly organized unions recognize an identity of interests between
employer and employee, and we give no countenance or support to any
project or enterprise that will interfere with the promotion of perfect
harmony between them." Sylvis expressed the same ideas at greater
length in a speech adopted as the preamble of the Molders Union: "In
all countries and at all times capital has been used by those possessing
it to monopolize particular branches of business, until the vast and
varied industrial pursuits of the world have been brought under the
immediate control of a comparatively small portion of mankind. Although an unequal distribution of the world's wealth, it is perhaps
necessary that it should be so. To attain to the highest degree of success in any undertaking, it is necessary to have the most perfect and
systematic arrangement possible; to acquire such a system, it requires
the management of a business to be placed as nearly as practicable
under the control of one mind; thus concentration of wealth and business
tact conduces to the most perfect working of the vast machinery of the
world. . . ." Capitalism is necessary; only its greed is bad. "There
is, perhaps, no other organization of society so well calculated to benefit
the laborer and advance the moral and social condition of the mechanic
of this country, if those possessed of wealth were all actuated by those
pure and philanthropic principles necessary to the happiness of all; but,
alas! for the poor of humanity, such is not the case. . . . What position
are we, the mechanics of America, to hold in Society? Are we to receive
an equivalent for our labor sufficient to maintain us in comparative independence and respectability, to procure the means with which to
educate our children and qualify them to play their part in the world's
drama; or must we be forced to bow the suppliant knee to wealth, and
earn by unprofitable toil a life too void of solace to confirm the very
chains that bind us to our doom? . . . There *is* not, there *cannot be*, any
good reason why they should not pay us a fair price for our labor. If
the profits of their business are not sufficient to remunerate them
for the trouble of doing business, *let the consumer* make up the
balance." [2]

There is evident here a wistful glance backward at the agricultural
equality, and a very reluctant acceptance of the new order. There
must be rich men; but let the masses at least preserve their old status.

[1] Powderly, *Thirty Years of Labor*, 35.
[2] *Ibid.*, 37–40.

If men are to gain wealth by the new order, they can divide that wealth among the workers. Labor can have at least a minor share in the process. It is the voice of those temporarily beaten and overwhelmed by the strangeness of the transformation.

Soon, however, the Civil War prosperity overtook the country; prices rose and wages with them. Men had but to ask to be granted. In the fall of 1862 many new locals were formed; from December, 1863, to December of the next year the number rose from 79 to 270. At the same time there reappeared the older trades' assemblies of the late thirties; beginning with Rochester, in March, 1863, they had by the close of the war spread to every important city, and they devoted their time to organization and agitation, to boycotts and publicity work, but not to aiding strikes directly. The unit was still, despite national organization in some trades, the city; when a central national body was to be formed there was a contest beteween the city assemblies and the growing national unions for its control. The employers, too, were busy organizing at this time, though as yet there were no collective agreements between them and the unions.

In 1864 the Louisville Trades' Assembly summoned a national trades' assembly to combat these employers' organizations. With a personalizing tendency comparable to the masters' hatred of "agitators" the convention accused the capitalists of banding together "for the express purpose of crushing out our manhood" and of assuming "to arrogate to itself the right to own and control labor." [1] and formed the International Industrial Assembly of North America to foil these attempts. They demanded an equal share of the wealth they created, favored conciliation and trade agreements rather than strikes, but provided for a generous strike fund. The assembly failed through lack of interest from the trades' assemblies on which it was based and through the hostility of the national unions, which preferred another individual unit of organization; but it illustrated the growing success of the unions. Meanwhile the number and strength of the national bodies was rapidly increasing; in addition to the molders, the machinists, and the printers, there were formed in the sixties strong organizations of locomotive engineers, cigar-makers, coopers, shoe-makers, and iron puddlers.

Before considering the successive attempts made to unite all these unions on differing bases of aim and of organization, and the struggle for dominance between the two persistent strains, let us stop to examine the general theories back of all this labor activity. The movement had

[1] *Finchers' Trades' Review,* Oct. 15, 1864.

by this time reached a position of comparative success; no longer a mere spontaneous protest against degradation, it could afford the luxury of a somewhat reflective and critical examination of its methods and aims. It was ready and eager to consider the social implications of its activities, with a view to extending them beyond the narrow limits of a living wage. Hitherto the social and political philosophy of the workers had been merely an application and adaptation of the natural rights theory of the Revolution; now their need was a philosophy that would furnish a social justification for labor activities in terms of the welfare of the community as a whole. Nor was it wholly a case of justification after the fact; nowhere is the presence of the second or social strain in American labor so noticeable as in the continued dissatisfaction expressed with the pure and simple unionism of private gain in economic competition, and the groping after an idealism to give a social significance to the workers' struggles. This philosophy was supplied in the nick of time by Ira Steward and his eight-hour theory, the dominant intellectual force in American labor down to the eve of the Great War. As John R. Commons says, "Steward's philosophy is what may be called the first philosophy springing from the American labor movement. Steward's contribution, in giving justification and shape to American labor's most characteristic demand, can not be overestimated and has not been sufficiently recognized."[1] The factor that caused the wide acceptance of this theory is the remarkable manner in which he combined the two characteristic strains, and formulated a program which while satisfying completely all those desires for individual improvement appealed also to the social interests of the workers with the assurance that thus, and thus alone, was the true welfare of society as a whole to be forwarded. All the more remarkable is it that in that age of abstract economic theory Steward was able to appreciate the importance of psychological considerations; it gives his theory a strikingly modern note. His acceptance of the wage-system, and even more the adoption of his ideas as the official philosophy of the A. F. L. have told against him for the modern worker, however.

The theory back of the revival of unionism in the fifties had been that which persistently reappears when the fear of unemployment is very strong. It is the theory the plumber goes on when he spends two hours upon a job requiring only one, or when he mends a leak in such a way that it will recur again in a short time. To economists it is known as the lump of labor theory; to workers, as the theory of "making

[1] *Doc. Hist.*, IX, 24.

work." It assumes that there is a certain definite and fixed amount of employment to be had which must in the workers' interest be made to last as long as possible and go around amongst as many as possible. It is well expressed in the resolution of a ten-hour convention held in Boston in 1852: "Wages are governed by the great law of trade—the law of supply and demand. . . . There is a certain amount of the productions of labor demanded by the wants of the community, and there are a certain number of laborers ready for employment to supply the demand. As the demand or the supply of laborers is in excess, wages will rise or fall. . . . A reduction of hours would be equivalent to diminishing the supply of labor." [1] This would at least keep wages up in the face of increasing immigration; if restrictions of another nature could be placed on the supply of labor, wages might even rise. Hence together with demands for shorter hours went limitation of the number of apprentices, efforts at keeping women and negroes from competing with the unionists, and attempts at restricting immigration. Such a policy worked to the immediate advantage of the unionists, but it obviously appeared detrimental to the interests of all others concerned. Just so soon as they felt they were no longer fighting for their very existence this troubled the consciences of the workers. And it was attacked with considerable success by the economists upon purely economic grounds.

Hence it was that the machinists, for instance, who in their first convention had resolved on shorter hours for the purpose of "making work," adopted Steward's justification for that policy in 1863 with great enthusiasm. For Steward proclaimed that reducing the number of hours not only benefited the men concerned; it also worked to the advantage both of the employer and of the community as a whole. And he inextricably knitted the individual and the social motives by pointing out that no workers could hope to improve their own condition until they also improved that of their poorest fellow-workers. One of the immediate effects of Stewardism was to transform the selfish trade-conscious unionism of the fifties into the class-conscious and barrier-breaking movement of the sixties.

Instead of making wages depend upon the supply, or capital, Steward emphasized the side of demand. It is the standard of living of the worker that dictates his wage, his wants and his desires, not any wage-fund. So long as this is low, wages will be low for all laborers. The problem is, how to raise this standard for the poorer workers. The an-

---

[1] *Doc. Hist.*, VIII, 131.

swer is through granting them leisure to develop new wants; through
shorter hours. Hence a compulsory eight-hour day.

"You are receiving," says Steward, "your scanty pay precisely because you work so many hours a day. My point now is to show why
this is true, and why reducing the hours for the masses will eventually
increase their wages. . . . The truth is, as a rule, that men who labor
excessively are robbed of all ambition to ask for anything more than
will satisfy their bodily necessities, while those who labor moderately
have time to cultivate tastes and create wants in addition to mere physical comforts. How can men be stimulated to demand higher wages
when they have little or no time or strength to use the advantages which
higher wages can buy or procure?"[1] As George Gunton, Steward's
foremost disciple, puts it, "Other things being the same, the cost of
(the worker's) living will be determined by the number of his habitual
wants. Thus the cost of producing labor is ultimately determined by
the socially accepted standard of living; that is to say, the state of material comfort and social refinement which is customary in, and thus is
determined by, the social status of the class to which he belongs, and
below which he cannot permanently go without being put to social disadvantages."[2] The problem, then, is "How can the social opportunities of the masses be enlarged?"

"My theory," answered Steward, "is, first, that more leisure will
create motives and temptations for the common people to ask for more
wages. Secondly, that where all ask for more wages there will be no
motive for refusing, since employers will all fare alike. Thirdly, that
where all demand more wages the demand can not be resisted. Fourthly,
that resistance would amount to the folly of a 'strike' by employers
themselves against the strongest power in the world, viz., the
habits, customs, and opinions of the masses. Fifthly, that the change
in the habits and opinions of the people through more leisure will be
too gradual to disturb and jar the commercial enterprise of capital.
Sixthly, that the increase in wages will fall upon the wastes of society,
in its crimes, idleness, fashions, and monopolies as well as the more legitimate profits of capital, in the production and distribution of
wealth. Seventhly, in the mechanical fact, that the cost of making
an article depends almost entirely upon the number manufactured,
is a practical increase in wages, by tempting the workers through
their new leisure to unite in buying luxuries now confined to

---

[1] *A Reduction of hours an increase of wages*, Steward, pamphlet, 1865.

[2] Gunton, *The Economic and Social Importance of the Eight-Hour Movement*, 1889.

the wealthy, and thus more costly because bought only by the wealthy." [1]

Thus it is to the interest of the employer and the public to unite in reducing the number of hours for the worker. "The increase in wages does not mean an increase in the price of the article produced, as do the 'strike' for higher wages when successful." As Gunton puts it, "Economic production absolutely depends upon social consumption, and the success of the employing class depends upon the extent of the consuming class. . . . Capital can yield increasing returns, *i. e.*, become a cheaper productive force than labor—only when it can produce on an extensive scale. . . . Since the laboring classes constitute seven or eight-tenths of the consumers, it is upon increasing their consumption —by means of raising the social life and wages of the laborer—that the market for capitalistic productions finally depends. . . . It will thus be seen that the economic interests of the employing classes are not opposed to, but are bound up with and *dependent* upon the social well-being of the laborer; that the success of the modern factory depends upon the comforts of the average laborer's home, and that the profitable employment of capital can only be promoted as the general rate of wages is advanced." [2]

In fact, ultimately "wages will continue to increase till the capitalist and the laborer are one. . . . The capitalist, as we now understand him, is to pass away with the kings and royalties of the past. In America every man is king in theory, and will be in practice eventually and in the good time coming every man will be a capitalist. The capitalist of today, however, is as necessary as was the king once, to preserve order. Nothing but a higher standard of popular intelligence can supersede the necessity of the one man power." But in the meanwhile Steward offers the traditional American ideal. "Without attempting to settle definitely how much common labor is worth,—for it is a broad question,—I will make the claim that no man's compensation should be so low that it will not secure for himself and family a comfortable home—education for his children, and all of the influence to which he is entitled by his capacity, virtue, and industry." [3]

But first and foremost the worker must remember that his wage depends upon the wage of his poorest fellow. The only path to self-help is through helping others. "Think of it, you mechanics, who affect social

[1] Steward, *op. cit.*
[2] Gunton, *op. cit.*
[3] Steward, Pamphlet, cited.

distinctions between the uncultivated laborer and yourself; on election day the capitalist and the common laborer unite to vote you down, and the rest of the year you and the shrewder capitalist unite and keep down and away from you the 'common, unclean laborer.' . . . In the production of wealth there is a king fact or law that rules all others and which may be called the north star of political economy; and it is this: that cheaper ways of doing things will always succeed against dearer ways. . . . Human muscular force must be made dearest, so that it can be driven out of the market and out of the world. . . . In the simple power of the cheaper over the dearer is contained the Divine or natural plan for making the selfishness of men serve each other, as soon as the wealth and intelligence of the more advanced part of them have given them the power to lift up the rest of the race. When selfishness is sufficiently enlightened, it discovers that its own personal interests can not be very well served without serving others. The universal power of the cheapest makes it absolutely impossible for any part of the human race to rise very much higher than the rest. . . . It is somewhat troublesome for the highest to pause in their pleasures and lift up the lowest; but they will be rewarded with more wealth if they do, and be punished with more poverty if they don't." [1]

It will at once be seen that this philosophy of Steward's is far more than a mere theory justifying shorter hours. It is a social philosophy: it lifts labor groups out of their comparatively isolated round of selfish strikes and trade exclusiveness and places them in closest possible relation to the wider group of workers, wherever they may be, of employers, and of the consuming public as a whole. It proclaims that not alone, but only in a group, as a united and coöperating body, can the workers hope to improve their position and secure their desired goal of an assured and relatively equal social status. It thus extended to a broader field that fundamental tenet of unionism, that in union there is strength, that some must forego immediate gain for the sake of the greater ultimate gain of all.

Hence it proved as successful as Marxianism in Europe in uniting and solidifying the laboring class. For Stewardism is essentially a gospel, a missionary philosophy; its only hope of success lies in awakening the workers everywhere to demand a higher standard. The early emphasis placed on an eight-hour day imposed by legislation soon passed; the eight-hour day itself was but a single means for raising that standard of living upon which social improvement depended. Hitherto one trade had sought to organize itself to increase its own bargaining power; now

[1] Steward, *op. cit.*, and *The Power of the Cheaper over the Dearer*, *Doc. Hist.*, VIII.

it was clearly seen that it was necessary to organize all trades, even the lowest, before any could rise very far. Thus it was that both of the great national bodies, the Knights of Labor and the American Federation of Labor, assumed as their most important task the organization of as many trades as possible; hence it was that the K. of L. was particularly interested in the common laborer, as that "cheapest" upon which the price of all labor depended.

Moreover, Stewardism was essentially optimistic. It believed that society was governed by a great "divine law" whereby all men if they resolved to help each other would ipso facto be raising themselves to the heights of prosperity. There was no limit to the goods to be achieved. The higher the wants, the greater the wages, the larger the scale of production, the cheaper the products; all in increasing ratio, it was believed. To start the ball rolling was bound to be hardest; once the eight-hour day prevailed, it would be easy to advance further. Steward had, indeed, no logical ground for stopping at eight hours; but then it is entirely misconstruing the force and the effect of Steward's philosophy to see in the emphasis on the eight-hour day, or, as some writers have done, in the legislative means to secure it, its most important aspect.

Stewardism was not revolutionary; it preserved the capitalistic system of production, and identified the interests of the employer with those of the worker. Most of the preambles to the constitutions of the unions of the present day, drawn up during the period when Stewardism was dominant, contain in some form this insistence on the identity of interest of the two parties, an insistence which seems strange to many contemporary unionists. But this did not mean what the modern employer means by the phrase, that the real interest of the worker is for the employer to make as large profits as possible; it meant that the controlling interest was that of labor, not that of capital. Whatever labor wanted was really best for capital, even though the latter was generally so obtuse as to desire some other end.

Finally, the most important factor in Stewardism for the present investigation is the remarkable way in which it succeeded in blending both of the tendencies that motivate American labor, the desire for individual advantage and the desire for social well-being. The workers must pursue the policy of strikes for shorter hours and higher wages, just as they had done before, while at the same time they could feel that they were satisfying their impulse to advance society as a whole which had hitherto proved rather disastrous to their private interests. Or, to look at the other side, they could go forth to aid all workers through organization and the institution of higher standards with the feeling that in so doing they were really improving their own position. Moreover, both types of men, those who were most interested in social as well as those interested entirely in private interests, could unite upon a common program and a common method. It is doubtful whether a social philosophy better calculated to appeal to the American labor movement in the stage in which it then was, that of a small minority that could hardly hope for any direct control of the ends of social action, could possibly have been devised: for it succeeded in combining those two forces that must be combined in any movement that hopes to achieve success.

The practical emphasis placed by the A. F. L. on Steward's philosophy is evidenced in the prominence in its literature of eight-hour doctrines. George Gunton, Steward's chief follower, author of *Wealth and Progress, The Economic Philosophy of the Eight-Hour Movement*, wrote in 1889 a pamphlet widely circulated as *The Economic and Social Importance of the Eighth-Hour Movement*. George E. MacNeill in 1890 wrote *The Eight-Hour Primer*, in 1893 the pamphlet *The Philosophy of the Labor Movement*. Lemuel Danryid produced *The History and Philosophy of the Eight-Hour Movement* in 1890. During the nineties the eight-hour movement was especially emphasized, and the fundamentals of Stewardism were so impressed into the workers' minds that they have largely continued to operate until the present day. Today the publications of the Federation bear the legend, "8 hours for work, 8 hours for rest, 8 hours for what we will," and the jingle composed by Steward's wife, "Whether you work by the piece or work by the day, decreasing the hours increases the pay." And even though the eight-hour day be now largely achieved, and the direct influence of Steward's gospel have subsided, the indirect and broader effects of it have been incalculably widespread.

It was just as this philosophy was gaining wide popularity that the labor movement took on its characteristic modern form, and became national in scope. We have seen how the International Industrial Assembly, founded on the local trades' assemblies, failed to materialize in 1864. Two years later another congress met at Baltimore, this time under the auspices of the national unions, and formed a National Labor Union. Powderly tells us that the leaders wished to engage in political activity, but realized that the men would not have it; they were concerned solely with the eight-hour question, then at the height of its agitation.[1] They deprecated strikes, seeking the "mutual confidence" of the employ-

[1] Powderly, *op. cit.*, 66.

ers, provided for the expenses of the Union, sought to further organiza-tion, and to reduce the number of the "botch apprentices." Next year they adopted a platform, and they held conventions until 1870.

At first the eight-hour day was paramount in the convention; it seems to have remained so with the members, for as the Union turned to political action it lost the interest and support of its members. In 1866, 1867, and again in 1870, the convention approved coöperation, but without en-thusiasm. The significant note in the conventions was the solidarity felt with the whole laboring class, influenced already by Steward's philosophy. In an address in 1867 A. C. Cameron of Chicago said, "What is wanted, then, is for every union to help inculcate the grand and ennobling idea that the interests of labor are one; that there should be no distinctions of race or nationality, no classifications of Jew or Gentile, Christian or infidel—that that which separates mankind into two great classes, the class that labors and the class that lives by others' labor. . . . If these principles be true, we must seek the coöperation of the African race in America." [1]   The Union accordingly not only welcomed colored and foreign workers; it extended sympathy to "the sewing women and daughters of toil of the United States," advocating "the same rate of wages for equal work for women," and resolving "to do all in our power to open many of the closed avenues of industry to women, and welcome her entering into just competition with men in the industrial race of life." [2]   There was even a resolution inviting the farmers to join, and the "common and unskilled labor to coöperate in our efforts to improve the conditions of the producing classes." [3]   This broadly class-conscious policy included even adherence to the recently organized International Workingmen's Society of Marx; it apparently broke down only where immigration and coolie labor were concerned.

The old American tradition was still strong. In the platform of 1867 it was stated: "We hold these truths to be self-evident, that all men are created equal, that they are endowed by their Creator with certain inalienable rights, that among these are life, liberty, and the pursuit of happiness; that to secure these rights, governments are instituted among men, deriving their just powers from the consent of the governed; that there are but two forms of government, the autocratic and the dem-ocratic . . . that the design of the founders of the republic was to institute a government upon the principle of absolute inherent sover-

---

[1] Cameron, *Address of the Nat. Labor Congress to the Workingmen of the U. S. 1867.*
[2] *Workingman's Advocate*, Aug. 27, 1870.
[3] *Ibid.*

eignty in the people, and that would give to each citizen the largest political and religious liberty compatible with the good order of society, and secure to each the right to enjoy the fruit of his labor and talents, that when laws are enacted destructive of these ends they are without moral binding force, and it is the right and duty of a people to alter and amend or abolish them, and institute such others, founding them upon the principles of equity, as to them may seem most likely to effect their prosperity and happiness. . . . We further hold that all property or wealth is the product of physical or intellectual labor employed in productive industry, and in the distribution of the products of labor. That laborers ought of right, and would under a just monetary system, receive or retain the larger proportion of their productions: that the wrongs, oppressions, and destitutions which laborers are suffering in most departments of legitimate enterprise and useful occupations, do not result from insufficiency of production but from the unfair distribution of the products of labor between non-producing capital and labor." [1] They accordingly advocated banking reform in the spirit of the early or Eastern greenbackism; and other reforms, such as education and the ever-present land problem.

But all these questions stirred the workers themselves but slightly. The leaders' persistence in running into politics finally drove them away. In 1866, after much discussion and opposition, a resolution for political action had been forced through: "Whereas the history and legislation of the past has demonstrated the fact that no confidence whatever can be placed in the pledges or professions of the representatives of existing political parties so far as the interests of the industrial classes are concerned; therefore be it resolved, that the time has come when the workingmen of the United States should cut themselves aloof from party ties and predilections, and organize themselves into a National Labor Party, the object of which shall be to secure the enactment of a law to make 'eight hours' a legal day's work by the National Congress, and the several state legislatures, and the election of men pledged to sustain and represent the interests of the industrial classes. . . . Where a workingman is found available for the office, the preference should invariably be given to such a person." [2] Political action was indeed tried, for the eight-hour day, where a lobby secured a law from Congress in 1868, for banking reform, and for other objects, with little success or result save the alienation of the trade unionists. In 1871 the Union

[1] *Doc. Hist.*, IX, 176.
[2] *Workingman's Advocate*, Sept. 1, 1866.

dissolved into a pure political party. A contemporary comment runs: "The leaders of the National Labor Union have learned nothing and it is to be feared will never learn to understand the labor question. All the great trades organizations having withdrawn previously, with the single exception of the miners, the congress can hardly be called a workingman's convention." [1] American workingmen, continues the observer, simply will not go into politics. This is confirmed by Powderly, who claims that demagogues and cheap politicians had repelled the workers from the National Labor Union. [2]

The history of the National Labor Union epitomizes the struggle that took place in the labor movement from 1870 to 1890. On the one side were those who, serving their apprenticeship during the sixties and seventies, had absorbed much of the spirit of that time, its general faith in reform by political action, in panaceas and in coöperation; this group comprised most of the leaders and a large minority of the workers, particularly the less skilled. On the other side were the great mass of the workers, still predominantly skilled craftsmen, for whom unionism meant solely more pay and shorter hours; this group took in the great national unions and their officials. Yet it must not be thought that the struggle can be phrased in terms of the social against the individual tendency; it was a question rather of method than principle that furnished the source of contention. The great strikes of 1877, and even more those of 1885-6, made it plain to the workers that in an industrialized community it was useless for them to rely upon either public or governmental support, or upon the compassion of the employers; thereafter the methods of business unionism steadily gained, while at the same time the self-centered craft unions came more and more to realize the necessity of organizing all the workers. The eighties, which witnessed the duel of the Knights and the Federation, saw a struggle, not between a humanitarian and a strictly selfish form of organization, but rather between an organization which attempted to combine a philosophy of coöperation, education, and general "reform," and a machinery designed with those ends in view, with the practical aims and methods of business unionism, and an organization whose philosophy and method were in close harmony. In the Knights the bond between those who wanted more pay and those who wanted to reform society was entirely artificial; to accomplish one end the worker had to forego the other, and the attempt to work for both resulted inevitably in failure. In the Federa-

[1] Copybook of Central Com., N. A. Fed., *Doc. Hist.*, IX, 360.
[2] Powderly, *op. cit.*, 90 ff.

tion, on the other hand, there was a natural and very easy progress from strict business unionism to the improvement of the conditions of the whole working class; it was necessary, not to turn about and face in another direction, but only to push those policies a little further which had already been successfully employed, in order to pass from the smaller to the larger goal. In the Knights, after a strike for a living wage, one was expected to engage in coöperation and in politics; in the Federation, one had only to go on and strike for the eight-hour day. And the event has proved how even those benefits which the Knights promised and which the Federation ignored if it did not oppose, have come about with the gradual development and unfolding of the principles lying back of the seemingly reactionary successful organization.

The National Labor Union had traveled further and further away from the immediate ends of the workers until it became in 1871 a political party; it marked the height of that second or crudely optimistic phase which we have seen recur in the history of the labor movement. It was but natural that the reaction should come upon its failure. The menace of industrialism, which had prompted the N. L. U., had only increased since 1866; consequently the great national unions, the Molders, the Machinists, the Coopers, and the Printers, united in 1873 in calling for a new convention that they might, "profiting by our dear bought experience, build up and perfect an organization such as was contemplated in Baltimore in 1866." [1] The new congress was to be a protection against "the rapid and alarming concentration of capital, placed under the control of a few men," which was bringing about "a rapid decrease of our power as Trade Unions in comparison with that of Capital," [2] and it was promised that it would not degenerate into a politician's paradise, but would "remain purely an Industrial Association, having for its sole and only object the securing to the producer the full share of all he produces." In the platform adopted when the Congress met in July the delegates protested against the "pauperization and degradation of the masses," advocated "a system which will insure to the laborer the fruits of his toil," and the "organization, consolidation, and coöperative effort of the producing masses, as a stepping-stone to that education that will in the future lead to more advanced action." [3] The congress shunned those questions which had led to the fall of the National Labor Union, restricting its attention to purely trade union matters such as

[1] *Workingman's Advocate*, May 3, 1873.
[2] *Ibid.*
[3] Powderly, *op. cit.*, 110.

apprenticeship, prison labor, and immigration. Although preferring arbitration to strikes, it made a provision, through financial support and effective publicity, for a strong protective policy by the congress.

What would have been the fate of this attempt at centralized business unionism had not the panic of 1873 occurred two months later it is impossible to conjecture. The Industrial Congress bravely held a meeting the next year at Rochester, and changed its name to the Industrial Brotherhood, but by 1875 there were few delegates left; the unions were too busy fighting their foes to think of federation. But the 1874 meeting is memorable for the adoption of a preamble so well expressing the spirit of the leaders of labor in the seventies that it was later annexed by the Knights of Labor as their own.

"The recent alarming development and aggression of aggregate wealth, which, unless checked, will inevitably lead to the pauperization and degradation of the toiling masses, renders it imperative, if we desire to enjoy the blessings of life, that a check should be placed upon this power and upon unjust accumulation, and a system adopted which will secure to the laborer the fruits of his toil, and as this much desired object can be accomplished only by the thorough unification of labor, and the united efforts of those who obey the divine injunction that 'in the sweat of thy brow shalt thou eat thy bread,' we have formed the Industrial Brotherhood with a view to securing the organization, direction, by coöperative effort, of the power of the industrial classes; and we submit to the world the objects sought to be accomplished by our organization, calling upon all who believe in securing 'the greatest good of the greatest number' to aid and assist us. I. To bring within the folds of organization every department of productive industry, making knowledge the standpoint for action, and industrial and moral worth, not wealth, the true standard of individual and national greatness. II. To secure to the toilers a proper share of the wealth that they create; more of the leisure that rightfully belongs to them; more society advantages; more of the benefits, privileges and emoluments of the world, in a word, all those rights and privileges necessary to make them capable of enjoying, appreciating, defending, and perpetuating the blessings of republican institutions." [1]

The persistent desire to retain the old status comes out in the ritual, where it is stated that "the great aim and object of our organization is to secure for the industrial classes that position in the world and in society to which they are entitled as the producers of the necessaries

[1] Powderly, 117.

and comforts of life;" the new Stewardism and solidarity of labor, in the statement, "The conditions of one part of our class can not be improved permanently unless all are improved together."[1] The indomitable idealistic spirit had crept in here, and as a result the trade unionists, still struggling to keep their heads above water, were far from enthusiastic. In summarizing these efforts to effect a national body Powderly interprets for us the general feeling of the average unionist: "It's no use in having so many organizations; we have our trade union and that is enough; we are not in favor of allowing our affairs to be discussed by those who know nothing about them, and *we will not associate with the common every day laborers in any organization of labor;* we do not object to meeting with them elsewhere, but to place them on the same level with ourselves is asking too much. Pretty soon they will want to take our places at the bench, and it is time to nip this thing in the bud."[2] The significant phrase here is "at the bench;" the skilled workers were soon to see the common laborer taking their places, not at the bench, but at the machine, which made a world of difference.

The hard times that set in with the panic of 1873 lasted till 1879; for the labor movement it was a time of stress and great searching of heart. Reduction of wages everywhere, if not actual unemployment, threatened to engulf the old national unions; the employers seized the welcome opportunity to attempt to break them up entirely through lockouts, blacklists, and other persecution. The movement was practically driven underground; this was the great period of secrecy and hidden rituals, for no man dared openly to lead in union activities when it meant virtual exclusion from employment at the hands of every master. Some it drove to predatory acts, to murder and arson. This was the time when the Molly Maguires, who speedily for the general public became the stock type of unionist, were pursuing their course of crime in the Pennsylvania coal fields. Others it forced into Marxianism and revolutionary socialism; still others into greenbackism and political reform. And some it led to abandon hope of securing any aid from the public at large, either in a general organization or a "people's party, and to concentrate their efforts upon building up a strong business unionism upon a "practical, non-theoretical basis."

It was in these years that the Knights of Labor, formed by Uriah Stephens amongst the Philadelphia garment workers in 1868, took shape and developed its "First Principles." There were many locals still in

[1] Powderly, 121.
[2] *Ibid.*, 127.

existence, remnants of the national unions of 1873, and locals which had never formed national organizations; out of this material Stephens was able to build up local and district assemblies, although, since he did not propose by immediate strikes to secure higher wages the members often left after a few months of seemingly ineffectual activities.   The original aims of the Knights, although kept secret, were very moderate. "It was not the intention to create an antagonism between labor and capital.   No conflict with legitimate enterprise was contemplated." [1] The first and greatest aim was education, and the formation of "a healthy public opinion on the subject of labor (the only creator of values or capital) and the justice of its receiving a full, just share of the values or capital it has created." The second aim was legislation harmonizing the interests of capital and labor, and making for better working conditions.   In accordance with these broadly social aims, the form of the organization was the antithesis of the exclusive craft union. This had failed to recognize "the right of all to have a say in the affairs of one.   It was because the trade union failed to recognize the rights of man, and looked only to the rights of the trades man, that the Knights of Labor became a possibility." [2]

The Knights recognized no craft, trade, or even industrial lines; it included all men, save doctors, bankers, and liquor-dealers, and was founded upon geographical, not functional, lines.   It thus appealed to the unskilled laborer, and just as surely tended to repel the craftsman; in this early period the only successful strike it could hold was in a locality like a mining camp where functional and geographical distribution coincided.   Otherwise it was only by political action, or by a general strike of all workers, that it could hope to secure results.   But this was to the founders an advantage, for they scarcely counted the strike as one of their weapons.

Stephens declared his ideals thus: "There should be a greater participation in the profits of labor by the industrious and intelligent laborer. In the present arrangement of labor and capital the condition of the employee is simply that of wage-slavery, capital dictating, labor submitting; capital superior, labor inferior.   This is an artificial and man-created condition, not God's arrangement and order, for it degrades man and ennobles mere pelf; it demeans those who live l y useful labor . . . What is the remedy?   Cultivate Friendship among the great brotherhood of toil; learn to respect industry in the person of the intel-

[1] Powderly, 149.
[2] *Ibid.*, 156.

ligent worker; unmake the shams of life by deference to the humble but
useful craftsman; beget concert of action by conciliation; confidence
by just and upright conduct towards each other; mutual respect by
dignified deportment, and wise counsel by what of wisdom or ability
God in his wisdom and goodness may have endowed us with. . . The
Knights of Labor builds upon the immutable basis of the Fatherhood
of God, and the logical principle of the Brotherhood of Man. Its work
is the complete emancipation of wealth-producers from the thralldom
of wage-slavery.' '[1]

These were the broad, idealistic, if not visionary, and generally social principles upon which the Knights set forth to aid the workers in
a contemplated campaign of education and legislative reform, culminating in a political party as the various local assemblies made the numbers sufficient.   With a few modifications the "first principles" of the
Knights, like the preamble they borrowed from the Industrial Brotherhood, represented the spirit of the late sixties when the first successes
of the new unions had given great impetus to the ever ready spirit of
social idealism.   But Powderly, the successor of Stephens as Grand
Master Workman, was destined to have many rude shocks from the
capitalists and the public whose philanthropic coöperation he sought,
and even more from the oppressed workers, who, beholding in his Order
a champion in armor come to deliver them, flocked to his banner and
eagerly placed powerful weapons in his hands.

The first rude awakening came in 1877.   The preceding year a convention of socialists, greenbackers, and Knights had been held in Pittsburg
to attempt the federation of all the elements in the labor world, trade
unionists, Marxian socialists, political reformers and the rest, which had
naturally come to naught through the effort of embodying these con-
tradictory aims in one group.   In the summer of 1877, however, the
industrial depression reached its lowest ebb; wages, already reduced to
the breaking point, were lowered one step further.   The result was a
spontaneous outbreak of strikes, starting with the unskilled railroad
workers and spreading like wildfire throughout the land, culminating in
three days of rioting and destruction of railroad property at Pittsburgh;
the militia were everywhere called out to put down the workmen, and for
the first time in American history Federal troops battled with strikers in
city streets.   The effect was instantaneous.   Stephens, and the leaders of
the workers in general, who since the sixties had been dallying with the
various social reforms in the confidence that they were championing

[1] Powderly, 161, 168.

"the people" against the tyranny of the newly-created capitalistic class, and that they had but to raise the banners for all good Americans to rally to the defence of the national tradition, had been offering the hand of reconciliation even to the capitalists. The answer they received was the erection of huge fortress-like armories throughout the industrial cities, the revival of conspiracy laws, and a willing acquiescence in the repressive measures of the blacklist and the lockout.

The result upon the worker was threefold. Immediately it sent a wave of solidarity and class-consciousness throughout the ranks; never was hatred of the capitalist and sympathy with fellow-worker so wide-spread in American history as in the next decade. Labor, which had been urged again and again to turn to politics, with no avail, united eagerly with the farmers' greenback party and in the next two years achieved substantial victories at the polls. But this political expression of the resentment of the workers soon burnt itself out; the greenback platform that bound them to the farmers became meaningless with the disappearance in 1878 of the premium on gold and the resumption of specie payment, the Democratic politicians managed to corral the positions and machinery of the Greenback Labor Party, and, perhaps most important of all, prosperity set in in 1879 and made economic action once more profitable.

More important ultimately than the immediate political direction given by the strikes of 1877 was the great impetus imparted to business unionism, that is, to an opportunist policy of rejecting the appeal to the public and to the reason of the capitalist in favor of taking all possible measures to increase the bargaining power of labor itself. The appeal of the workers had been met by bayonets; it was obviously impossible to put faith in generous policies which could not hope to be effective until a long process of education had taken place. These ultimate aims were not rejected; they were merely postponed while the workers were insuring a roof over their heads. Indeed the "first principles" of the Knights, retained many loyal adherents even while they were being relegated to the background as practical measures of immediate protection and relief. But it cannot be gainsaid that, in spite of the persistence officially of the social philosophy of the Knights, the strikes of 1877 marked the turning point at which the mass of the workers definitely foreswore a primary interest in social reform for the grinding business of pulling themselves up slowly by their own efforts. Not until they had made a clear and a secure place for themselves within American business itself, until they could stand up to the capitalist and say him nay, would they again, as a settled policy, seek to transcend the framework of business life.

The attitude which thus became ascendent, in its resolve to proceed one step at a time as well as in its note of some further aim lying hid, biding its time, is to be found in the testimony of Strasser of the Cigarmakers before a Senate Committee. Strasser had been a Marxian; he was with Samuel Gompers the leader of the "new" or business unionism.

Q. You are seeking to improve home matters first?

A. Yes, sir, I look first to the trade I represent; I look first to cigars, to the interests of the men who employ me to represent their interest.

Chairman: I was only asking you in regard to your ultimate ends.

Witness: We have no ultimate ends. We are going on from day to day. We are fighting only for immediate objects—objects that can be realized in a few years.

By Mr. Call: You want something better to eat and to wear, and better houses to live in?

A. Yes, we want to dress better and to live better, and become better citizens generally.

The Chairman: I see that you are a little sensitive lest it should be thought that you are a mere theorizer. I do not look upon you in that light at all.

The Witness: Well, we say in our constitution that we are opposed to theorists, and I have to represent the organization here. We are all practical men." [1]

When in Rome do as the Romans do, especially if one be bent upon overthrowing the Roman citadel!

Though as we shall see this business unionism ultimately captured the Knights, it was in the new and the reorganized older national trade unions that it first became powerful. It is significant that Strasser was elected president of the Cigarmakers in the very year of the great strikes. He and the president of the New York local, Samuel Gompers, impressed by the failure of a strike of their own in 1877 against the tenement house system, resolved to recreate their union, and later if possible the entire labor movement, upon the lines of the strong British trade unions. In the convention of 1879 they had their way. The international officers were given complete control over the local unions; an immediate gain in members was sacrificed, through the institution of high membership dues, to a large protective fund; and an extensive benefit system was introduced to hold the union together when hard times, hitherto the death of all previous American organizations, had made the prospect of immediate advancement uncertain. Moreover, the central officers were empowered to transfer funds from a strong to a weak local. As a consequence of this

[1] Quoted in Commons, II, 309.

policy, the union increased from 2,729 in 1879 to 14,604 in 1881.[1] Slowly but surely, although it was not until the emergence of the A. F. L. in the late eighties that the movement became general, the national unions reorganized upon the model of the cigarmakers, encouraged as they were by the good times following 1879 to extend their policy of strikes and boycotts.

Meanwhile the effect of the 1877 strikes upon the Knights of Labor had been more doubtful. Officially the Order denied all connection with the strikes; they played no large part in their methods. Actually many members took part in them, and thereafter, for all its high principles, the Knights became an aggressive and protective body. Moreover, for those strikers who were largely unskilled and unconnected with any national organization, it was the easiest course for them to declare their adhesion to the Order in a body, though their motives might not include a single one of the rather middle-class aims for which the Order ostensibly stood. Throughout its history the Knights were recruited largely from such locals, which passed within and without the fold with equal celerity and facility; the usual procedure was first to declare a strike, and then afterwards, as a source of strength and prestige, to join the Knights for such period as might be advisable. Theoretically a highly centralized body, the Order never seems to have maintained the firm hold upon its members which the elaborate benefit systems and the fairly representative character of the conventions of the national unions gave them. The whole organization, in fact, was modeled somewhat on the lines of the soviet system of Russia: Local Assemblies, comprising all the trades in a given locality, sent delegates to the District Assemblies, and these in turn were represented in the General Assembly, which thus, lacking any direct contact with the locals, could not appreciably influence their action. This state of affairs made for sudden and large accretions in membership in time of stress and just as rapid falling off when no more was to be gained; but, and herein lies its importance, it was the only method whereby, outside of strong industrial unions, the semi-skilled and the unskilled could be reached.

The direct result of the 1877 strikes upon the Knights of Labor was to bring about that national organization that rivalry between the Philadelphia and Pittsburgh District Assemblies had hitherto prevented. A convention at Reading in 1878 became the first General Assembly, adopted the preamble of the Industrial Brotherhood, and declared for the lifting of the veil of secrecy, which was finally done in 1881. The specific measures proposed were, the establishment of bureaus of labor statistics,

[1] Quoted in Commons, II, 308.

the establishment of coöperative institutions, productive and distributive, the freedom of the public lands, employers' liability, the weekly wage, mechanics' lien laws, "the substitution of arbitration for strikes, wherever employers and employees are willing to meet on equitable grounds," the abolition of child labor under fourteen, of prison labor, the securing of equal pay for equal work for both sexes, the eight-hour day, and financial reform. These measures all obtained a certain allegiance from the workers, who would undoubtedly have welcomed them all; yet Powderly confesses that the whole preamble and its hangover of ideas from the sixties represented the notions of the founders and leaders, and not those of the men themselves. They advocated pure trade unionism as much more successful in strikes, whereas Stephens and Powderly placed all their faith in educative measures.[1] Almost the only point of the "first principles" that really attracted the workers was its class-consciousness, typified in its mottoes: "That is the most perfect government in which an injury to one is the concern of all"[2] and, "When bad men combine, the good must associate, else they will fall, one by one, the unpitied sacrifice in a contemptible struggle."[3] The Knights were strong, when they were strong, because of this universality of appeal; yet their strength was exerted rather upon the unskilled who looked eagerly upon them from without than upon those who from within realized the structural weakness of the Order.

The years following the centralization were mainly occupied with strikes conducted by the District Assemblies. Growth was comparatively slow, from 20,000 in 1879 to 50,000 in 1883,[4] with almost as many withdrawals each year as new members. The question of politics as a method of carrying out the legislative ends of the Order, was finally and characteristically disposed of by leaving the decision to the local assemblies. During this period old unions were reorganized and new ones formed, which, on attaining maturity, left the mother order and formed national trade unions of their own. The strikes, despite the obvious unsuitability of the Knights' structure for such tests, were largely confined to a single trade, and were almost uniformly unsuccessful; the Telegraphers' strike of 1883 was typical. The fact that this was a period of prosperity when the national trade unions were generally gaining their demands made this a particularly heavy blow at the Order's popularity. Powderly, who

[1] Powderly, *op. cit.*, 272.
[2] *Ibid.*, 245.
[3] *Constitution of the Knights of Labor*, 1878.
[4] Commons, II, 343–344.

had succeeded Stephens, though personally bent on putting into practice his coöperative ideas, was compelled in 1883 to confess that not coöperation but strikes was what the members wanted. And when these failed it was to the boycott that the Order turned.

The industrial revolution first made its appearance on a large scale during the Civil War; yet it was productive, in the labor movement, of organization largely in the semi-skilled trades. For thirty years thereafter the craft unions were practically dominant. It was not till the eighties that the country became really industrialized, that railroads were extended to every hamlet, and that factories sprang up in great numbers. And it was not till the eighties that labor organization and industrial unrest became a really potent factor in our national life. After the great outburst of the mid-decade labor settled back into the relatively stable form from which it has but recently started to emerge.

The prosperity of the early eighties waned in 1884, and did not recover until three years later. Wages were on every hand reduced, but, unlike earlier depressions, not very much unemployment resulted. This, together with the increased strength of the unions, resulting in part from the adoption of the benefit system and in part from the natural growth of industry, sufficed to keep the organizations above water and to give them great fighting strength. Many strikes, the first resort, having failed in 1884, the Knights turned to boycotting and achieved considerable success with this formidable weapon. But in 1885 conditions improved a trifle, and at once strikes broke out spontaneously throughout the country. It was the unskilled, the lumbermen, the lowest-paid railroad workers, those whom no trade union would accept, who burst forth in a universal outcry for better conditions. It could hardly be said that the Knights of Labor, though the direct gainer, was the cause of these industrial conflicts; they rather came as spontaneous protests, and then, after the men had struck, they affiliated with the Knights. The employers, taking alarm, generally forced a second strike to beat the newly formed union. Thus the shopmen of the Union Pacific Railroad prevented a wage reduction in 1884, joined the Knights, and had to strike again. A similar strike, supported by the railroad brotherhoods, occurred on the roads controlled by the notorious Jay Gould. The next year would have seen a further general strike had not Gould met the Knights and concluded a bargain with them. This dramatic event, in which Powderly conferred on equal terms with the most powerful and the most feared capitalist in the country, inspired among the workingmen in all parts of the country respect and delirious admiration for the Knights of

Labor. Here at last was a powerful protector; at once they struck and appealed to the Order for aid. It was estimated that the Order probably contained as many as five million members! Congress and the state-legislatures went out of their way to conciliate this labor vote. Never, not even in 1877, had such a wave of solidarity and hatred for the "capitalists" passed through the labor ranks of the country; men declared themselves ready to give sympathy, money, even their lives to aid their fellows. They spurned the very idea of arbitrating when they belonged to such a powerful organization.

To the outsider the Knights of Labor seemed destined to become the dominant and exclusive labor organization in the country. With an actual membership in 1886 of over half a million, and a reputation worthy of ten times that size, the Order seemed invincible. But none knew better than Powderly himself, in the midst of his pride over becoming a figure of national importance, that at bottom the Order was far from a success. None of the new members cared the slightest for the principles for which it stood, principles that hesitated to employ the strike at all; few of them had any direct or lasting connection with the Knights. It was just at this crisis that the Order proved its inherent unfitness: in spite of all the emphasis it placed upon education, it was unable to accomplish any real discipline or training of the thousands who had literally forced themselves into its ranks. There was nothing to bridge the gap between the pure self-interest, which had led the men to join, and the social idealism of the leaders and their first principles. The two strains would not merge; and so the Knights gave way to another organization in which they would. Even in 1886, at the very height of the power of the Order, the workers had repudiated such a baseless social idealism and clung to the methods of business unionism; it was but a question of time before they would desert to an organization whose structure corresponded more closely with their aim.

That structure had already been started. In 1881 there had met at Pittsburgh a small body of delegates to form the Federation of Organized Trades and Labor Unions of the United States and Canada, all members of trade unions and some of them disgusted with the poor showing of the Knights. The body was organized on the model of the Trades Union Congress of Great Britain; its aims were to be, like that body, an organ of publicity and propaganda, and it was hoped to establish an American replica of the Parliamentary Committee of the British congress.[1] The call had emanated from the same men who had already undertaken to

---

[1] Commons, II, 319.

reconstruct American unionism on the British basis; Gompers took a prominent part, ran for president, and was defeated only because of his intimate association with the socialists. But, far more important, he was made chairman of the Committee in the Plan of Organization. A contemporary writer in the *Pittsburgh Commercial Gazette*, with partisan intent, states: "Mr. Gompers is the leader of the Socialistic element, which is pretty well represented in the Congress, and one of the smartest men present. It is thought that the attempt will be made to capture the organization for Mr. Gompers (for president) as the representative of the Socialists, and if such an attempt is made, whether it succeeds or not, there will likely be some lively work, as the delegates opposed to Socialism are determined not to be controlled by it. If the Socialists do not have their own way, they may bolt, as they have always done in the past. If they do bolt, the power of the proposed organization will be so seriously crippled as almost to destroy its usefulness." [1]

But Gompers withdrew to save the organization, and it adopted a declaration of principles that has to this day remained in the constitution of the American Federation of Labor. "Whereas, a struggle is going on in the nations of the civilized world between the oppressors and the oppressed in all countries, a struggle between capital, and labor, which must grow in intensity from year to year and work disastrous results to the toiling millions of all nations if not combined for mutual protection and benefit; the history of the wage-workers of all countries is the history of constant struggle and misery engendered by ignorance and disunion; whereas the history of the non-producers of all ages proves that the minority, throughly organized, may work wonders for good or evil; it behooves the representatives of the workers of North America, in Congress assembled, to adopt such measures and disseminate such principles among the people of our country as will unite them for all time to come and to secure the recognition of the rights to which they are justly entitled, and conforming to the old adage, 'In Union there is strength,' the formation of a Federation embracing every trade and labor organization in North America, a union founded upon a basis as broad as the land we live in, is our only hope. The past history of trade unions proves that small organizations, well conducted, have accomplished great good, though their efforts have not been of that lasting character which a thorough unification of all the different branches of industrial workers is bound to secure." [2]

[1] *Proceedings, First Session, Fed. of Org. Trades and Labor Unions.*
[2] *Ibid.*

The objects were declared to be the encouragement and formation of trades and labor unions, of national and international trade unions, and of trade and labor assemblies and councils, and to secure legislation favorable to the interests of the industrial classes. To this latter end there was instituted a legislative committee to serve as a lobby, on the British model. The platform included incorporation of unions, to protect their property, compulsory education, abolition of child labor, uniform apprentice laws, the eight-hour day, ("Grasp one idea, less hours better pay") protection from prison labor, from immigrants, and from the truck system.[1]

But the congress had little success with legislation, and by 1884 it was decided to abandon British inspiration and to embark on an extensive eight-hour program. The report stated: "This much has been determined by the history of the national eight-hour law—it is useless to wait for legislation in this matter. In the world of economic reform the working classes must depend upon themselves for the enforcement of measures as well as for their conception. A united demand for a shorter working day, backed by thorough organization, will prove vastly more effective than the enactment of a thousand laws depending for their enforcement upon the pleasure of aspiring politicians or sycophantic department officials." Accordingly the congress abandoned its purely advisory character by resolving on a general eight-hour strike for May 1 ,1886, and called upon the Knights of Labor to coöperate with them.[2]

The reasons for this resolution put through in spite of the smallness and the general indifference of the members, were complex. The Knights, first of all, gained their power through strikes for a retention of wage rates; if the trade unions took up the eight-hour strike, so popular a few years before, they could greatly increase their prestige. That this actually resulted is shown by the great increase in membership and in locals in the next two years. For the majority, the eight-hour day appealed as an aid in "making work;" but Stewardism was rapidly gaining strength at this time, and it is of the essence of Stewardism that it merges, in practice, with the make-work theories. Thus in 1882 the two motives were blended in a speech in the convention: "The eight-hour day will furnish more work at increased wages. We declare it will permit the possession and enjoyment of more wealth by those who create it. It will diminish the power of the rich over the poor, not by

[1] A. F. L., *Proceedings*, 1st Convention.
[2] *Ibid.*, Fourth Convention.

making the rich poorer and the poor richer. It will create the conditions necessary for the education and the intellectual advancement of the masses. It will not disturb, jar, confuse, or throw out of order the present wage system of labor. It is a measure that will permanently increase wages without at the same time increasing the cost of production of wealth. It will decrease the poverty and increase the wealth of all wage laborers. And it will, after a few years, gradually merge the wage system into a system of industrial coöperation in which wages will represent the earnings and not (as now) the necessities of the wage laborer." [1]

The Knights of Labor was at the height of its meteoric career. Powderly had little faith in Stewardism, or the eight-hour in general; he was, besides, rather jealous of the Federation. Nothing was done about coöperating in the general strike, and just before May 1, 1886, he sent out a secret circular advising against it. But the workers in general knew nothing of this secret disapproval, and flocked to the Knights in greater numbers than ever. In March a great strike broke out on the Gould lines, marked by almost as much violence as those of 1877; before this had been settled, the eight-hour strike began. The unions, deserted by the officials of the Knights, were nevertheless successful in securing large reductions in hours in many trades; but they never forgave Powderly for his lack of support. And on May 3 occurred the Haymarket bombing in Chicago, which caused an instant revulsion, not only on the part of the great mass of the American people, but on the part of the workers themselves. As Gompers put it, "The effect of that bomb was that it not only killed the policemen, but it killed our eight-hour movement for that year and for a few years after, notwithstanding we had absolutely no connection with these people." [2]

The Knights of Labor subsided almost as rapidly as it had grown. In the beginning of 1887 it had grown to 700,000 members; in 1890, but 100,000.[3] By 1887, too, the bulk of the membership had shifted from the unskilled workers of the cities to the small tradesmen and artisans of the country towns, those who were attracted more by its general policy of uplift than by the benefit offered by strikes; and in the early nineties it became allied with the Farmers' Alliance and the Populists, replacing Powderly in 1893 with J. R. Sovereign, an Iowa farmer. In its decline it remained true to its "first principles;" and the fact that it

[1] A. F. L., *History, Encyclopedia, and Reference Book*, 215.
[2] Industrial Commission, *Report*, VII, 623.
[3] Commons, 482, II.

was to the farmers that it made its appeal reveals not only the persistence of the ideal of Jeffersonian democracy, but even more how this ideal, in its original form, had ceased to be, as it had been in the eighties, the aim of the worker. The effect of the industrial revolution and of the great mass of foreign labor, which had no traditional affiliations with Jeffersonianism, could not be better illustrated than in the strangeness with which the following statement of the traditional American ideal, which in 1865 would have aroused a burst of enthusiasm, fell upon the ears of the unionists of the nineties:

"The order of the Knights of Labor is not so much intended to adjust the relationship between the employer and the employee as to adjust natural resources and productive facilities to the common interests of the whole people, that all who wish may work for themselves, independent of large employing corporations and companies. It is not founded on the question of adjusting wages, but on the question of abolishing the wage-system and the establishment of a coöperative industrial system. When its real mission is accomplished, poverty will be reduced to a minimum, and the land dotted over with peaceful, happy homes. Then, and not till then, will the Order die." [1]

The workers preferred the more immediate gains to be had from the national trade unions; they flocked to them in increasing numbers, and the history of the decade from 1885 to 1895 is a history of the growth of the American Federation of Labor, which had changed its name from that of Federation of Organized Trades in 1886, at the expense of the Knights.

The rapid decline of the Knights of Labor did not mean that all the workers lost returned to a state of disorganization. Rather it signified that they had withdrawn bodily from the Order to found national unions of their own, on the Federation model. The Knights, as we have seen, had recruited its membership from men to whom not its first principles but its strike policy had appealed, and these men furnished a fertile soil for business unionism. Back in 1879 permission had been given to "sojourners" to join one local assembly that they might later organize assemblies "of their own trade." Moreover, it was resolved that "trades organized as trades may select an executive officer of their own, who may have charge of their organization, and organize local assemblies of the trade in any part of the country, and attach them to the D. A. controlling said trade . . . that trades so organized be allowed

[2] General Assembly, Proceedings, 1894, 1.

to hold delegate conventions on matters pertaining to their trades."[1] This meant that business trade unionism was allowed to form national unions within the Knights; and as time went on the strictly workingman membership came to be organized in District Assemblies which were all but in name trade unions. The first of these was the window-glass workers, but soon other trades, in addition to those which like the miners were by their nature industrial and not general, joined the order in a body. Old trades unions, like the Knights of St. Crispin, the strong shoemakers' union of the sixties which had been greatly weakened by the introduction of machinery, were taken over and reorganized. In 1881 D. M. W. Thompson wrote: "I am sorry to say that I found very few of the principles of our Order in practice. In fact, there seems to be a general ignorance, or disregard of the principles of our organization. The older ideas of the former trade associations seem to predominate and control the actions of the locals generally."[2]

In 1884 permission was given to form national trade assemblies, and, after a set-back with the rush of the unskilled in the next two years, this movement proceeded rapidly. By 1887 there were at least 27 national Trade Assemblies,[3] and P. J. McGuire of the Federation could rightly say, "The Knights of Labor are now taking lessons from the trade unions, and are forming themselves on National Trade District lines, which are simply the skeletons of trade unions without their flesh and blood."[4] As business unionism thus grew in great strides in the heart of the Knights, the Trade Assemblies one by one broke loose, formed international unions, and joined the A. F. L. This movement was caused both by a natural affinity to the Federation unions and by a growing disaffection for the Knights' principles, and by the bad name which the Order had gained from the events of 1886. Moreover, the Knights of Labor by their aggressive tactics drove the Federation into open warfare and scabbing, and when it became impossible to belong to both organizations there was little doubt which side the trades would espouse. By the early nineties, when the Knights definitely disappeared as a labor organization, it was no longer a question of business unionism versus social idealism; it was merely which type of organization was best suited to the universal spirit of business unionism.

What, then, are the reasons for the non-success of the Knights of La-

---

[1] *Proceedings*, 1879, 72.
[2] *Philadelphia Journal of United Labor*, May, 1881.
[3] Commons, II, 428.
[4] *Carpenter*, Oct., 1887.

bor? Are they that the craft and not the industrial union must be the basis of a strong labor movement? Are they that the workers prefer their private advantage and the gains which exclusive craft business unionism gives them to the more social and disinterested aims of improving the conditions of the entire community? Both answers have been given, but neither, it appears after a careful investigation, is justified. As to the first the Order never stood for industrial unionism in any sense; the local assembly was not made up of all the workers employed in a given industry, but was mixed and corresponded to what is known in the Federation as a "labor union," a body of workers made up without regard to either craft or industrial lines. The only organization within the knights, before the growth of the trade assemblies, which was made industrial by its regional distribution, was the assembly of the coalminers; and far from proving that the industrial union is valueless, this union, which joined the A. F. L. in 1890 as the United Mine Workers of America, has become the strongest union in the Federation.

As to the second answer, we have seen that the basic fault with the Knights of Labor was not that it tried to combine the self-interest of the workers' desire to gain a more stable and more equal status in society with the idealistic aim of raising every one to a better position through general political and social reform, but rather that it made no attempt at all to combine and merge them, and to create an educative situation in which the broader would inevitably develop out of the narrower motive. This the A. F. L. with its underlying principle of Stewardism, which linked the good of one group up directly with the good of all, was able to effect, though only after a long and arduous training. The Knights' structure failed because, like the cosmopolitanism of the eighteenth century in international relations, it failed to take into account the solid foundation of group interests and group loyalties upon which it must ground itself. The industrial structure is not centralized, but federalized; and to control it effectually labor must organize on parallel lines. The only state of industry with which the Knights of Labor was equipped to cope was the homogeneous farming community, or else, by a political general strike, with society as a whole.

Not only had not the industrial revolution progressed far enough to bring about a real solidarity of interests in all classes of labor, but even if it had the structure was unsuited. The unskilled could not be effectually organized until the growth of large bodies of capital and the subdivision of labor had brought vividly home to the craft unions the truth of Steward's contention that only by raising the lowest could the highest hope to raise themselves. The Knights' structure was thus either belated or premature.

Moreover, we must not overlook what was brought forward by knights themselves as the gravest defect of their order, the extreme centralization which concentrated great power in the hands of executives who, as it happened, were out of touch with the wishes of the rank and file. The District Assembly was given supreme power over its Local Assemblies, and the General Assembly over the District Assemblies; while the general officers were elected at two removes from the workers. Consequently, in view of a situation affording little flexibility to adjust specific situations (there was the same constitution for every local and district assembly) and but slightly democratic and responsive to the control of the membership, it was to be expected that serious internal troubles would arise. Thus in 1894 a large number of delegates, including National Trades Assembly 135, the miners, were locked out of the General Assembly and withdrew to form a rival Independent Order of the Knights of Labor of their own, adopting a constitution " which was so framed as to prevent the general officers from exercising autocratic power, as they have been and are doing in the old Knights of Labor, for the purpose of continuing themselves in office." [1] Powderly was severely attacked for a number of his actions, and in general a strong reaction against a central body with great powers favored the looser structure of the Federation.

We have thus far traced the general development of ideas in the labor movement from its industrial beginnings in the Civil War period until the American Federation of Labor arose into a dominating position in 1890. Thereafter, interesting and varied as were the events that marked the history of the unions, the type tended to remain quite stable; everywhere business unionism under the aegis of Samuel Gompers was dominant. Inasmuch as it can hardly be claimed that even today the type has been superseded, and as such business unionism seems to represent a fairly permanent stage in American labor history, it is requisite to pause here and undertake, more fully than has hitherto been done, a careful consideration of the aims, the philosophy, and the implications contained in the activities of that type of group individualism we have called business unionism.

[1] *Official Handbook, Independent Order of the Knights of Labor*, 1896.

8. BUSINESS UNIONISM—RELATIONS WITHIN THE GROUP

OUR modern industrial civilization rests largely upon the theory of the freedom of contract. When a man has a piece of goods which he has made he takes it to another, and the two freely bargain upon the price to be paid for it; what that price shall be is determined by the amount of the commodity available and the eagerness with which the second individual desires to secure it, and must under no conditions be the subject of political interferences on the part of the government, under penalty of entirely disorganizing the machinery of production. This theory has been also applied by those who desire to employ workmen, with the approval of the vast majority of the community, to the commodity which those workmen have to dispose of. Those considerations which govern the price and purchase of the raw materials necessary to the process of manufacture have been kept in view with regard to that essential raw material, human labor. In buying bales of cotton the purcashing agents of a textile mill secure the lowest quotations for the quality they desire, while the cotton brokers seek to dispose of their cotton to the highest bidder. Likewise the boss in charge of hiring hands gives jobs to those who will accept the lowest wages, while workers, if they are in a position to choose, secure employment at the factory that offers highest wages. If the price of cotton rises so high that it is no longer profitable to manufacture cloth, the demand is stopped and brokers with cotton on their hands are forced to lower their prices. If they fall so low that it becomes unprofitable to grow it, the growers cease to supply any, and the manufacturers are obliged to increase their offers. Similarly, if a man asks too high wages, mills are free to shut down until he will accept lower pay; whereas if the mills offer too low wages, the men are free to withdraw their labor—individually—until the offer is raised. This—so runs the theory—would result in the permanent withdrawal of a number of workers from the industrial field and from this world, did they not have the foresight, imitating the planter who in similar circumstances reduces his acreage and the supply of cotton, to reduce the supply of laborers through abstention from the consequences of marriage. Thus automatically the supply of raw material is adjusted to the demand, and a free bargain necessarily being to the advantage of all parties concerned—else why should they enter into it?—the general welfare is promoted by the beneficent laws of political economy. It was advantageous to the cotton planter to sell his cotton at the price he did, else why did he engage in the business of growing it? It was of advantage to the worker to sell his labor for the wages offered, rather than to starve, else why did he not starve? To suggest, as some did—for there are unfortunately always malcontents—that a divine plan whereby most men could not afford to purchase cotton shirts might not be preferable to a more human arrangement whereby the amount of cotton grown and manufactured was adjusted to the number of cotton garments required to clothe the community properly, was almost as blasphemous as to suggest that the wages paid might bear some relation to the cost of living.

Unfortunately for this theory, cotton brokers, desiring neither to accept prices offered nor to engage in another occupation, found it to their advantage to engage in agreements among themselves to keep the price of cotton at a certain level; and in other commodities the same considerations prompted the formation of corporations to control the entire supply of that commodity and thus secure higher prices. This policy has been in America notably successful, from the point of view of those who initiated it, in the raw materials of iron, copper, and anthracite coal, for example, to say nothing of manufactured products. Hence in this particular the theory has been forced to give way before facts, and the Supreme Court has lately authoritatively established the new principle as an integral part of that body of practices known as "good business."

This principle, even then quite familiar in industrial life, was the policy which triumphed with the American Federation of Labor. The first principles of the Knights of Labor had been pushed aside as irrelevant to the realities of American economic life by the rising industrialism of the seventies and eighties; the workers, then, would adopt a policy that was "practical" and in accord with good business. They would accept the business régime, and seek by approved business tactics to acquire just as good a place in the business structure as they possibly could. Their antagonists had no scruples about their duties to the community at large, or to any particular portion of it; for this, it must be remembered, was the era of "The public be damned." To the newly arrived immigrants, who flocked to our shores in such numbers in the eighties, true Americanism seemed to mean the forgetting of those amenities of life which had softened the daily toil of the peasant in Europe, and the impatient plunge into that orgy of business enterprise and perilous rate-wars and price-cutting which makes the eighties stand out as in some respects the most typical and least creditable era of American industrialism. With the captains of industry and finance, who were at that period enjoying perhaps more of public favor than ever before or since, regarded everywhere as the truly great citizens of the Republic, it is not hard to understand how the workers, after a last lingering glance at the agricultural democracy vanishing over the western horizon, should feel rather a just pride than a sense of disappointment that they were at last becoming hard-headed business men. For the worker has ever desired to be equal to the majority of his fellows; and when the psychology of America had changed from that of the thrifty farmer to that of the enterprising business man, the aim of the worker underwent a quite similar transformation. It was in this very decade that the American labor movement took shape and became what it is today; and no observer can afford to overlook the fact that the modern worker has a priceless heritage of victories and set-backs, of patient tiresome organization crowned by a grudging recognition in collective bargaining. He has risen, as assuredly as ever did a Rockefeller or a Carnegie, to his present position solely by his own unaided efforts; it is he who should be the true hero of "Up from the Depths." And today, even though he recognize that changed times demand changed policies, he will not do aught in word or deed to reflect upon the acts of those who in the formative period of modern unionism won for him that measure of economic freedom he may now enjoy.

Nothing in a sense can be more typical of the general spirit of labor during this generation than the address with which President J. W. Sullivan, of the New York City C. F. U., welcomed the A. F. L. convention of 1895. And nothing could be more typically "American" in the sense of the word that calls to mind mushroom boom towns, Western boasters, and the push and go of business enterprise. "We run the largest local business enterprise in the American continent. This enterprise is to 'bull' our labor market. We succeed. We keep wages up right along, 25% above the level they would be were employers to have their way. In some cases we put them up 50%. We thus retain for our own use half a million dollars which without our unions would go to enrich capitalists and monopolists. $26,000,000 a year! That's our joint dividend, no less. We retain this wealth justly because we produce it. We retain it because we have the power to do it. We are well-organized, well-disciplined, well-led. We boast therefore in our chosen leaders the greatest Captains of Industry in this metropolitan center. Their equals in this community can not be named." [1]

This revelation may not especially appeal to those today who do not find bulling any market a particularly inspiring act, yet it marks a distinct epoch in labor history. The same note, with a greater emphasis, however, on the purposes for which this process is being carried on, appears in a pamphlet of the early nineties, Dyer D. Lum's *Philosophy of Trade Unions*. "The trade union is a business, matter-of-fact institution, responding to personal needs, living in the present for the present, and not concerned about its status in the millennium. Born of the New, it instinctively opposes the Old Civilization. . . . Trades unions are not system-builders—sufficient unto the day is the evil thereof, and tomorrow will find a new relief for picket-duty. Self-interest is not only the fundamental law of our being, but it is the incentive which has lifted man from the animal into the sphere of the human. . . . The present struggle for shorter days of toil is not based on any sentimental desire 'for the other fellow,' but for self alone. We want a higher standard of living, and to secure this self-interest becomes mutual interest, to wring from privilege a greater opportunity. . . . Our selfishness has broadened into mutualism."

And looking back upon the history of the movement to which he had given so much unselfish toil and of which he could rightfully claim the proud title of leader, Samuel Gompers in 1915 epitomized that spirit when he said: "The American Federation of Labor is guided by the history of the past. It draws lessons from history in order to interpret conditions which confront working people so that it may work along the lines of least resistance to accomplish the best results in improving the conditions of the working men, women, and children, today, tomorrow, and tomorrow's tomorrow, making each day a better day than the one which went before. This is the guiding principle, philosophy, and aim of the labor movement.

" We do not set any particular standard, but work for the best possible conditions immediately attainable for the workers. When these are obtained then we strive for better. The working people will not stop when any particular point is reached; they will never stop in their efforts to obtain a better life for themselves, for their wives, for their children, for all humanity. The object to attain is complete social justice." [2]

[1] A. F. L., *Proceedings*, 1895 Convention.
[2] Gompers, *The American Labor Movement*, 1915.

Thus it was that business unionism came into the ascendant in the American labor movement, and has for some thirty years remained fairly stable and permanent. Yet there are elements contained within the very heart of business unionism which as time has gone on have so increased in importance that they seem about to force a readjustment and a realignment of forces. What these elements are it shall be the purpose of the present analysis to bring out.

Business unionism regards itself as a great corporation which has one valuable commodity to sell, the labor of its members. This labor it is its aim to sell at the highest possible price, a price including not merely money wages, but also returns in shorter days and improved working conditions in general. Thus the primary aim of the business union is to engage in a business transaction with the employer, and in that transaction to secure the best possible terms. All other activities carried on, though they may also possess attractiveness and utility on their own account, are at bottom valued chiefly as a means toward the attainment of strong bargaining power. The employer has on his side the power of discharging individuals, of depriving them of the means of securing a livelihood; the workers have the power to withdraw their labor, and to deprive the employer of the chance to make profits on his manufactures. These are the forces manipulated by the leaders on both sides; the employer can threaten discharge, and can keep as large a supply of labor available as possible, while the worker can see to it that all labor acts as a unit, and thus force the employer to come to his union for his hands. Around this simple basis revolve nearly all of the measures and policies which have characterized the activities of both capital and labor throughout the era of business unionism.

The situation thus closely resembles the armed peace which has been the basis of international relations. In the everlasting jockeying for position the leaders on both sides, just as the diplomats of Europe, are constantly demanding more and more preparedness, greater and greater armies, more and more powerful fighting machines. Neither industrial leaders nor diplomats actually desire conflict; neither consider a strike or a war as good in itself. Yet their whole strategy depends upon being able to threaten such conflict, to show that in case it should eventuate they would possess the advantage; and it cannot be said that either industrial leaders or diplomats have any profound antipathy to that state of affairs which so much occupies their thoughts. Specifically, the strike is not valued in itself by the leader of the business union, and if he can get what he desires without it, he most assuredly will accept a peaceful settlement of the bargain. Strikes are but incidents in the jockeying for power; they are entered upon by one side or the other, when victory seems assured, for the sake of improving their bargaining power. Yet the leader of a business union would be utterly at a loss if he were not assured that, even though he never need to strike, back of him there lay the power of the organized workers; just as in the war of steel and gold no diplomat of China or of Peru, however astute, can hope to secure great advantages for his country. What the worker has won, he has perhaps won justly; but he has won it, not because his demands were just, but because he had the power to enforce them. This truth, albeit subject to considerable limitations, has been at once the basis and the lesson of business unionism, indelibly burned into the mind of the worker through long years of bitter struggle.

The aim of the business union, to attain a strong bargaining power, to become a fighting machine that can be used by its leaders to enforce its demands, has naturally called into being a type and structure of organization admirably suited to just that purpose. This aim implies a well-disciplined army that can be called upon to act as a unit— when necessary, to fight, when necessary, to preserve the peace and keep its agreements, and to be ready at all times to enforce a diplomatic victory through action on the economic field. This function to which business unionism has adapted itself has determined the relations which obtain within the union group, and has raised the old problem of democratic control versus efficiency of action. For the same body of workers who must serve as the disciplined army is also the body that has formulated the demands and that stands to win or lose in the conflict. There is thus a constantly recurring struggle between the forces of discipline and authority and the popular will, a conflict punctuated by the insurgence of the rank and file and the installation of new and more responsive leaders. Nevertheless, as will be seen, it does not appear that on the premises of business unionism any permanent solution to this problem can be found—assuredly none has yet been discovered— and this is one of the factors which bodes ill for the permanence of business unionism as a type. It seems impossible to reconcile democratic control with any kind of army.

To lead such an army as the typical business union presents there have naturally come to the front leaders peculiarly fitted by nature and temperament to perform the functions required of them. Thus it is manifestly impossible to form a correct judgment as to the real desires and aims, the real wishes of the workers from a consideration of the type of leaders who are developed, and to judge the purposes of the entire group by those of the captains. The function, not the free desires of the workers, has led to the survival of a certain type; and the whole purport of this volume has been to maintain that the function depends quite as much upon the industrial structure and upon the aims of the employers and of society in general, in short, upon factors hitherto quite beyond the workers' control, as upon the desires of the workers themselves.

To lead an army, to haggle with powerful employers on the basis of threats of force, requires an aggressive leader, a close bargainer, a shrewd diplomat, a dominating personality, capable and perhaps quite fond of exercising personal authority—in a word, it requires a man remarkably similar to those captains of industry who by their exercise of the same qualities have elevated themselves in the industrial struggle. To the qualities necessary to wrest a fortune from nature with one hand while fighting off one's fellows with the other, however, the leader of the business union must add a facility in oratory and persuasion, a talent for winning the support of the workers and their personal loyalty; he must approximate those arts by which the politician appeals for public approval. Hence it is not surprising that labor history reveals some leaders who have forsaken the workers for the business game, or who have become politicians and aspirants for public office; nor that the desire to lead their fellows to victory at the polls should always appeal more strongly to the leaders than to the rank and file. It is not surprising that some leaders have even conformed to the type of the despised "demagogue," and have sought their own advantage rather than that of their men. The genuine cases of such action have, of course, been seized upon by the employer as typical of the whole number, and nothing is more common than for our press to treat the labor leader and the "self-seeking agitator" as synonymous terms. It would be unkind to suggest that possibly the employer, at a loss to comprehend the motive of disinterested service to one's fellows, interprets the state of mind of the labor leader on lines smilar to that of his own, and being out to win for himself at all costs naturally supposes that all other men would do what he would do in their places; it would be cruel to question whether possibly those labor-leaders whom he regards as "good" and moderate and fair-minded might not possibly be those who had proved themselves most susceptible to official flattery and promises of private advancement. Taking all these factors into consideration, we may hazard the opinion that the small number of genuine demagogues and the great majority of disinterested leaders and patient self-sacrificing personalities to be found at the head of the labor movement is a real tribute to the persistence of the social idealism to be found therein. Nor must we forget that all labor leaders are ultimately responsible to the workers whose representatives they are, and that no one is quicker than the worker to detect sham and trickery and any trace of disloyalty. It is true that occasionally a union will keep in power a man who has been proved venal; but no such man, however useful he may be as a military leader, receives any personal respect or loyalty from his union. And how many large corporations can with a clear conscience deny the imputation of any trickery in their own counsels? The business union, we must remember, is proud of being an American business organization.

But after all it is never the dishonest and insincere who merit the honor of condemnation; it is the sincere man who is mistaken and wrong. Those workers most opposed to the policies of some of the present leaders of the Federation do not question their sincere attachment to the interests of their fellow-workers as they see them. They claim rather that the function which the business union performs has tended to develop leaders peculiarly adapted to the conditions amidst which the business union was generated, and that now that these conditions have been considerably altered those leaders are by inertia of office continued in power when they might, with greater advantage to the workers, be replaced by other and younger men who would be more responsive to new situations. It is in fact incontestable that many leaders of the Federation and of some of its unions are "war horses," men who have grown grey in the service of their fellows, trained in the bitter struggles of industrial warfare, habituated to certain types of activity and policy and unable to visualize any other state of affairs than that in which the fighting of their younger days has been spent. They are, claim the younger men, victims of a war-psychology which makes them unable to imagine a state of peace or the policies necessary to one.

Such leaders are continued in office largely from a sense of personal loyalty and obligation; it would be shameful to turn out a man who had given his best years to the service of his fellows when he might have risen high in the industrial world. And quite naturally they use the large powers which the constitutions of most unions give them to further those policies which they feel to be best and to keep down and suppress those workers who they feel are foolishly counseling courses which cannot but result in harm to themselves and their fellows. It is but little wonder that Mr. Gompers, whose early associates were Marxians, who spent years struggling against the desires of his small body of followers to break into the political field, who sees the American labor movement at its present strength largely as a result of just such wisdom, should look with disfavor upon efforts to form a distinct labor party, even though it might well be that the very growth of organized labor and other industrial changes had materially altered the situation. Moreover, a labor leader is not and cannot be an actual worker at the bench or in the shop; he is somewhat elevated above the level of the men who have to struggle for their daily bread, and while this eminence undoubtedly gives a broader view and a more philosophic outlook upon society as a whole, it at the same time necessarily causes the loss of some of that sympathetic insight into what are the basic desires and aspirations of the workers' hearts. The responsibility of an executive position rather dampens the desire of the young worker to rush into battle and hazard all on one chance; the leader is apt to have a tremendous respect for the power of his capitalist opponents, and to tend to overestimate rather than to underestimate the weakness of his own side.

All of these considerations will serve, for example, to explain the conduct of the officials of the Amalgamated Association of Iron, Steel, and Tin workers, whose action, or rather whose lack of activity, was the immediate cause of the failure of the great steel strike of 1919.[1] Their experience had included probably the bitterest struggle which has ever been waged in between organized labor and organized capital, and they displayed the results in their most extreme form.

With this type of leader developed through the natural demands of business unionism, the business union has not really known what to do with the accretions of power which have constantly been coming to it. It is rapidly approaching the time when it will hold within its hands the power to determine general social policies, if indeed it does not already do so; in an industrial country like England it is the great unions which seem to be the seats of real political authority in those matters in which they care to intervene. The British trade unions decide on matters of foreign policy, and Lloyd George wisely decides to adopt the same course. At the Spa conference, in July, 1920, it is significant to note, it was neither the skillful arguments of Herr von Simon, the diplomat and politician, nor the economic reasoning of Herr Stinnes the coal king, but the blunt ultimatum of Herr Hue, the leader of the coal miners which had final weight with the Allies. This growing power of organized labor is no-

[1] W. Z. Foster, *The Great Steel Strike.*

where realized, least of all by the leaders of business unionism in America. They have been trained in but one field, and as their weapon grows in power and range they do not know how to use it in any other. It is as though the President of Switzerland, in the midst of vexatious boundary disputes with Italy, should suddenly find at his disposal the combined armies of Russia and Germany. Small wonder if under such circumstances he persisted in annexing Italian territory, even though in so doing he precipitated a world cataclysm. The business leader instinctively preserves the rules of the game he is playing, but with his added power he plays it to the very limit—he is conservative in that he does not desire to alter the general economic structure, but he is ready to press more and more exhorbitant demands which cannot but eventuate in the economic change he deprecates.

Such is the typical leader of a business union. The type of group relation developed is quite suited to him; it is that type we have already noticed as characteristic of American institutions and as dominant in American business organization, the responsible executive relation. It implies leaders with large powers of discretion and of action, but equally weighted with the burden of heavy personal responsibility. Pick a man and give him full control, carry your union card and pay your dues; but let him know that if he fails to deliver the goods he will be ruthlessly discarded. This is the pioneer, the fighting type of organization; and competitive business is essentially of a fighting nature. It is the Andrew Jackson type, the tribune of the people; it underlies the popular movements for the commission form of government, for the short ballot with executive appointments, for the recall of elected officials, for the replacement of judicial officers with commissioners endowed with great discretionary powers,—in a word, it is that theory of government which Roosevelt represented and which goes under the general name of "progressive." And the world has but just been treated to a supreme example of the way in which America rejects those who after accepting authority and responsibility fail to live up to their promises, in the person of her Chief Executive himself. President Wilson's largely personal rule was quite in accord with the principles of American progressivism, or responsible executivism; and had he succeeded the country would have resounded with his praises. But for divers reasons he failed, and seemingly no one is too poor to add to his opprobrium. Indeed, the fate of President Wilson, great as he is, might suggest to the critic the limitations of the theory upon which he acted.

Be that as it may, this is the type of internal relation which has obtained in business unionism: a willing obedience so long as the leader got what the workers demanded of him, an angry revolt when he failed. The first result of this policy is that the leader strives earnestly to get what the workers want; and the second is that he is quite apt to use all of his powers of persuasion to make them want what he can get. Particularly in times of transition, when perhaps a large minority seriously questions the aims of the leader, he is prone to pursue those aims all the more vigorously, just as the reply of the leaders of Germany during the war to those who questioned whether peace might not be preferable to conquest was to pursue with increased vigor a policy of military conquest. It is much easier to engineer a strike for increased wages than to elaborate all the tiresome details of a real plan of social reconstruction, or even of permanent collective bargaining, just as it is much easier to secure peace with victory than a real league of nations.

To the executives thus elected to carry out their demands the workers entrust great power over the formulation of policy, and even greater powers of influencing public opinion have been assumed. In the matter of collective bargaining, the leaders have almost a free hand; in the vital matter of strikes, it is usual to entrust to them the power both to call and to end them. Most unions indeed require a strike vote to be taken before a strike can be called; but no strike benefits can be obtained, which means that no strike can be successful, if the president and the executive committee do not approve, while it is customary to vote for a strike and leave the declaration to the president when he may judge the time to be ripe. And in most of the older unions, such as the railroad brotherhoods, the president can order men back to work at his own discretion. As a result, once a strike has received general approbation the matter has definitely left the hands of the workers and depends almost entirely upon the wisdom of their leaders; the army, resolved upon war, divests itself of its democratic control, and loyally submits to the will of its captains.

Moreover, the officers enjoy considerable power over the conventions through their ability to decide upon the eligibility of delegates and to exclude those from locals which they can declare, for financial or other reasons, not to be in good standing. This furnishes a convenient method for getting rid of men who may possibly cause trouble on the convention floor; it was used at the Nashville convention of the United Garment Workers, and resulted in the withdrawal of the excluded delegates and the formation of a new union. The executive committee, usually made up of men of the type described, can generally revoke the charter of any local which it disapproves, particularly in case of an unauthorized strike. Besides this direct power, it is the custom to send as delegates to the conventions and to the A. F. L. conventions the officers and leaders of the local unions, from motives of loyalty and of habit; and these are apt to form a willing support for the officials and to crush any opposition from the younger and newer men. Moreover the elaborate systems of benefits most business unions have built up, generally with the conscious intention of strengthening the organization and holding the membership together in unfavorable times, are only too successful in accomplishing their purpose, and in preventing action on the part of locals which might meet with opposition from headquarters. The radical worker derides such unions as "coffin societies," and will have in his organization no stabilizing benefits; but he pays the penalty in shifting and temporary membership, and has to resort to constant strikes to hold any men at all.

In spite of this great power exercised by the officers over the members of the union, in large part perhaps because of it, there is a constant struggle going on between the leaders backed up by the older and less aggressive members, and the younger and more active "rank and file," a struggle which has become more and more acute with the growth of a new spirit and a longing for new methods and measures among the latter. Periodic revolts and the election to office of the leaders of the opposition are common occurrences; yet it is no less common for the new leaders soon to become as conservative as the old ones, and with office to assume the vices of authority. A case in point is the International Association of Machinists, of which the present (1920) administration, elected as radicals over the "conservative" incumbents, are now being themselves assailed by a large minority, which in many locals is a majority, as too conservative. It appears exceedingly hard in one man to unite the qualities of a successful general and strategist and a humble representative of the wishes of the majority; only exceptional individuals like Sidney Hillman seem able to do it.

If one is led to the comparison of a great army by the type of leader which business unionism elevates to power, and by the relations which he enjoys with the group, the analogy becomes irresistible when one contemplates the men themselves and their spirit of group solidarity. The success of an army depends fundamentally upon that elusive something, its morale; upon the amount of cohesion and unity and fixity of purpose which it displays, the amount of whole-hearted coöperation and mutual confidence and trust which permeate its members. Similarly the success of a business union depends upon the amount of group cohesion and solidarity. And this spirit, this morale, can be developed, just as in an

army, through two radically different policies: through the authority
and the external discipline of the central organization, and through the
subtler and more elusive spontaneous spirit coming from the whole
membership.

The first method, that of authority and external discipline, has been
often tried by labor leaders; it is perhaps natural to the dominant type
of personality which we have seen emerges in the business union. Hence
we have seen how the business union has developed an elaborate machinery well fitted for giving those in power control over the policies
and the opinions of the members, and methods of securing support from
every local. The disciplining of unruly members, outlawry and expulsion, the revocation of the charter of a local which will not agree
with the others or the president, or its suspension, refusal to allow its
delegates a voice in convention, treatment of members not in good
standing as scabs with no rights, exclusion from closed shops,—all those
methods built up to protect the union worker against the lower standard of the non-union man which can be turned against an unruly member of the group—these and many other methods are employed by the
leaders to secure solidarity and discipline. Revolt of a large number
and the formation of a new union is seldom resorted to, since it gives
too excellent a chance to the employer to play one union off against
the other and profit by the division amongst the workers. This was
tried in the mines of the West between the A. F. L. and the Western
Federation of Miners when it was affiliated with the I. W. W., and has
recently been resorted to by employers in the split between the Amalgamated Clothing Workers and the United Garment Workers, an in-
significant A. F. L. organization. The length to which the leaders of
business unionism will go to endeavor to enforce discipline was shown
in the outlaw railroad strike of the spring of 1920, when Mr. W. G. Lee
of the Trainmen actually united with the employers to call for an injunction against the men he claimed to represent, and suspended many
locals with thousands of members.

Yet despite all this machinery of authority and discipline, in time
of real crisis the officers discover how powerless they are to force cohesion on their men from above. When a local has been strong enough
to develop a system of strike benefits of its own, as many of the large
and radical locals have done with precisely this end in view, it can
safely defy its national officials and disregard their frantic efforts to
remain in control of the situation. This has been well evidenced in the
series of so-called "outlaw" or unauthorized strikes following the arm-

istice, in which the rank and file revolted against leaders who no longer represented their own aspirations, and struck on their own accord.

The longshoremen, the printers, the coal-miners, the railroad workers, to name but the most prominent, were able to revolt with impunity, even in the highly disciplined railroad brotherhoods, for they well knew that no officer would long allow to remain outside of his union such large and essential bodies of the workers in the industry. For labor leaders with no one to lead make a sad and sorry spectacle, and many an officer who would otherwise be tempted to get rid of unruly followers is reminded that after all he owes his position solely to the fact that he represents the workers who retain him to look out for their interests. Moreover, when locals are expelled from their national body and from the A. F. L. the state and city federations are quite apt to disregard this action entirely and extend aid and fellowship to those whose disgrace they well know will be but temporary.

No, morale, in a union as in an army, is hardly to be forced from above. No methods of German discipline were able to restore the lost morale of the Austrian troops in the last years of the war; no policies of discipline and expulsion are going to develop that solidarity of labor upon which the ultimate success of its aims depends. The morale of a labor organization is a natural and spontaneous outgrowth of the unity of purpose and the community of interests which binds all the workers together against their common antagonist. No army, unless it be an army fighting to defend its very hearth and families from the desecrating invader, can equal the solidarity and group-mindness of the labor union. Where the aim is such as all the members instinctively recognize to be their own, there is no need of any external discipline; so powerful is the social impulse even among the despised and unlettered "foreigners" and "hunkies" that they would no more think of preferring their immediate private advantage to the good of the group, and of proving traitor to the confidence placed in them, than the soldier would of deserting to the enemy for increased pay. When, as in the recent steel strike, the issue is clear beyond peradventure of doubt, Republican and Socialist, craft unionist and industrialist, A. F. L. leader and Sidney Hillman, join against the common foe and share their money and their strength. It is such experiences, such waves of sympathy transcending the ordinary limitations of petty quarrels, that make many workers believe that even an unsuccessful strike is of inestimable advantage to the labor movement—and thus pave the way for the transformation of business unionism. That individual responsibility for the welfare of the group, that moral indignation at the traitor or scab, which business unionism calls forth for its own fighting purposes, is so strong that it is futile to attempt to restrain it or hold it within bonds. It is sweeping business unionism irresistibly along towards something far broader and more inclusive.

In brief, it can be said that the business union displays all of the military virtues, loyalty, comradeship, courage, mutual sympathy and aid, and, it must be added, many of the military vices. It is at bottom an army, an army which gives orders to its leaders and follows those leaders so long as they lead it to victory and no longer.

Even such a cursory survey of the type of relations obtaining within the business union reveals the essential instability of its general status, and the elements that are at work in its very heart bidding fair to transform it into something else. The business union in accordance with its function tends to assume the structure of the compact and well-disciplined army; yet the business union is vastly more than an army, it is a body of men seeking greater freedom and greater opportunity, banded together to help one another in their quest. Its leaders, its aims, its methods, are all ultimately determined by the rank and file. The motive of self-interest alone might counsel the perfect development of the army, but the motive of social idealism, fostered and strengthened by the development of those very virtues necessary to the army's success, comes into conflict again and again with the strictly military organization; and on such occasions it is not the motive of social idealism that gives way.

There is thus at the present time a marked tendency away from excessive centralization to a more democratic control, and at the same time a shift in emphasis from the fighting function of business unionism to a function more directly applicable to the industrial structure. The type of labor leader now in the ascendent is not the type made prominent by the fights of the nineties; that generation has for the most part passed away. The J. W. Sullivan who boasted of bulling the labor market would not be received today with loud applause by any union. Leaders are coming to regard themselves as the representatives and spokesmen of their men, not as their rulers. The work of officers in former days was largely to organize and create their union, but now that unions are large and flourishing and the founders have disappeared from the scene the sense of proprietorship or paternal regard has vanished. The old convention, held once a year to give the successful organizer backing and popularity, the convention that was often hand-picked by the president, is in most unions becoming more and more infrequent. This tendency is well typified in the Firemen, which held annual conventions from 1873 to 1888, then changed to biennial conventions, and in 1910, shifted to triennial ones. Some unions have not held a convention for twenty years. The legislative function is at the same time vested in the entire membership, who have a referendum on all important questions and in some cases elect their officers directly. New measures are introduced by individual locals, and thus cannot be railroaded off the convention floor. Those leaders who have not recognized the coming of the new day have been suddenly enlightened by the revolt of the rank and file, and, in most cases, they have come to realize the necessity of voicing the aspirations of the workers if they are to retain their positions of leadership. The development, under various names, of shop committees, with its consequent bringing of unionism nearer to the atmosphere of the daily toil, has been influential in a more democratic direction. And finally the so-called "new unionism" of the garment trades, which arose as a revolt against all those features in business unionism which were least democratic and least adaptable to the general sense of social idealism, is by its example exerting a powerful influence in favor of control directly by the workers of all union matters, and the development in the workers of the power and ability to handle successfully even larger questions.

Coincident with this shift away from the exclusively military organization is a tendency towards relinquishing the purely military aim of business unionism. The industrial organizations against which war must be waged are constantly extending their sphere of influence, and the organization of employers is proceeding with great rapidity. Thus self-interest dictates an ever widening and ever more inclusive organization, while the spirit of class solidarity is every day receiving new impetus. It is characteristic of the labor movement that the change from craft to industrial unionism is urged not only by strategic necessity, but also by the ever widening area of coöperation and loyalty. And the resulting industrialization of the business union makes possible a function which the old union never contemplated and could not have accomplished if it had, the development of more and more of actual control over the operations of the industry itself. It is perhaps too early to hazard a prediction, but recent events and tendencies seem to point to a gradual shifting of stress from primary interest in fighting to secure higher profits on the sale of labor—the business motive—to interest in problems of industrial function and production, in the actual control of the industry. Many unions have become interested in educational problems along industrial lines, and are desirous of replacing the present chaotic system of new workers by some plan which will insure greater skill. Some have gone so far as to envisage the necessity of training their workers for the assumption of more and more responsibility as they are given larger and larger shares of control over industrial conditions. One can even see traces of the development of a new type of leader— the industrial expert, not the mere fighter, the man who can discuss with coal operators the complex problems of coal production and distribution, or with railroad managers the best methods of efficient operation, or with clothing manufacturers the means of getting rid of the seasonal nature of that industry to insure steady production. The miners, the railroad men, and the clothing workers have already secured the services of such experts. And with the new leader is coming a new organization—for fulfilling industrial function, not merely for bargaining power alone. But the most significant factor about this new tendency is that it does not involve, as all such more social and productive tendencies, like, for instance, the coöperation of the sixties, did in the past, the abandonment of trade unionism, the turning away from tried and successful methods, the suppression of the root instinct of the labor movement, the desire for immediate improvement of status; but that it is the natural outgrowth of the normal and almost inevitable development of business unionism itself. As we shall later, as labor organization grows more and more complete, such a transformation seems bound to follow, and nothing short of an almost unthinkable eradication of the labor movement itself seems to stop it. As the propounders of the Plumb plan said, such developments seem the only possible policy from a business standpoint.

Of course, such a development will be very slow, and may very likely be influenced in its course by other and at present unforeseen factors. For instance, if the employers unite to crush the labor movement, and follow the lead of the Steel Corporation in their anti-labor policy, the union will be forced back into a purely military organization, and all considerations will have to give way to those of fighting strength. There are certainly very few industries today where the workers are in any degree fitted to assume any great share of control of the larger aspects of the business. Yet that growth of knowledge of the processes of production is not utterly remote; the modern movement among employers to give a large amount of shop autonomy, undertaken at the behest of efficiency engineers with a view to increased production, will undoubtedly greatly hasten the development of a sense of responsibility. In fact, the double strain, by no means confined to the workers, is bound to operate in the future increasingly on the side of the employers also; and in some such coöperation as seems to be approaching in England it is probable that the new unionism will develop—coöperation forced by the power of labor, but at the same time voluntarily accepted by the employer. Nor have recent experiences tended wholly to confirm the traditional belief in the superhuman sagacity and efficiency of the American business man, which would make his replacement impossible. How long it may take, no one can tell; but that sooner or later some such state of affairs will come to pas is a prediction as safe as any that can be made in the complex processes of human affairs.

9. BUSINESS UNIONISM—THE RELATION OF THE GROUP TO OTHER GROUPS

So far we have been considering the relations which obtain within the business union, between its members, and between the rank and file and the leaders. But important as these are for an understanding of the labor movement, it is the larger social relations, the relations between the union group and other groups, and between the union and society as a whole, that are of primary importance for our fundamental problem of social responsibility. And here also while examining the business union we may discover within its aims and policies the germs of new and different purposes.

If the analogy of the business union to the business corporation be correct, then in its relations to other groups it will tend to approach the same type; its aim will be that of any business body, to corner, so nearly as possible, the entire supply of the commodity in which it deals and to boost prices to "all the traffic will bear," for the profit of its members. This monopolization of labor, and, if you will, the consequent "labor profiteering," is the aim of all business unionism, in so far as it is business unionism and nothing more, just as it is the aim of every business enterprise in the country; that is, just in so far as it remains "respectable" and "American." And just as the business man is amazed when he is accused of profiteering, and in bewilderment asks since when it has become wrong for a man to make as big profits as he possibly can and at just what point a fair profit becomes profiteering— for has not the ability and the standing of the business man from time immemorial (which means from the time of the introduction of free competition some two centuries ago) been judged solely by the size of the profit he can obtain?—just so the business union is at a loss to understand criticism which seems to misjudge the basic principles of business use and wont, and to be utterly subversive of the foundations of true American initiative and enterprise. And it can hardly be gainsaid that one who does not thus admit the right of a labor union to obtain what wages it can through economic pressure, one who believes that "the public" has preëminent right to protection against excessive wages— such a one must also admit that the profits of business corporations and even the august law of supply and demand itself must submit to social regulation and control. For better or worse such a one questions the entire economic system erected upon the basis of private profit.

For out of the individualism which is the basis of modern economic theory has grown a new individualism, an individualism in which the unit or individual is no longer a single man, as it was in the days of Adam Smith or Jeremy Bentham, but a group of men forming a single legal person. These bodies of men are the real units in industrial life; society today is far too large and far too complex and integrated for the single individual apart from some group to count for much. No man would think of setting up a steel mill in opposition to the U. S. Steel Corporation; no single individual would think of setting up one at all. Similarly no man would hope alone to get a higher wage or shorter hours from that company. Industrial relations today obtain between great aggregations, between the Steel Corporation and the A. F. L., not between isolated individuals.

Nevertheless, while the unit has radically altered since the heydey of economic liberalism, the type of relation has remained the same. It is still an individualism—in the sense that each group is out to serve its own interests with little thought for those of any other, save as they entertain the optimistic and comforting belief that what is best for the individual is *ipso facto* best for society in general. The business man points with pride at his affluence as betokening the prosperity of an entire country; similarly the unionist maintains that anything increasing the well-being of his group *ipso facto* is of advantage to society. This may well be true; but a robber chieftain might easily make the same claim for his band—Robin Hood did.

Yet the business union is not inspired exclusively by this spirit of group individualism; its purposes are constantly transcending the narrow group aims which consistency would require, and are stretching out to include more and more of society. All those influences at work within the industrial field, which have been exhibited above in their relation to the internal organization of the union, are exerting even greater pressure toward the enlargement of the area within which individualism has given way to group coöperation. The history of trade unions, in fact, is in great measure the history of the enlargement of the scope and jurisdiction of the union, an enlargement which, in accordance with the dual strain of the labor movement, usually starts from reasons of self-interest, and then grows greater to include social idealism also.

It must not be understood that within the group self-interest has been in any sense replaced by or abandoned for a social and coöperative motive; that the worker has agreed to disregard his own advancement and immolate himself that his group may prosper, after the manner of patriotic devotion to a mystical State. Such men there assuredly are; but if such men were all there would be no labor movement. So to interpret our contention were totally to misread the basic principle we are advancing. It is rather that modern conditions have made it necessary, in order to serve best the interests of the individual, to serve also, and perhaps first, those of the group. Within the external frame of individualistic relations there has come to be a merging of the individual and the social, so that instead of being at cross purposes the two are in fundamental harmony. What conflict remains is between immediate and permanent interest; just as in an army it is to the ultimate safety of the soldier to obey his commander's orders, though at times his immediate security may seem to lie in flight. There is a constantly growing field within which this identification of interests holds. This is the lesson of business unionism, even as it is the theory of Steward.

The essential individualism that has inspired the external policy of the business union is clear when one investigates the history of its relation to other groups. Primarily this comes out in the attitude of the business unionist toward membership. Whom would they admit to their body to enjoy the fruits of their exertions? In almost every case, with women, with negroes, with foreigners and aliens, the first impulse was to exclude them entirely and retain for themselves the jobs and the wages; this springs from the instinctive make-work philosophy of the insecure laborer. But in every case it soon became apparent that they would be far better off if they retained their monopoly by absorbing competitors than if they left them outside; they could hardly hope to exclude them from all employment. Self-interest finally impelled inclusion; and then, in accordance with the principle of the double strain, those very men who had most opposed such inclusion became most eager to aid all those possible. Where self-interest did not say nay, social sympathy was quick to express itself.

Consider the question of admitting women. Back in the convention of the National Trades' Union in 1836 a committee on female labor reported that woman's place was in the home, and that indulgence in factory work injured both themselves and the male operatives. "As an evidence of the injurious tendencies the female system has upon the male operatives, we will take the societies composing the Union of Philadelphia and Vicinity; for example, of 58 societies, 24 are seriously affected by female labor, to the impoverishing of whole factories, and benefit of none but the employers. It is presumed that this is a fair criterion to judge of other sections of the union; and from all these calculations there is evident reason to believe, that some of the different branches of operative mechanics will in time be superseded by female operatives to the entire exclusion of the males, and the consequent introduction of dissipation, indolence, and crime." [1] From the thirties to the sixties the bulk of the factory operatives in New England were women, and no attempt was seriously made to organize them; where women tried to enter men's trades they usually met with similar attempts at exclusion or even with strikes. As late as 1850 the cordwainers of New York provided in their constitution that no woman should work in any of the shops they controlled unless she were a member's wife or daughter, although in general the New England cotton and shoe trades were so largely in the hands of women that organization was forced, to prevent competition with the men.

But when it became apparent that women could not be kept in the home the more far-seeing organizations urged their inclusion, the national officers usually having to force the matter upon reluctant locals. In 1867 the printers recommended to their locals the organization of separate locals for women; in 1875 the Cigarmakers' convention admitted women. The Knights of Labor, for all its inclusive humanitarianism, did not admit them till 1880; while the Federation both admitted them and encouraged their organization from the very beginning. Of late years the old antagonism has almost entirely passed away, and the slogan "equal pay for equal work" has become popular, not only because of its advantage to the men, but even more because of genuine sympathy and solidarity with the woman worker. In 1912 the only unions specifically excluding women were the Barbers, the Switchmen, the Molders, the Potters, the Upholsterers, and the Paper Makers; though in the nature of the case many others were exclusively male. [2]

Precisely the same general tendency may be observed with regard to the admission of negroes, though here the question is somewhat complicated by Southern race prejudice and the desire of the Northerners to fraternize with the blacks after the Civil War. They were excluded until their use as strike-breakers and their general low wages necessitated their organization; then a real desire to improve their condition manifests itself. In New Orleans, Galveston, and Savannah unions of colored workmen engaged along the waterfronts were in the early eighties ad-

---

[1] *National Laborer*, Nov. 12, 1836.
[2] See F. E. Wolfe, *Admission to American Trade Unions*, 1912.

mitted to the city trades assemblies on an equal footing with white unions.[1] The idealistic movements of the sixties and seventies, and the Knights which grew out of them, declared of course for solidarity with the negroes; the Knights' convention at Richmond in 1886 was enlivened by many manœuvres of the Northerners to force this equality on their Southern confrères. Powderly combined with a genuine humanitarian interest in the blacks an intelligent appraisal of the workers' best interests when he said: "Southern cheap labor is more a menace to the American toiler than the Chinese, and this labor must be educated." [2] The Federation admitted the negro from the beginning, but the difficulty of organizing the unskilled Southern worker and the prejudices of the local unions, which in all matters of admission are most conservative and most short-sighted, united to keep him out until fairly recently. In 1910 the unions which excluded negroes were the Wire Weavers, the Shipbuilders, the Switchmen, the Maintenance of Way Employees, the Telegraphers, the Railway Clerks, and the four Brotherhoods; but constant efforts are made in the A. F. L. convention to secure the abandonment of these restrictions.

What has obtained with women and with negroes has also obtained with foreigners and alien immigrants; the policy has been to keep them out if possible, to organize them if they are already here competing with American workers. Where a union like those amongst the glass trades is highly organized and through the closed shop can exclude whomsoever it will, and is much troubled by the importation of foreign workmen, it may impose initiation fees as high as $500 upon the alien; others exclude him entirely. Ever since the Albany molders in 1858 united to import European strike-breakers, the history of American labor has been full of struggles to keep the market from being flooded by unskilled workers at the instigation of employers to whose advantage it is, in the words of a recent writer in the *New York Evening Post*, to have "something like 105 men for every hundred jobs," men with no aspirations after an American standard.[3]

In 1869 the anthracite operators threatened to put an end to their labor troubles by importing coolies from China; a shoe manufacturer in North Adams, Massachusetts, actually did bring over Chinese cobblers who cost but a dollar instead of three dollars a day. The National Labor Union naturally protested; and largely as a result the Burlingame treaty

---

[1] Commons, II, 310.
[2] Powderly, *op. cit.*, 658.
[3] July 12, 1920.

was negotiated. Three years later a cutlery works brought over coolies at $18 a month; but these attempts were all too patently subversive of American standards to succeed in the East. Yet it is suggestive that at the time the agitation for exclusion was at its height, District Assembly 49, the radical and advanced New York organization of the Knights of Labor, presented in the General Assembly a resolution that "special efforts be made to organize the Chinese," which was rejected by a vote of only 95 to 42.[1] Chinese were formally excluded in 1882.

The idealism which persisted in regarding America as the home of the oppressed overcame self-interest in 1878, when the section of the old preamble of the Knights opposing "servile races" was omitted, on the ground that it was "best not to insert anything in the preamble which could be construed as opposing any section of humanity." Powderly's comment is typical. "While it was a beautiful sentiment which actuated the men who gathered at the first General Assembly, and while it appealed to the best instincts of the membership at large, it was found to be in direct opposition to the best interests of the members of the order. The basic principle on which the order was founded was *protection*, not protection from the manufacturer or employer alone, but from our own avarice, our weakness, and from cheap workmen also. Theoretically it sounded very well to extend a welcome to all to share in the protection to be derived from organization, but it was discovered that to carry out this practice would load the country down with men to whom the American laborer could extend no aid, and who were too ignorant to help themselves." [2]

But while the workers had general support in their efforts to exclude Orientals, they could not hope to keep out Europeans also. In 1869 manufacturers began advertising abroad for labor; in 1872 Polish immigration on a large scale started, in 1877 after the great strikes Hungary was canvassed, and in the eighties commenced the flow from eastern and southern Europe. At first the worker, in his desire to emulate the business man and prove himself a good American, demanded a "high protective tariff on labor"; but the gentlemen who upheld protection for manufactured articles waxed eloquent over the shame of destroying the sacred asylum of liberty, confident that labor was no simple commodity like steel or cloth. The Knights managed in 1885 to get a law, modified two years later, prohibiting the importation of contract labor; but otherwise the unionists, unable to prevent the influx of foreign workers, turned

[1] Powderly, 426.
[2] *Ibid.*, 429.

to the next best policy and decided to organize them. The futility of attempting exclusion when we realize that even by 1886 but 21% of the workers of Illinois were Americans of the old stock,[1] and that today in our basic trades like steel and coal over sixty per cent of the workers are aliens, is quite obvious. So, save in a few highly skilled trades, the unionists have long ago abandoned the hope of keeping the foreigner either out of the country or out of their union; and have set to work to carry to the ignorant worker from southeastern Europe the gospel of unionism. So successful has this policy been that today the very men brought over by large corporations to furnish a willing and docile supply of labor are denounced as foreigners, aliens, and revolutionaries, and they have proved themselves, in struggles like the steel strike of 1919, fully the equals of the native Americans in loyalty and solidarity. Indeed, it is hardly too much to say that it is with these newer workers that the most vital force in the entire labor movement is to be found today.

In each case, then, the business union has at first sought to down its rivals, and then, finding it more advantageous, has admitted them to partnership and coöperation. Hence in this particular the business union has come to be unlike its prototype, the business corporation. The latter strives to absorb or amalgamate into a trust or monopoly, and then to put down and destroy any competitor; but the union throws wide its doors and allows, nay, implores, all workers in a given industry, and all those who desire to work in it, to come into the fold. If it be a monopoly, it is not an exclusive monopoly; sad experience has taught it the futility of exclusion, which injures those who exclude as much as those excluded.

Has the business union, then, escaped the danger to which the medieval guild succumbed, of becoming a closed corporation to deprive others of the chance to make a livelihood? Despite tendencies and conditions which have made the danger very great, up to the present it has, and there seems to be little likelihood that as time goes on it will become more exclusive. The crucial question, of course, is that of the relation to the new and younger worker, the question of apprenticeship. We have seen how the masters of the last century utilized the old craft apprenticeship laws to dispense with the highly paid journeymen, and how they excited the antagonism of the skilled artisan through their dependence upon "botch mechanics and apprentices." This abuse of the apprentice system by the masters in the early days provoked a strong and a natural reaction and a strict regulation by the union of the numbers of apprentices; and it was this question that formed perhaps the most powerful

[1] Illinois Bureau of Labor, *Report*, 1886, 227.

incentive toward the collective agreements and conciliation that mark business unionism. This limitation is at bottom based on the make-work philosophy, but there are other elements involved. The Industrial Commission of 1901 reported "the chief motive which influences the unions in shaping their apprentice rules is the desire to maintain their wages by diminishing competition within the trades. The only other motive which is not included within this formulation is the desire, for reasons which may be classed as artistic, to prevent the lowering of the standard of skill. This feeling can not be supposed to exert more than a minor influence upon actual policies." [1] Motley, however, in his study of the apprentice system, believes the latter motive, " the instinct for workmanship," to be much stronger than was supposed in the days before the application of social psychology to the workers.[2]

But what has contributed more than anything else to the breakdown of the apprentice regulations has been the growing industrialization and specialization of work, which has replaced the old skilled craftsman with the unskilled machine-tender, who needs no arduous training to become a strike-breaker. Here again limitation of membership spells ultimate ruin; and perhaps the dominating spirit today is that expressed by the Amalgamated Clothing Workers when they voted, not to restrict membership, but to seek the 44-hour week that their friends and relatives in Eastern Europe might be able to come to America to get work.

Indeed, there is even growing the recognition that the union must do more than merely admit the workers to its ranks; it must substitute for the old apprentice system a modern method of technical education. Among many of the older skilled unions the man or boy who desired to learn the trade or advance in it had to leave the union and become a scab until he had acquired sufficient proficiency to meet the union regulations; but in the newer industries, particularly among the garment makers, efforts are being made to train and educate the members after they have joined the union. The establishment of labor colleges at Boston, at Seattle, and elsewhere indicates the trend of the times. That the admission of new members to a trade needs some sort of social regulation is admitted by most observers; it is within the realm of possibility that industrial education will in the future be placed in the hands of the unions themselves.

In their relation, then, to other groups seeking membership within the union the business unions have gradually abandoned strictly business

[1] *Report*, v. 17, p. 53.
[2] J. M. Motley, *Apprenticeship in American Trade Unions*, 1907.

principles because it has proved better business policy to do so. The same can be said of its relations with other groups with whom it comes into contact. Take for instance the bitter jurisdictional disputes that from time immemorial have marked craft unionism, disputes between crafts with conflicting claims over certain branches of work. These have in the past often led to scabbing on the strikes of fellow-workers in the most callous disregard of union standards; they have generally resulted from changed processes and the improvement of industrial technique, and occur whenever, for instance steel ships replace wooden ones, or electric locomotives steam engines. Here selfish group interest certainly operates to the exclusion of wider sympathies and ideals; it is largely because of such a dispute between the trainmen and the maintenance of way workers that the Brotherhoods have withheld their strength from the A. F. L. Yet this is one of the most potent causes making for industrial unionism, either openly, or disguised as "blanket agreements" or trade departments. Craft rivalry has served only to discredit the business union in the eyes of the younger worker; for the area within which group coöperation and loyalty now obtains far surpasses the small limits of any one craft.

Even graver charges of regard only for group interest can be brought against those highly skilled business trades which employ helpers or assistants and pay them directly; in these cases it is not too much to say that the worker thus placed in the position of employer to some one beneath him has behaved precisely as the employer he censures, and has passed on with interest the ruthless treatment he has received. It was formerly the practice, before machinery revolutionized the trade, for every glass bottle-blower to furnish a boy to help him at his work; and it is to the shame of the workers that they vigorously opposed the application of child labor laws to these helpers. Moreover, the treatment accorded by unions to the labor in their own offices has not always been such as they would desire to have meted out to them. Such phenomena are marks of the dominance of the business ideal and of the selfish motive to the exclusion of all other considerations.

Finally there is the attitude of the craft unionist toward the unskilled; nor is it very different from what we have already observed. The interests of the latter have generally been protected only when economic circumstances have forced it as a measure of protection to the skilled. Yet there have always been waves of sympathy that have extended far outside the single trade. As we have already seen, the business unionism of the eighties and nineties developed under the ægis of Steward's philosophy because that philosophy so well represented the merging of the desire to improve the workers' own condition with the desire to aid their fellows. It became the essence of union principles that only by raising all could any one be raised; and, though in practice often disregarded, this principle has with the development of flavoring industrial conditions come to have more and more appeal.

It is claimed that the Knights of Labor failed because it sought to enroll the unskilled; but while to some extent the case this is not strictly true. Not because it tried to interest skilled workers in men about whom they cared little, but because the unskilled were not strong enough for successful organization—this is the truth in the contention; and had the Knights organized industrial rather than mere labor unions it is still a question whether it might not have succeeded. Its failure, in spreading the conviction that the unskilled were impossible of successful organization, undoubtedly set back their cause.

The Federation, too, has latterly shown much concern for the unskilled, both in its large industrial unions and in smaller so-called federal labor unions. Particular activity followed the challenge of the I. W. W. But in general, as a part of the growing tendency toward industrialism, the unskilled are being absorbed into unions as rapidly as they can successfully menace the organized workers; and once in they become part and parcel of the great army of loyal workers.

Finally business unionism betrays its essential group individualism in its relations to political parties. Here it is its policy to utilize them as means to the attainment of its own group ends; to develop efficient lobbies, and while disclaiming any broader social outlook to vote for one candidate and oppose the other according as he favors or opposes the measures labor desires. But this is but typical of the American political system which regards parties as the means whereby individual and group interests can be harmonized into socially effective organizations.

These examples of the relations between the business union and other groups in the community are sufficient to make clear the nature of that group individualism in accordance with which its actions are regulated. But the most important relations of all are those that concern business unionism and society as a whole, and which obtain between it and "the public", taken in its most general significance as society organized for purposes other than production, the chief of which economically is consumption. And here the business union acts just as do other business corporations; when weak it is quite willing to implore public aid and sympathy, just as weak industries crave either large grants of land, like the railroads, or high protective tariffs, like the steel mills. But when the union has grown strong and powerful, while still preserving its special protection where its interests are thereby furthered, it is prone to insist on its private rights and independence where such interference by society would militate against them—again in a way not entirely dissimilar from a business corporation. Thus the unions of Australia when they were weak demanded compulsory arbitration, or the interference of "the public" in industrial disputes to enforce upon employers higher wages and standards; and so long as this resulted in the lifting of sweated trades to the level of the general laboring population, they were most enthusiastic in favor of this new instrument of securing their interests. But when the arbitrators refused to grant standards higher than those generally observed, the unionists went back to their own method of strike and indifference to public arbitration, and as a consequence in Australasian industry, just as in Canada and wherever they have been tried, compulsory arbitration laws are unenforceable.

While not monoplies in their attitude toward other groups of workers, seeking to include all competitors where business corporations seek to exclude and destroy them, the business unions are monopolies in their attitude toward employers and "the public." In comparison with other monopolies, they are apt to be more powerful and considerably less vulnerable than all but the very strongest trusts. Legally the latter seem almost impregnable, while against unions injunctions are easily obtained, but legal and actual vulnerability are two very different things, and it is considerably easier to force a small group of employers to surrender their property and their means of production should they refuse to serve the public (a course actually taken recently in Italy) than it is to force a great body of workers to become productive. This question verges on our fundamental problem, and will receive later consideration; here we but point out the monopolistic nature of the business union.

We have already seen the attitude both sellers and buyers of labor take toward outside mediation and arbitration—accepting it when it strengthens their position, rejecting it when, as in the case of Mr. Gary in the 1919 steel strike, it bids fair to weaken it. This attitude is typical; the business union, like the business man in general, operates for profit and not for any "sentimental" desire to serve the community. That would hardly be "good business." Hence the business unionists aim to get what they can and let the consumer pay; as one leader recently expressed it, if the employers do not make enough money they can easily "pass the buck" to the public. Most workers now recognize that a continual rise of wages which the employer can use to send prices up is useless as a permanent measure of relief; but even the most intelligent and enlightened know that by strikes they can manage to keep themselves a little ahead of the game, and until other relief is at hand they persist in the tactics of business unionism.

Business disregard of the welfare of the community resulting from an eye on the main chance may even develop into that extreme type known as predatory unionism, in which the workers in a monopoly unite with the employers to boost prices. The activities of "Skinny" Madden and Brindell of the building trades form a good example; others are the willingness of transportation corporations and other public utilities to utilize the increased pay they offer their workers as an argument toward the securing of higher fares and rates. Such a policy is merely an offensive and defensive alliance between business organizations for the better control of the trade.

This attitude finds further exemplification in the readiness of some business unions to find an excuse for breaking their contracts when it is no longer advantageous to them to keep them. In general of course the sanctity of contracts as a cardinal business principle is rigorously adhered to, as the only possible basis upon which collective bargaining can operate; but certain discrepancies between labor and other commodities prevents a too rigorous application of contract law and custom. Labor, unlike other articles for whose supply contracts are made, can not, as yet, at least, be attached for debt, or non-fulfillment of agreement. And whereas the business man who undertakes obligations which subsequent conditions render impossible to fulfill can always clear himself by declaring himself insolvent and going through bankruptcy procedure, the labor union which makes an agreement to work at a wage which a rapid rise in prices later reduces to less then sufficient to support its members has no means of liquidating its assets and starting out afresh. If contracts between unions and employers were made enforceable by law, as many advocate, this would be tantamount to reviving in new form the old imprisonment for debt. One solution might possibly lie in the establishment of a bankruptcy court for labor contracts; another, in making real instead of monetary wages the basis of collective agreement. Be that as it may, the lack of any means of freeing the union of obligations which it has become impossible to fulfill is the direct cause of nine-tenths of the so-called "broken contracts" which have not first been broken by bad faith on the part of the employer. That there does exist a residue of cases where group interest and freedom from penalty lead unions to violate contracts can not, however, be denied; it is one of the consequences of group individualism.

But the direct clash between the interest of the business union and that of society occurs in the use of labor's main weapon, the strike. The worker never strikes against "the public" or the consumer; but the nature of his weapon obliges him to injure the employer through the consumer. Direct injury or sabotage he rarely resorts to; but his weapon by its very indirectness necessitates the injury of the public. Thus the contention is true that every strike is to the immediate disadvantage of the consumer, and that its use is always attended by loss to the community. But in placing responsibility it is not so clearly recognized that it is not the side that begins the strike or lock-out that is alone to blame for the cessation of production. Preference of individual group interests to the interests of the community is the direct cause of industrial warfare, but the employer who prefers higher profits to granting any demands of his workers is placing his own interests ahead of the public need for production just as surely as is the group of workers who prefer higher wages to that same production. A strike and its resultant loss to the consumer is caused and continued just as much by refusal to accede to demands as it is by persistence in making them, and for precisely the same reasons: the worker prefers to see the public suffer rather than accept or continue a low standard of living, and the employer prefers it to accepting lower profits. This holds true in both strikes and lockouts, and is entirely independent of the particular group whose demands precipitated the conflict. The strike is the logical result of the system of group individualism; it can pass away only when that system does. In this similarity established between the actions of capital and labor, no invidious comparison, of course, is intended, nor any justification; the condemnation often bestowed upon the course of labor by the editors of public opinion is merited, so far as it goes, and is a promising sign. But it must be clearly realized that this condemnation cannot be voiced against the members of the unions without at the same time applying to every business man and organization; for it is a condemnation, not of individuals, but of the entire theoretical basis of modern business structure. The union that strikes to prevent a reduction of real wages is doing precisely what the mill does which shuts down when further operation would be unprofitable; and the same approbation or condemnation visited upon the business man who, running the chances of periodical hard times and losses, makes as high profits as he can while he can, must be applied also to the union which, exposed to the same danger of unemployment in bad times, extorts what is can from employer and public while it can. Neither workers nor employer *wants* to curtail production; yet in the modern economic organization he *must*.

Public opinion has today reached the stage where in certain industries it calls "public utilities" it refuses to allow the employer, even to his loss, to curtail his service to the public. Municipal transportation and power supply is supposed to belong to this class, as of course do all those services carried on directly by the government; and it has been suggested that a similar enforcement be directed against the workers in such public utilities. Aside from the non-existence of bankruptcy laws for labor, it is exceedingly difficult to find any line of demarkation between, say, the supplying of light and the supplying of moving pictures, which will define just when an industry is a public utility and when it is not. Why, for example, is it more essential that men in the post office be not allowed to strike than men in the coal mines? or that trolley lines be forced to supply service than woolen mills clothing? The nature of the employer and the form of organization in the industry bears no relevance to the necessity of the service to the public.

Thus in this most important of all relations the business union reveals its dominance by the philosophy and ideology and methods of group individualism. It is like any other respectable corporation. "The steel industry," runs the recent Interchurch report on the 1919 steel strike,[1] "is being run for the making of profit, and not primarily for the making of steel as the country needs it, and it favors (a) spells of idleness during which the country and the steel workers pay for the maintenance of idle machinery and later (b) spurts of long hours, high speed labor." Without pausing to ask who on earth ever supposed the steel industry was being run "primarily for the making of steel as the country needs it," we could add, "The business union is being run for profit, and not primarily for the production of commodities as the country needs them, and it favors (a) periods of enforced shut-down during which the public suffers and (b) high wages which add to the cost of living for everyone."

"But," say the loyal members of the Federation who do not yet realize this similarity of aim, (though they are growing fewer every day) "you forget that the worker is acting only in self-defense." As-

[1] *New York Times*, July 28, 1920.

suredly, the worker would starve if through strikes he did not enforce
a living wage; but so by the same token would the employer who made
no profits. When does a fair profit become profiteering? When does
self-defense become depredation against the public? The man who
admitted that in prosperous times the business man who is not making
huge profits and the laborer who is not making huge wages are incompetent, was but drawing the logical conclusions from our system of
group individualism.

What, then, is the cause of this general sense of irresponsibility
towards the community or its needs, of the absence of any sense of
obligation toward society, which is the characteristic note of business
unionism? Why has group individualism become dominant, threaten-
ing the very basis of social and industrial existence and eating the heart
out of the great industrial machine which the last century created in
Western civilization? We have now arrived at a position where we
are able to analyze the causes of the condition we regard as dangerous.
At bottom it is the very necessity of the individualistic economic system upon which that civilization rests; capitalism, fully developed,
would thus seem to be cutting its own throat. The purpose determining the structure and methods of the union is the same as that determining all business and economic activity everywhere: the desire for
profits, if possible with resulting benefit to society, but first and last,
for good or for ill, the desire for profits.

Yet there is a still further reason why the business union is irresponsible: whereas the capitalist is directly responsible to the community,
in that he possesses the power and control of the physical means of production, the worker is primarily responsible to, and is urged to be loyal
to, his employer's profits, and only secondarily to the community or
its needs. Whether or not production will continue or will be suspended
is vested legally in the capitalist and owner of the factory; that is the
meaning of the great principle of private property on which contemporary civilization rests. If a strike threatens it is for the employer
to decide whether the loss to his pocket-book or the loss to the public
will be preferred; but for the workers the decision is between loss to
their pay-rolls or loss to dividends. The employer is in direct relations
with the consumer, he receives his remuneration from that consumer.
The worker is but indirectly related to the consumer; not the purchaser
but the employer remunerates him. It is exceedingly difficult to build
up or to expect a feeling of loyalty and responsibility to be developed
between two parties whose interests, as are those of employer and em-

ployee, are in many respects antithetical.   And if the worker sees that the community does not hold the employer, who is in direct relations with it, responsible for failure to supply service; if he sees Mr. Gary lauded and praised instead of being charged with deliberately curtailing the production of steel, if he sees no complaint against the mill-owners who shut down because they cannot get the prices they want, he is not likely to be over-solicitous of restraining his demands and refraining from securing them by strike, of "loyally" helping his employer make large profits, on the plea that he must operate the industry for the good of the community.   Efforts to create a feeling of loyalty and responsibility to the employer are, in fact, regarded by the workers, and generally, it must be confessed, quite correctly, though sometimes inadequately, as the efforts of the employers to save themselves and their profits.

For it is to his profits, not to the public, that the capitalist wants the worker to be responsible.   That would imply making of the worker a partner in the industry, and granting him real control over its direction; and it is one of the cardinal tenets of good business that the worker is in no wise a sharer in the enterprise.   The business belongs to the Company or the owner, not to the workers in it; and the former alone are responsible for its conduct.   The employee has been carefully made to feel that his personal fate is negligible and of no account.   "You're fired," says the foreman; "it's easy enough to fill your place."   "If you do not wish to accept these wages," says the suaver superintendent, "there are plenty of men who do."   Raw materials to be had in one market are useless if there is more in another cheaper one.   Under such conditions, with labor just as responsible and just as capable of responsibility for the conduct of the industry as the pig-iron or the coal, it is not much wonder that the workers do not develop a loyalty to the interests of the public or of anybody outside themselves.   Before they can be expected to regard themselves as coöperating in the efficient service of the community they must be given some opportunity to coöperate and serve.

Yet, in spite of all these unfavorable conditions, if there exist some strong general social purpose the business union will respond.   The impulse is not lacking; it is the opportunity which rarely comes.   During the war the unionists of every land, hardened and practical business men though they were, responded almost to a man to the call made upon them.   They would work efficienctly and well so soon as they felt that the object of their endeavor was to further aims far greater than the swelling of dividends. In countless speeches and articles they learned that they were the men behind the men behind the guns, that upon them ultimately rested the safety of their friends and relatives in the trenches and their own homes and families. The whole community suddenly awoke to perceive that they, the workers, were important and indispensable members. It was no longer, "If you don't like it you're fired." It was "Men wanted at high wages with good conditions." The community expected the workers to do their duty and gave them an adequate remuneration for doing it; it is no wonder that they responded nobly and well. Despite all the conditions militating against such efficient functioning, as the need increased the workers loyally outstripped it.

But when peace broke out, it was no longer a question of "making the world safe for democracy" or working "for King and Country" or "Pour la France"; instead it was a question of "getting back to normal." Perhaps just because of their taste of efficient production for service as a motive rather than the profit of the stock-holder, the workers in all lands are far from enthusiastic about swelling their employers' dividends. No longer does the press speak of "rewarding the faithful worker"; its tune has changed to an exhortation to all good citizens to come out and put down through strike-breaking the "autocracy of labor." Attempts like the Plumb plan to formulate a method, however imperfectly, whereby the railway men may work together toward the efficient operation of the roads as a public utility, and thus carry over into peace times the stimulus and spur of the war period when they were operated on that basis, are met with the cry of "rank Bolshevism." It is no wonder that the unionists do not feel the same enthusiasm in "ensuring the supremacy of American business" as they did in fighting the armies of the Kaiser; it is no wonder that they see little incentive to work hard for their employers if they can have a good time without it. To many competent observers it has indeed appeared, as Mr. Laski said, that the mainspring of the capitalistic system, the willingness of the worker to work for the gain of the capitalist, has indeed snapped.

The experience of war time teaches again the old lesson that any knowledge of the history of the labor movement can not fail to corroborate, that the workers are eager and anxious to do their work faithfully and well, with a view to the well-being of the community as well as to their own interests, if the community will but respond to their overtures and grant them the conditions of efficient functioning. During the war nothing was too good for our munition-makers and ship-builders, because we realized that the better their conditions the better they would work and produce. Today it is "pampered labor" and "unwonted luxury." When responsibility is expected of the workers, they have responded; when the community has rejected their social idealism and scornfully delivered them over to the mercy of their employer, disillusioned they have been forced to conform to the group individualism which rules society.

For the public feels no reciprocal responsibility to labor for the responsibility it demands of it. When it fears for its supply of some commodity it threatens troops and injunction, and swarms out to put down strikes to the great joy of the employer; but has it ever done anything for the worker which he has not forced it to do by his own exertions? It protects any employer who wishes to start a new business against the competition of foreign manufacturers, even though in so doing it may double or treble the cost to itself; but has it ever protected the weak laborer from the competition of unskilled immigrants?

Frank Morrison, Secretary of the American Federation of Labor, and a staunch business unionist if there ever was one, said recently: " The workers will not concede that the community has any purpose or intention to render justice to the workers should it force itself into participation in industrial relations. On the contrary, its only object in forcing itself into these relations is to prevent the workers from taking advantage of natural conditions to better their economic condition . . . a right which the community holds sacred when applied to property. . . . The community's interest in the worker is founded upon its own desire for the worker's commodities, and not upon any belief in the rights of the worker; its concern is not with the wages paid to the workers or the conditions under which they work, but rather with the continuous operation of industry so that its wants may be supplied without interruption. After these wants have been supplied it is a matter of no concern to the community what becomes of the worker." [1]

This is the worker's conception of the community, based solely upon the bitter experience of the past. This is the "community" in the sense defined, society organized as consumers, the political machinery through which society functions. It is incontestable that this "community" is controlled by capitalistic interests which through legislature, court, and press secure that the interests of those with a stake in the country, business men and employers, shall be followed. The "community" also claims that this at the same time makes for the best interest of all

[1] *New York Times,* July 18, 1920.

the workers. The latter doubt this. They honestly believe that the dice are loaded against them, that the government is hostile to them and has no concern for their interests. They believe that the "community" desires low prices even if it means starvation wages. They believe that it desires the stoppage of strikes no matter what the justice of the strikers' claims. They believe that it cares not a whit what becomes of them so long as its wants are cheaply filled. And it would indeed be very hard to prove that the workers are not right.

The blame, if blame there be, for the irresponsibility and selfish regard for group interests which the business union in common with the business man displays on occasion must be laid squarely at the door of society at large. It has acquiesced in a social philosophy that has made such things possible; it cannot assail labor unions without assailing its own standards and its own acts. And that small professional group who are comparatively detached from industrial conflict, that remnant left over when labor and capital have been subtracted, to whom editors and professors appeal with sublime hope for impartiality, the "community" in this sense has only its own selfish disregard of the workers' desires and hopes and its unthinking subservience to the interests of the employing and business classes to thank if the workers in their struggle to improve their conditions are too busy to consider the inconvenience their acts may cause for the clerk or the preacher.

10. BUSINESS UNIONISM—ITS IDEAL AND ITS IMPLICATIONS

THE ultimate aim of the labor movement is the attainment of security and an equal status in society; business unionism seeks to realize this aim through the organization of a monopoly in labor and the selling of this labor, as a business proposition, to employers in exchange for a secure and improved status. Business unionism thus has a special ideal and aim of its own toward which it is tacitly if not consciously working, a state of affairs which if achieved would represent for it the best possible society.

This ultimate aim includes, first of all, the complete organization of the trade. Collective bargaining is successful just so far as it is in the power of the union to control all the workers in a given field. If any large proportion remain outside, the union is exposed to their competition, and finds it impossible to carry on a successful strike so long as the employer can secure as many men as he wants at his own pay. Bargaining power is effective only as it is effectively backed up by the power to withdraw services. The aim of every union, no matter what its conscious philosophy, if it desires to secure any concessions from the employers, is to attain that ideal of the unionist's heart, the fully organized trade. Revolutionary or predatory unionism, which, like the I. W. W. repudiates all contracts and agreements, of course does not find this essential; the I. W. W. aims rather by swift forays and guerilla attacks to force the employer out of business. Even the I. W. W., however, hope eventually to attain complete organization, and in business unionism this is the goal of the workers' hopes. This does not necessarily mean the closed shop; the closed shop is not an end in itself, but a means to the attainment of organization. A union which like the railway brotherhoods, or the clothing unions, has practically organized the whole of its trade cares very little indeed whether the shop be closed or open, whether, since there are scarcely any non-unionists, they be discriminated against or no. Such a union knows that every worker will want to join the union, and that a genuine open shop, a shop in which there is no discrimination against the unionist, speedily becomes a union shop.

But complete organization necessarily means far more than the organization of a single trade. When the worker was still a skilled artisan the craft was the important division; the cobbler, the carpenter, the mason—these were the economic units, and the cobbler's outfit, the carpenter's kit, were the tools and means of production. But today the cobbler is replaced by the great shoe factory, subdivided into thirty or forty distinct trades; and for the production of shoes not one but all of these processes are necessary. The modern tool is not the instrument of the handicraftsman, but the great factory and all that concerns its supply. The organization of the worker to control it must follow the tool; and today in most industries the tool is rapidly broadening out from the single machine to the entire factory. The persistence in these conditions of the older separate trade unions, organized in days when trade distinctions were far more vital than they are today, each trade with its separate agreements well-timed by the employer to terminate at different intervals, and thus prevent the occurrence of a strike of all his hands at one time; all these conditions weaken the separate trades, and give rise to that situation in which half the workers are "scabbing on the job" while the other half are out on strike. Suppose that the collective agreement in the coal mining industry expires, and the operators refuse to renew it save on lower terms: a situation which normally produces a strike. The miners down tools, but the operators rush more or less skilled strike-breakers from all parts of the country and manage to get out some coal. If the stationary or hoist engineers will only strike too, the affair will be a success, because the engineers will be exceedingly difficult to replace. But they have a contract that runs for two more years; they will not go out, and the strike is lost. After such an experience the miners recognize the great advantage they would gain if the engineers were only in their union and could if necessary be withdrawn to increase their bargaining power. Is it any wonder, therefore, that the coal miners have organized an industrial union that includes all those who work in or around coal mines?

All industries, of course, are not yet so fully industrialized in structure as coal mining; in most the separate trade lines persist in a significant form. But in order to organize an industry completely into one great group it is not necessary for all craft distinctions thereby to be obliterated. Precisely the same result can be obtained if the industrial union is a federation instead of a highly homogeneous body. To all intents and purposes the four railroad brotherhoods act as a single unit in any important question; during the war they united with the ten A. F. L. unions of the less skilled railroad workers to form what is known as the fourteen railway unions, and it is clear that while not sacrificing their autonomy these fourteen trades for all practical purposes form a single industrial group like the National Union of Railwaymen of Great Britain. The garment workers, though industrially organized and including even the office clerks and the draymen and truckdrivers who handle their product, preserve for certain purposes the separate trade divisions of cutter, presser, baster, and so on. The building trades have become a unit with their "building trades councils"; the past year saw the most "craft autonomous" of the A. F. L. unions unite in a joint national committee to manage the steel strike as a unit. The A. F. L. Trades Departments are increasing in importance. The "blanket agreement," in which all the crafts in a given industry bargain and strike in unison and combine their grievances is growing more and more popular. All of these are signs of the realization of labor that in order to carry out their ultimate aim of complete organization and effective bargaining power they must in some way organize themselves with the entire industry as a basis.

This is the first aim of business unionism; the second, paradoxical as it may seem, is for the complete industrial organization of the employers. The latter have in most fields been quick enough to organize for themselves; we saw, for instance, how the blacksmiths' and molders' unions of 1859 were called forth directly by employers organizing against labor. Many industries are in the hands of so-called trusts; that is, not every mill or factory is amalgamated into one large corporation, but in the industry there is one great company that by its size and power dominates all other and acts as their spokesman in all important matters. Such is the U. S. Steel Corporation, for example. Most other industries are united into trade associations that exercise a controlling influence over their members, speak for them in time of strike or labor difficulty, and effectually if not legally limit prices by agreement. These range all the way from the close concert of action in the meat-packing and the anthracite coal trade to the less organic and more competitive trades. Natural economic reasons, the unprofitableness of unrestricted competition primarily, have prompted this virtual centralization. These associations have taken over the function of bargaining with the union that on its side controls the industry; collective agreements are generally made between associations of workers and associations of employers, not with individual employers. No single company can afford to grant better conditions and higher wages than others; the competition would kill it. And no single company is strong enough to get better terms from the union; if it were, they would be speedily enjoyed by all the others.

But there are some industries where the unit is relatively small, and here the union itself desires an employers' organization with which to deal. In the clothing trade, in the soft coal trade, for example, shops and mines are fairly small and competition is bitter; a separate bargain with each would be wearisome, and a series of never-ending shop strikes would not be worth the small advantage that might be gained in some places. In collective bargaining it is thus to the interests of both sides to organize completely and deal as units with the drawing up and acceptance of wage-scales and other agreements. The garment unions have thus forced organization on the reluctant employers; but now that it has come, few would care to return to the ruinous days of cut-throat competition for labor. The building trades similarly have forced organization for builders for purposes of collective bargaining.

The development, then, of business unionism according to the lines it has marked out for itself, provided that development could continue in the direction of least resistance with no outside interference, would logically result in the formation in every important national industry of a group comprising all the employers and another group comprising all the workers, bargaining together on a basis of equality, making treaties and concluding agreements. It would be a balance of power in which the undue growth in strength on either side would cause dislocation and friction. It would be a business partnership between two groups for the continuance of the industry, in which one, as it were, would be the active and the other the sleeping partner. Such an ideal has already been practically formulated in England as the Whitley Joint National Councils; incidentally, what it might mean for the rest of the community is foreshadowed in the provision in the constitutions of a number of the Whitley councils already established in England of means "for the joint maintenance of selling-prices."[1]

Within this structure the aims of business unionism would continue to function. Security of employment—the first great end of the labor movement, the only safeguard against the haunting dread of starvation—would be the first achievement the unionists would seek. To obtain this, the unionists would insist, as they grew in power, on taking over all control over the "hiring and firing" of men; on allowing their dismissal only for proved incompetency or dishonesty, and then only if some other provision were made by the employer or society whereby it would

[1] *American Labor Yearbook*, 1920, 358.

be certain they would not suffer.   The lack of any such provision and the working class consciousness and solidarity, together with sad experience, in industries like the garment trades where the union has a certain amount of control over dismissal, are the direct causes of the unions at times forcing the retention of inefficient or incompetent workers; as in the federal service the lack of any pension system has led humane department officials to retain on the pay-roll men whose years of faithful service have made them incapable of further labor.

But in addition to this virtual assumption of control over the hiring and firing of individuals, business unionism in its search for security from unemployment as it grows stronger will vigorously protest against the business methods of laying off hands when trade conditions slump or prices and demand falls off.   In the history of the labor movement the great strikes have always taken place—in 1877, in 1886,—when the employers at the close of a period of prosperity have sought to reduce their labor force; and it is not too much to say that the greatest gain the labor movement has ever made, commonly overlooked in the presence of more spectacular considerations, is the way in which the unions have forced the mills to keep on their men in slack times.   The modern superintendent shows that a large reduction is sure to mean a strike; he realizes that it will cost less to keep his men on than to precipitate a complete shutdown.   As business unionism with greater organization attains greater real control over industry, it will demand that the supply of labor be no longer considered as a raw material to be bought and sold in smaller quantities in time of decreased output, but rather as a fixed charge upon the industry.   The capitalist does not burn down his factory or allow it to rust and rot during hard times; just so, the business union claims, he must maintain his labor force in good condition also.

Not only does the union object to hard times; it condemns the seasonal character of all trades which run by spurts and starts.   Already the coal miners and the garment workers are protesting against the type of management that allows high speed overtime production when prices are best, followed by unemployment and idleness when they decline; the system that postpones as late as possible the production of coal until the fall and winter when men will pay more for it than in spring and summer.   And of course in thus calling for continuous employment and production the worker is directly contravening the interests of his employer, which as we have seen lie in a very flexible labor supply capable of delicate adjustment to the state of the market.   Compelled to maintain a fixed amount of labor, the employer will lose great opportunities for the sudden amassing of profits in time of need or the freedom from the charges of surporting men in time of surplus. Many employers do not like to throw their men out of work, especially if they adopt the benevolent paternalism which regards the giving of employment as a laudable charity; and some even hesitate to dismiss them at a direct loss to themselves. But no employer today ever carries this benevolence very far; in the words of a recent trust president when shutting down his woolen mills, "We can not afford to keep men on without a certain number of orders."

Finally, with continuous steady employment assured, the business union will seek a high standard of living, just as high as it can extort when it comes to making treaties with the employers' organization. No business man ever voluntarily curtailed the golden inflow of profits so long as they lasted; no business man, though he might assert, and assert it truly, that he was "making so much money he didn't know what to do with it," ever thought of making less. He rather went on to prove his assertion by inordinate luxury. Not even Henry Ford, philanthropic and well-disposed as he is, inclined to let his employees share to some extent the gold mine he has discovered, has yet proposed to make machines at cost. And no business unionist will ever stop, if he has the power, raising his wages just as high as he possibly can. The only limit to the size of the "fair day's pay" he asks is the limit to his power to secure it. Labor is insatiable; it will never stop in its demands until it is forced to by some outside power.

Such is the ideal of respectable and conservative labor unions, an ideal not clearly seen as yet by all advocates of economic opportunism, but yet the ideal to which all the tendencies of business unionism point as its logical development and full flowering. This is the ideal type of the business union, the "perfect" union. Partnership with capital, security of tenure, ever increasing wages—such is the outcome of collective bargaining. But it is not the whole picture. Such an apotheosis of the business union has several further and highly edifying implications, implications which on the whole do not tend to relieve a scene otherwise fairly sombre enough.

For the utopia of the business unionist is a rigid and static society, a society made up of dozens of great antagonists in pairs, eyeing each other in every industry jealously and bitterly, a society incapable of adaptation either to the genuine needs of the community or to any changed process of industrial technique. It is a society based on a precarious balance of power which renders any change possible only at the price of a terrific industrial struggle. Just as for the past century the map of Europe could be changed to correspond with newly awakened nationalistic and commercial exigencies which had been wholly dormant in 1815 when it was laid out, only through the dreaded course of war; just as the seething mass of eastern Europe and the Hapsburg Empire could only attain that realignment without which life was intolerable to its inhabitants through precipitating a deadly and destructive struggle over the entire globe: just so the utopia of the business union would prove an iron cage preventing the free development of social and economic forces.

For business unionism ultimately means stagnation. As both sides, organized labor and organized capital, grow in power, collective bargaining is extended to more and more minute details. Agreements necessitate a more and more complicated regulation of rates, wages, scales, and conditions, a regulation exceedingly difficult to work out and agree upon, and even more difficult to change. Hoxie gives an excellent account of the increasing elaborateness of these details. "The employer is constantly endeavoring to reintroduce individual bargaining and to force down the wage rate and to increase the exertion and output for a given wage by indirect and specific encroachments on the existing status, for instance, by slight changes in method and process, by creating conditions which require slightly greater exertion or irregular home work and overtime; by division of processes and redistribution of work, by changes in tools, by changes in mode of payment, and by arbitrary fines and exactions. These changes for the most part have the effect of increasing work or reducing pay. In the absence of clearly defined standards they are easy to introduce and are often introduced so as to result in reductions without knowledge of this effect by the workers, and the individual worker alone is usually too weak, even if he does recognize their effect, to resist them. It is a method of forcing workers to compete against one another without their knowledge. These encroachments mean, therefore, undercutting and a progressive reduction of wage rates, and conditions of employment.[1]

"The only way to prevent this is to have all the incidents of work and pay most minutely and clearly specified and this specification rigorously maintained. . . . Many minute and harassing specifications are laid down especially in regard to kinds of work that may be done, by each worker, modes of doing work, times and modes of payment, deductions and exactions, times of beginning and ending of work, ma-

---

[1] Hoxie, *Trade Unionism in the United States*, 257.

chinery, materials, objectionable work, etc. . . . It is evident that these standards can not be maintained effectively so far as *all* the workers are concerned if the employer is allowed to adopt at will changes in methods and processes of work. Such changes make it possible for the employer to create new tasks and jobs for which no standards or uniformities have been established, to lop off parts of the work from the old standardized classes, along with laying off the workman himself, and in both ways to create new classes of workers with new conditions of work, and perhaps lower rates of pay for all the members of the group, to prevent the degradation of skilled workers and the introduction into their midst of subgroups in which competition exists, they must prevent the introduction of such new conditions of work— the creation of new tasks and jobs and new classification of the workers— except under their control and under conditions that will secure on the new jobs conditions of work and pay uniform with the old. . . . Hence, in part, the union tendency to resist new trades, new machinery, new methods and processes." [1]

The agreements in some industries today are the product of months of labor and comprise whole volumes of figures and stipulations; it is said that in the Lancashire cotton trade experts give their entire lives to the working out of such scales, and even then but imperfectly understand the great mass of detail. When it is remembered that each major provision represents a compromise arrived at only after hours of argument and expostulation; that at any time disagreement in the formulation of a new contract may mean a complete tie-up of the industry; that any new process or method would irrevocably wreck the entire list;—it is no wonder that both employer and worker come to the conclusion that new inventions or changes would cost far more in the process of readjustment than they would ever be worth. Such a condition means of course the curbing of the initiative of both worker and manager, the rejection of new inventions and more efficient methods, and in general the reëstablishment of all those restrictive and deadening regulations which marked the decay of the guild control of industry. The only way out of this economic stagnation would be the replacement of collective agreement, which is a treaty making process, with all of the faults and none of the virtues diplomacy displays, by a process of genuine legislation: the careful adjustment of new conditions and new processes to the needs of the worker. But such a process implies a genuine control by the worker over the actual conduct of industry, and that industrial control far transcends the limits

[1] Hoxie, *op. cit.*, 290.

of business unionism. Here again business unionism contains within itself the tendencies which will make it inevitably develop into something quite different. With all the processes and standards minutely determined, the workers would subside into a state of contentment and self-satisfaction; the determining of complicated agreements would not interest them. All such matters the business agent would tend to, and insure the steady supply of wages whether the worker was busy or idle, whether times were good or bad. His union would of necessity become a bureaucracy which denied him any effective voice or responsibility; and the employer, with every interest in keeping him from demanding more and more, would probably adapt a policy of benevolent paternalism and charge the cost up to the community. Visions of a capitalistic state on some such model levying tribute on the more undeveloped portions of the globe are quite familiar, thanks to Mr. Hilaire Belloc and others; if the days of the grandeur (and decline) of Rome were imitated in this respect, history might well repeat itself also in the *panem et circenses* to the unionists. The unions would be the most conservative groups in the country, as they were when the guilds reigned, with no social idealism, no sympathy or regard for any group outside their own small circle. Status they would have achieved, status equal to their fellows; like the French rentier peasantry they would be permanently satisfied with the status quo so long as they could suck more and more profits out of the owner of the industry. Equality, yes—but no liberty and no social or even class solidarity—nothing but prejudices.

This picture is purposely extreme; not for a moment do we believe that such a state of affairs is either desired by any man, unionist or capitalist, or that it could ever come to pass. Surely in our exposition the inconsistencies, the opposing tendencies, must be already apparent. Yet such a state has been closely enough approached in a very few conservative unions, notably the glass workers, the pattern makers, and, till a few years ago, the railroad brotherhoods, to give us food for thought. The purpose in thus sketching an ideal or completely developed business unionism, by following the logical implications of the aims and principles on which the business union of today operates, has been to reveal both the inadequacy of those ideals and the impossibility of business unionism developing very much further along the lines it has hitherto traversed.

For this has been the sum and substance of our contention throughout the examination of the conservative or business trade union. It can never achieve the ideal which it has set for itself, because in the very progress toward that goal it is bound to transform itself into something very different indeed. Business unionism, in fact, carries within itself the seed of its own destruction, and it is now our task to sum up those tendencies which make it not only possible but highly probable that the group individualism which to a large extent characterizes the union movement of today is through the fuller development of its present motives and aims destined to be transformed.

Business unionism is based on a balance of bargaining power. Bargains can only take place between equals. That is why the unions have insisted on collective rather than individual bargains, in which the employer's power is so markedly disproportionate to that of the worker that to use the word bargain at all is a mere travesty. But suppose the power of the organized workers grows until it is the employer who is the weaker; suppose he becomes so much the weaker that his function is but to agree to whatever terms the workers are willing to grant? What then becomes of the collective bargain, and of the business ideal founded thereon? Many manufacturers are already complaining of what they call the "autocracy of labor," by which they mean of course that control of the industry is passing from their hands to their employees, and that they can no longer run their own business to suit themselves. As a matter of fact, with each new advance towards its business goal, with each new accretion of strength, the business union tends to upset the balance of bargaining power upon which, like the peace of the system of theoretically equal and independent European states, its treaty power and processes depends.

In the first place, complete organization, that goal of the business union, implies, as has been seen, under modern industrial conditions, if not a single great industrial union, at least a single federation of unions acting as a unit for each large industry or vocation. This means that the workers would cease to think and act in terms of their particular job or trade, which necessarily tends to obscure their vision of the industrial process as a whole, and think and plan rather for the entire productive unit. The hoist engineer, organized as a separate craft, thinks only in terms of the hours, wages, and conditions pertaining to that craft; but organized as a part of all the other workers in or about the coal mine, the whole body of United Mine Workers, in the normal course of considering wages and hours, is led to regard them as they affect and are affected by coal mining as a whole. Hence they have been naturally drawn to consider the further and more fundamental causes of their insecurity and low standard of living, and to assail the inefficiency and waste entailed by methods of operation in jumps and spurts. A single craft neither desires nor can presume to dictate any general industrial policies; but a union organized on the industrial basis is not only brought face to face with the necessity of exercising direct control over the conduct of the enterprise, but as it grows in power it will inevitably be led, whatever its proclamation of adherence to the pure milk of business unionism, to assume more and more of the functions of the present employer. Under these conditions it is not surprising that thousands of unionists at the present day are consciously abandoning business unionism, and instead of a simple demand for a division of the profits are putting forward a demand for an increasing control and regulation of the conduct of the industry. And with the motive of individual advantage thus necessitating a great emphasis on the purposes and processes of production, the double strain is placing greater and greater emphasis on the social consequences and implications of production.

Thus it can confidently be predicted that if the unions increase in power they will of necessity tend to assume more and more of direct control over the industry; just as confidently it can be said there is no limit to their demand for a higher standard of living. Mr. Gompers has said, as has already been quoted, "We do not set any particular standard, but work for the best possible conditions immediately obtainable for the workers. When these are obtained then we strive for better. The working people will not stop when any particular point is reached; they will never stop in their efforts to obtain a better life for themselves, for their wives, for their children, for all humanity." [1] In this opinion he finds himself at one with William Z. Foster, secretary treasurer of the National Committee for Organizing Iron and Steel Workers during the recent steel strike. "It is idle to say that the trade unions will rest content with anything short of actual emancipation. For they are as insatiable as the veriest so-called revolutionary unions. In the measure that their strength increases, so do their demands. They have sent wages up: 2, 3, 4, 5, 6, 7, 8, dollars per day, and hours down: 12, 11, 10, 9, 8, 7, 6, per day with all kinds of other concessions sandwiched in between. And now they are more radical in their demands than ever before in their history. Permanently satisfied trade unions under capitalism would be the eighth wonder of the world, outrivalling in interest the famous hanging gardens of Babylon. They would be impossible. With its growing power, Organized Labor will go on winning greater and greater concessions, regardless of how profound they may be." [2]

[1] Gompers, *The American Labor Movement.*
[2] Foster, *The Great Steel Strike*, 257.

With these two men, the leader of the so-called conservative wing of the American labor movement and a representative of the more radical section of the orthodox body, in perfect agreement as to the real meaning of the slogan " A fair day's work for a fair day's pay," any notion that the business union would ever stop if it had the power to extort more from the employer is quite futile.   Even if, as was suggested above, the employers' and the workers' organizations united to increase joint profits, with every gain of strength the workers would demand the lion's share.   And with this insatiable appetite for more meeting them at every turn, with all control of "their own business" taken out of their hands, through minute regulation or through actual control by the worker: it would indeed be foolish for the capitalists if they did not urge some form of nationalization or other scheme that would give them a secure and permanent income.   It is a question at present whether most of the stock-holders in the railroads of this country really would not prefer government operation and control with a guaranteed rate of interest to the present prospects of increasing rate regulation and "labor domination."   In England, where the labor movement has attained much greater power, there are many industries that would thus welcome the advent of what is called "state capitalism." Those captains of industry who have latterly become rather captains of finance would lose interest in the operations of the stock markets so soon as the demand of the worker for security had put a stop to the possibility of flexibly adapting industrial conditions to the business market.   And any such proposal for nationalization with or without control by the unions would of necessity entirely transform the aims and functions of the business union.

The growing power of the business union and of the labor movement in general will either continue to be exercised solely for the interests of the group, or it will broaden its aims so as to include in addition to the group interest the comprehension of the needs of society as a whole, of the consumers in general.   If this power were exercised for purely selfish interests, society would be forced to place upon it some sort of restrictions and limitations, such as are now thrown about public utilities.   It might even go so far as to penalize strikes solely for group interests.   But where the worker is denied the right to strike, the most conservative business unions becomes *ipso facto* revolutionary and lawbreaking, seeking to change at least certain aspects of the social system; and once shaken out of its shell the business union would be forced to embark either politically or otherwise into still further policies which, inasmuch as they could necessarily be social rather than group, would so transform the business union as to make its features unrecognizable. This is the penalty for attempting to curb by legal means the actions of the labor movement; when *all* activities and policies become "subversive," the workers will naturally have no scruples in choosing the most advantageous, and thus legal assaults upon radicalism prove only to be boomerangs.

On the other hand, even if the political government made no such attempt at social regulation, the possession of power is an almost irresistible temptation to use it. It is an immensely salutary educative force, tending to call out aims much more fundamental than those comprised in collective bargaining. With the interest and thought of the worker centered on production as a social function, he will, if it seems more advantageous to himself and to the consumer, stop at no change in the economic structure of society that he has the power to effect. If the wage-system meets with his disapproval, he will replace it by some other more efficient method of production; if the private ownership of the means of production and the right of property itself fall under his censure, he will supersede them with other forms of control and other types of rights.

That even the most conservative unions are in no sense bound to the safe and sane principles of business unionism it requires but a slight acquaintance with the events of recent years to convince. The unions of Great Britain, especially the so-called "Big Three" or "Triple Alliance," of the railwaymen, the mine workers, and the transport workers, are at present enjoying so much power that they literally have not awakened to its potentialities. Relying on general public disgust with parliamentary government as carried on by khaki elections and coalitions, they have appointed themselves the tribunes of the people, and sought by direct action to attain purely political ends. They have attempted to make their voice felt in both the foreign and the domestic policies of the British Empire; and, it is edifying to note, the British government generally decides to abopt a certain course of action fairly soon after the Big Three have demanded it in a pronunciamento. To many, even to those who approve the individual policies which the British unionists are seeking to enforce, this seems fraught with the utmost danger; but its significance here is merely to make plain how the control of very large power can lead business unions outside their own private interests to demand sweeping changes in the social structure. For it was but ten years ago that the British unions were notoriously conservative and dominated by group individualism, even more so than those of our own country. But then occurred reorganization and new inspiration from the industrialists, and today the British unionists hold in their hands inestimable opportunity for either good or ill.

Or take the example of Germany. After the Kapp revolution it was Karl Legien and the conservative unions who held the only real power in the country. The Ebert government was preserved, but it was preserved only because the unionists wanted it. The general strike that defeated Kapp put in Legien's hands the virtual dictatorship of Germany; he gave the power back to Ebert, but he realized, and the German unionists realized, that it was he and not Ebert who dominated the situation.

Or if we turn to America itself, where the relatively slighter strength of the labor movement has tended to restrain both the assumption and the exercise of power, we have but to consider how the Plumb Plan, worked out by Mr. Glenn Plumb and his associates as a purely "business" and "practical" solution to the railroad problem, with never a thought as to possible underlying social theories, was taken up by the conservative railroad brotherhoods, in America the very type of the business union, and adopted by a ninety per cent majority. The conscious aim of efficient and economic operation for the fulfillment of the needs of the community is assuredly a far cry from the older aims of business unionism.

Therefore, from all these causes, from the assumption of more and more control over the actual conduct of industry, from the demand for greater and greater returns that will make it more profitable to the employer to submit to social regulation and its attendant social guarantee of income, from the simple growth of power itself, the business union will find itself in a situation where its original aim of collective bargaining for the profits of industry will be far transcended. Just as surely as the community is bound to become more and more industrialized, the labor movement is bound to grow in strength, in numbers, and in power. We are prone, perhaps, to regard the industrial revolution as an event that occurred in England in the century between 1750 and 1850, and later took place in other lands in a much shorter time. This impression is totally erroneous. The industrial revolution did indeed start in England about 1750; but it has kept up ever since, growing more and more extensive, more and more intensive, and more and more rapid in its movement with every year. Far from slowing up, the industrial revolution is proceeding with greater and greater acceleration. And until that revolution halts the labor movement will continue to grow in numbers and in power; and with its growth the transformation of business unionism will be inevitable.

The business union, then, according to all present indications, will continue to grow in strength. That strength will be exerted in channels that are anti-social unless it is allowed to function through channels socially directed toward social ends. This is the sum and substance of our investigation of the typical union of the last twenty years, the business trade union.

11. INFIDELS AND HERETICS—ALIEN PHILOSOPHIES AND THEIR EFFECTS ON THE AMERICAN LABOR MOVEMENT

BEFORE continuing with our examination of the new unionism to which the typical business union of the last generation seems to be approaching, both in order to comprehend it fully and to make our survey of the various philosophies and attitudes that have come into prominence in the American labor movement at all adequate, we must pause for a moment to consider the effect on the old traditional American agricultural ideal of democracy of the great mass of foreigners from other lands and other intellectual atmospheres and traditions, and of the alien philosophies originally developed to meet conditions quite different from those obtaining in the United States. These are the infidels—those who, born in another faith, steadfastly refuse to be converted to the true doctrine of the Fathers of the constitution, the faith which, for all the higher criticism bestowed upon it in recent years, certainly remains in its fundamental dogmas the faith of the great body of American workers. Then there are also the heretics—those whom, just because they have turned apostate and after having once been in the fold have gone astray, the mother church persecutes even more bitterly than the infidel who, after all, is hardly to blame for his misfortune of being born in another community.

In general the great and tremendous influx of foreign immigration, a labor phenomenon that no other country has ever experienced in such a diversity and to such an extent, has exerted little direct but great indirect influence on the development of labor ideals and ways of thinking. The absorption of the great stream of aliens into the native American movement has been most remarkable, when the fact is considered that some sixty per cent of the workers in our basic industries have been born in other lands. There is already little discoverable difference between the attitude of the descendents of the immigrants from Northern Europe, the Irish, Scotch, German, and Scandinavian, and that of New Englanders who came over in the Mayflower; and, alarmists to the contrary notwithstanding, the younger generation, and the great majority of the older generation, of workers from the south and east of Europe have already adopted most of the virtues, together with most of the vices, of the American type of mind. But in certain of our great cities, where the foreign-born congregate together in colonies of their own, there is enough group sentiment left to cause the development of philosophies that have become rooted in the homeland whence the group has come.

The immigrant comes from a stratified society in which class consciousness has been drilled into him for centuries back. He belongs to the lower class, to the peasantry, generally; not for him is it to aspire to take his place as an equal among the lords of the earth. He must toil and labor as his forbears toiled and labored; he may, indeed, cherish hopes of raising his entire class to a somewhat better position, but that he should rise out of his class is unthinkable. But when he arrives in America he believes all this will be changed. There are there no classes, no peasants, no masters; he does not exactly expect to pick up gold in the streets, of course, but he still looks upon America as the land of wonderful opportunities. American democracy is seen through a rosy haze which, perhaps, leads the simple peasant of Sicily or the harassed Jew of Poland to expect more than it can possibly give. Of late years there have come, of course, disturbing reports back home that all is not quite so glorious as it has been painted; but nevertheless the immigrant still feels, and feels rightly, that in certain respects at least America must be preferable to the conditions under which he has been living.

But when he arrives in the slums of our great cities, or in some squalid mining or mill town, he is doomed to the disillusionment that follows every too optimistic hope. The real benefits America offers, those intangible things that only time can bring home, seem to him remote, and may even fade away in the distance with his disappointment in the hope of material prosperity. His wages are indeed more in a week than he formerly earned in a month; but so are prices, and in exchange for the free life of the peasant he has the unceasing monotony of factory or mine labor. True, he is immune from the incursions of the Tsar's Cossacks, free to do what he will; but if perchance he live in Western Pennsylvania this freedom may seem somewhat unreal. If he has not expected too much, he will assuredly be satisfied, and voice, as so many of our newly made Americans have voiced, the gratitude which he feels toward a land that, with all its faults, offers opportunities undreamed of in Eastern Europe; but if he has, and most immigrants fall into the latter class, he will be the prey of disillusion.

This disillusion can have two effects. It can breed a frank and somewhat bitter cynicism, which determines him to play the game as Americans play it, to beat them if possible, and to rise to the top in the ruthless methods of business. Thus he becomes absorbed in the American labor movement, follows its shrewd business methods, and extracts all he can from his employer. If he is successful, he rises, in some small way at first, to the employing class himself, and far outdoes the native American in grasping and driving oppression; the sweatshop contractors were nearly all just this type of successful immigrant.

Or the sense of disillusionment instead of throwing the foreigner headlong into the business struggle, may lead to a total rejection of the whole American theory, in its business or its trade union formulation, and send him to radical theories born of the conditions of the lands he has left and well nourished in his new country. In industrial matters, he says, America is far worse than the monarchy I came from; all governments are alike, and must give way to something else. His foreign birth emphasizes the class consciousness he already feels; if he is an Italian or a Jew or a "Hunky" he knows that the people on top regard him as of almost another species from themselves, and with an ill-concealed disgust despise him for being different. He becomes, quite naturally, a revolutionary, inspired by a fanatical doctrinaire social idealism. It is the "system" that is to blame, the great, impersonal octopus reaching out everywhere to seize him with its tentacles; somehow, he feels certain, if only the system were thrown off or destroyed or broken up (he is not quite certain just which term applies) than all his problems would solve themselves. Just a simple remedy, a single law or two, and his vision of America as the land of golden opportunity would then come true. Since the solution seems so utterly and absolutely simple to him, he cannot but feel that those who do not enthusiastically embrace it are conspiring with the system to keep him down; organized labor, in its indifference to his remedy, must be corrupt and bought by the capitalists.

So the more intelligent young foreign-born worker may become a revolutionary of one persuasion or another, and sets off on his crusade only to be confirmed by opposition in the rightness of his views. But the majority of the workers are perhaps too unintelligent to do more than follow any leader who appears to offer them hope of relief from their present discontents, and thus are readily absorbed into whatever orthodox business union thinks it worth the trouble to organize them. The immigrant, it must be remembered, is not apt to be the skilled laborer from the foreign city; the purveyors of hands for American industry have generally been careful to make sure that he is the simple peasant. And workers tinged with revolutionary ideas are not apt to emigrate; they are too much interested in effecting social change in their own land. Yet by the same token when the unskilled workers are approached by a radical leader they willingly respond; they are in no wise attached to the principles of the constitution or to any other foundation of the modern society.

For all these reasons alien philosophies, and in particular the class conscious theories of Marx, appeal mainly to those already class conscious, and gain a foothold in the fairly homogeneous immigrant centers rather than in localities where native American stock is predominant; though, it must be confessed, certain revolutionary philosophies are a marked exception. But these are quite different from orthodox Marxianism, and represent an indigenous growth. The history of Marxian socialism in the United States is the history of the attempted "Americanization" of a philosophy that from the start was recognized as something alien to the tradition of the great body of American workers. "In Europe," says one of the foremost of its leaders, "the socialist movement sprang up in the midst of the native population and adjusted itself to the economic and political conditions of each country quite mechanically and without effort. But in the United States the situation was altogether different. It is estimated that no more than ten per cent of the members of the Socialist Labor Party, during the period described (1877–1900) were native Americans. All the rest, including the most active and influential leaders, were men of foreign birth, insufficiently acquainted with the institutions, customs, and habits of the country of their adoption, and frequently ignorant of its very language.

"In these circumstances the pioneers of the movement soon realized the hopelessness of their task to effect radical social and economic changes in this country by their own efforts, and henceforward they considered it their special mission to acclimatize the movement and to leave its further development to the American working men. The endeavor to 'Americanize' the socialist movement is the main key-note of the activity of the Socialist Labor Party throughout its entire career." [1]

In fact, socialism appeared in the United States as a German product, and found by far its largest support here among the German element. Of late years the Jews, for whose welfare and aid the Socialists alone seemed to have any genuine care, have likewise become its enthusiastic followers. And, although its members are eager to deny it, and point to the fact that at the first convention of the present Socialist Party

[1] Hillquit, *History of Socialism in the United States*, 5th ed., 193.

in 1901 only 25 out of 124 delegates were foreign born, and that the average of enrolled membership is 71% native,[1] it is impossible not to admit that socialism, or at any rate the Socialist party, has hitherto had no special appeal for the worker of American stock. The very fact that its strongholds are in New York and in Milwaukee, and in mining and mill communities of the East, all places where the foreign-born are very strong, emphasizes the distinction between Marxianism and the American democratic tradition. But the Socialists are also quite right in insisting upon the "American" nature of their theories and their following; for if to be "American" means to have the support of a great body of American workmen today, then Socialism assuredly can make good its claim. It is American industry itself that has become foreign-born, until there has almost developed a servile race in the country.

Of course, the leaders of Socialism are by no means in the same situation as their followers. They are, for the most part, intellectuals inspired with a passion for social justice, and they naturally comprise some of those whose ancestors were suckled on the pure milk of Americanism; they regard Socialism, with perhaps certain modifications, as the consummation of American democracy. They are sincere converts of whom Socialism is very proud, and they have been of inestimable service to her. Moreover, perhaps the majority of the million voters whom the Socialists have been able to attract vote as they do, not from a conviction of the inherent truth of the Socialist dogmas, but largely as a matter of protest and resentment against the other large parties. The same could probably be said, with less assurance, of large sections of the trade unionists. Socialism during the last twenty years has been the one possible alternative to the continuance of things as they are upon which any large number of men have agreed. The convinced Socialist, who worships his Marxian Bible, is even today largely confined to the worker out of touch with the main body of the American Labor movement. Nothing can make this more plain than the respective attitudes which the A. F. L. and the Socialist Party adopted towards American participation in the war.

The socialist movement in the United States falls naturally into three periods, before 1877, the period of the Socialist Labor Party, 1877–1901, and that of the present Socialist Party. The first two periods represent almost entirely agitation among the German-speaking workers. Before the Civil War, Weitling, a refugee of 1848 and a combination of Marxian and Utopian, carried on a paper and spread certain Marxian ideas;

---

[1] Hillquit, *History of Socialism in the United States*, 5th ed., 309, 357.

and in 1857 a Communistic Club was formed in New York. With the International Working-Men's Association, founded in 1864 by British unionists to regulate the international labor supply, and the scene of much of Marx's work, the National Labor Union, under the influence of Sylvis and with the motion of restricting the evils of free immigration, expressed its sympathy, and even elected Sylvis as a delegate; but he could not go without funds, and his death in 1869 stopped all further interchange between American and European labor. In 1868 the German workers in New York formed a General German Workers' Union, which first joined the National Labor Union, but in the next year joined the International as Section 1 of New York, and adopted Marxian principles. Soon there were sections in Chicago and San Francisco, of various foreign nationalities; in 1870 there were over 30 sections and some 5000 enrolled members, which, to gain the attention of the American movement, supported a number of strikes then in progress. In 1872 the North American Federation of the International was formed, and the next year the General Council was transferred to New York. The last conference of the great International at Philadelphia in 1876 was a perfect failure. The truth is that the Germans were quarreling among themselves, while alarm at the Commune of 1871 and the amusing antics of Section 12 under two feminist agitators, Victoria Woodhull and Tennessee Claflin, had either scared or laughed away the American support that at one time seemed about to attach itself to the Socialists.

Nevertheless, in 1874 A. Strasser, the cigar-maker who was later to figure as a pioneer of pure and simple business unionism, formed the Social Democratic Working-Men's Party out of several of the old sections of the International; this organization participated in and captured the Industrial Congress of 1876, and in the same year formed a national party which in the next took the name of the Socialist Labor Party, with doctrines of strictest Marxianism. In 1879 this party had almost 10,000 members, which, however, had shrunk four years later to a bare 1500.[1] The anarchist movement of the eighties drew from their ranks. and had almost annihilated them at its collapse in 1886, The Socialists, too, looking with envious eyes on the success of the Knights of Labor and the American Federation, sought both to get their aid in political action and to gain control of them; but, for all their dallying with the Socialists in times of depression, such as the 1886 Henry George campaign in New York, the unionists, so soon as business picked up,

[1] Hillquit, *op. cit.*, 207.

turned a deaf ear to them. By 1896, however, the Socialists had 200 sections, and had managed to secure control of several city federations, notably the Central Labor Union of New York, the United German Trades, and the United Hebrew Trades. These latter had been organized through the efforts of the Socialists in the spontaneous revolt of the Jewish garment workers in New York against sweatshop conditions; in gratitude they have remained largely socialist ever since. In 1893 the Socialists captured District Assembly 49, the New York branch of the Knights, and helped defeat Powderly; but a quarrel soon broke out between the essentially rural Knights and the Socialists.

In the Federation socialism was represented by a respectable minority. In 1881 six out of the hundred and seven delegates had been declared socialists; but the great struggle did not come till 1893, when Gompers was defeated for reëlection and a plank calling for "the collective ownership by the people of all means of production and distribution" was referred to the constituent unions. Next year it was quietly dropped in the midst of heated discussion over Socialism, and thereafter the Socialists averaged about one quarter of the membership of the conventions. By 1895 the Socialists, having antagonized both Knights and Federation, sought to form a trade union of their own, and set up the Socialist Trade and Labor Alliance, modeled exactly on the type of the Knights. While they were able to gain at the outset the Central Labor Federation of New York, and the United Hebrew Trades, the Alliance, as an attempt to utilize the trade union movement for political purposes, was an utter fizzle. The total vote in 1898 was 82,204; the movement had no influence on the American workers.

In 1899 a split occurred in the Socialist Labor Party; the seceding majority joined several other groups under Eugene V. Debs, and after a little difficulty with utopian colonizers formed in 1901 the Socialist Party. By abandoning the strict impossibilism of the older organization and adopting more opportunistic and reformist tactics, the socialists have been able to secure as many as a million votes.

Why has the socialist movement in the United States remained a thing apart from the general movement, having, indeed, many adherents even within the business unions, but depending mainly upon the immigrant populations of our great cities? Why has it remained more doctrinaire and orthodox than almost any other socialist party, so much so that during the war it was left almost alone to adhere to the anti-militaristic principles of the International? It has the proud distinction of remaining faithful to its principles in time of peril, but that very loyalty meant that it was out of touch with the main body of American labor. Why has not socialism taken on American form and feature, as it has been acclimated in England? Why, since America is the land where capitalism has traveled further on its Marxian path than in any other, has socialism so failed here?

Fundamentally, it is because its ideology and its aims are quite foreign to the American spirit and tradition of a democracy of equality. To accept Marxianism, it must be swallowed whole; and though American labor readily accepts the class struggle, it is quite unable to contemplate the utopia of the orthodox socialist. The American distrusts the state and all its ways with the bitterness of a century and a half's rule by politicians; the efficient German bureaucracy, with its nicely graded and adjusted scales of ability, is to him incomprehensible. He is not at all averse to a collectivism; group enterprise, from the days of de Tocqueville, has been a characteristic of America. But that the group to take over the means of production should be the government —for he recognizes no such entity as the "State"—those cheap politicians, those unsuccessful lawyers—well, a Shonts may be bad enough, but he is not going to take his chances with a Tammany Mayor. Socialism, as government operation, leaves him utterly cold because he has never in his experience met with such a thing as the German bureaucracy or the British Civil service, and if he had he would reject a system that merely substituted an aristocracy of ability for an aristocracy of wealth or birth. He wants no aristocracy whatsoever. Hence it is that, while he may advocate collective ownership and operation, he is indifferent to any proposal to make the group the government. In this the American worker is at bottom syndicalistic, as the A. F. L. conventions have repeatedly revealed; and syndicalism, we may remember, originated in a country which has enjoyed some fifty years of rule by politicians. Socialism will never be able to conquer the American tradition unless it abandons or greatly weakens its emphasis on the "State."

But if the American is not a national socialist, neither is he an anarchist in the sense in which the Latins of Europe may become. Not that he is particularly averse to the use of force (to which, strange irony, are committed those who are revolting against the employment of all force!) but he has no stomach for that particular variety which comprises stealth and conspiracy and dynamite. He prefers force open and above-board, a few broken heads, perhaps, but essentially the economic force of the strike. Occasionally workers will suffer from the delusion that the bomb is their only recourse, as happened a few years ago with the bridge workers; but that is the exception that proves the rule, and is invariably the result of the influence of a particular leader.

In the eighties, indeed, there arose a real anarchist movement; but it comprised only those elements which the Socialist Labor Party then drew from, together with a few intellectuals. In 1881 there was formed in Chicago a branch of the International Working People's Association, the so-called "black international," composed of seceding sections of the S. L. P., under the leadership of Johann Most. It held a convention in Pittsburgh in 1883 which issued a most inflammatory proclamation calling on workers to employ all means, especially force. It achieved national importance as a result of the Haymarket bomb of 1886, which, though almost certainly exploded without the knowledge or the consent of the I. W. P. A. officers, was certainly the logical deduction from their proclamations. The Black International, and with it anarchism, disappeared utterly from American labor; and the net result was to turn the conservative business unions, whose eight-hour strike was directly ruined by it, as far as possible from revolutionary sentiments.

At this point it might be well to mention the most recent of the alien philosophies, the Communist and the Communist Labor Parties, splits from the emergency convention of the Socialist Party at Chicago in August, 1919. They are slight organizations produced by the reaction of Russian events on souls too impatient with the conservativeness and opportunism of the orthodox Socialist Party; the latter is merely an organization of discontented "left-wingers" who want more action and excitement, mainly from the northwest, (Minnesota, Oregon, California, and Ohio) but whose principles differ very little from orthodox Marxianism—they are merely reformers seeking the pure gospel. The former is or was composed of about 30,000 members of the seven Slavic federations of the Socialist Party, Russians whose leaders desired to emulate their countrymen, and the Michigan delegation which, after calling the new party, found itself hopelessly overruled. These leaders who did not bother to consult their "followers," drew up a platform calling, in a little stronger language than usual, for the socialist aims, and preferred the "mass strike" to political campaigning. Obviously, neither group is worthy of serious thought as part of the labor movement.

What, then, has been the net result upon the American labor movement of these various foreign philosophies? Undoubtedly the greatest effect has been to increase class consciousness and class solidarity. The theory of the class struggle has been that part of Marxianism that has made the strongest appeal to the American worker; and the feeling of class consciousness marks nearly all the newer unions today. Socialism, besides, has probably done much, in the hold it has been able to get in the A. F. L., to aid in the tendency toward the breaking down of craft lines.

Moreover, socialism and collectivism have made it easy for the worker to favor the application of a certain amount of state socialism—minimum wages, health insurance, pensions, and the like—which without its influence would probably still be regarded by the workers with the same suspicious eye the employer preserves for it. From legislation freeing labor from special disabilities the A. F. L. lobby has thus been easily led to legislation directly in its favor.

But, on the other hand, these foreign radicalisms have undoubtedly increased the general conservatism of the American labor movement. It has often been afraid to adopt and propose policies that it otherwise would have enthusiastically endorsed for fear of being branded with the stigma of "socialistic." This fear of "socialistic tendencies" has been all the more potent in that they are generally identified with the clearly alien element of the community who seem not yet thoroughly "Americanized." For the native worker of older stock, socialism or radicalism of any sort has come to be identified with the squalid slum and the unskilled labor which in his pride he is apt to despise. As distinct from these "ignorant foreigners" he is a business man, and he prides himself on his ability to vote the Republican ticket with the most successful business man in the land. And, it must be confessed, a good deal of this attitude has crept into the immigrants themselves. They have everywhere been taught, and in many cases they have finally come to believe, that socialism is one of the things that along with the full beard and the peasant shawl must be discarded in the process of Americanization: to become a conservative business man is somehow much more "American" than to remain a radical.

If the history of American labor has revealed any lesson, it is that the American, while quite willing to embark upon political action to secure the aims and needs of his trade union, is utterly opposed to any political action seeking to accomplish primarily political control of economic conditions and disregarding those unions. Any political party that he will whole-heartedly support must be the servant of the union movement, must supplement it, not take its place. The efforts of the Socialists in their Socialist Trade and Labor Alliance to imitate Germany in making of the unions an instrument for the furthering of party aims came to a sudden and complete collapse. If American workers are to remain what they have been in the past, any labor party they form must be firmly based upon and completely controlled by the strong unions, and its program must emphasize primarily trade union control and organization.

Hence the radical philosophies based on Marx have almost entirely remained in the hands of foreigners who, however they may have become a very large factor in American industry, have remained as yet outside the traditions of the American labor movement. They have remained essentially a philosophy of protest and revolt, and it is hardly too much to say that as yet they have presented no program, political or industrial, at all practicable in the face of American conditions and the psychology of the American worker.

* * * * * * * *

But while orthodox Marxianism has never gained a real hold on the American labor movement, there has been a spirited native revolt against the business union—a revolt taking its beginnings in the Western Federation of Miners, and developing into the I. W. W. The presence of the I. W. W. and its failure to transform the American labor movement directly are alike significant. So intriguing in theory with its doctrines of the industrial state and its generous social unionism, so revolting in practice to minds brought up in traditional ways of thinking, by reason of its extreme predatory character, it has nevertheless exerted, and probably will continue to exert, an important if indirect influence on the older business unionism.

The Western Federation of Miners was organized in 1893 as a result of the Coeur d'Alene outbreak among the metal miners of the west. These sturdy pioneers were for the most part Americans of the old stock, bred in the old frontier tradition and impatient of the restraints of Eastern industrialism. They had been engaged in independent gold and lead mining, and when the advent of capitalism created large companies and reduced them to wageworkers, they banded together, in the spirit of the Vigilance Committees, to protect their rights from aggression. On their side were all the traditions of the wild and woolly west; on the other, all the strength that capitalism can gain in newly developed lands, like South Africa. Strikes of extreme bitterness and deadliness followed swift upon each other: Coeur d'Alene in 1893, Cripple

Creek in 1894, Leadville in 1896-97, Salt Lake and Coeur d'Alene again in 1899, Telluride in 1901, Idaho Springs in 1903, and Cripple Creek again in 1903-04. The state governments were wholly in the hands of the mine-owners, and this heightened in the miners the profound disgust with political government that pioneering conditions had fostered. They thought at first of capturing the state legislatures, and used much of the ideology of socialism; but they put more trust in economic action, and seriously discussed the purchase and operation of mines. They had done well enough before the advent of the capitalist, and they would do well enough without him again.[1] Their union, which took in all workers, waiters, lumbermen, and the rest, in some respects recalls a union of "all good citizens" to clean up the disreputable elements; for the Western Federation organized a Western Labor Union of which it was by far the largest member. Their methods were rough and ready, and involved none of the business tactics of the older unions; William D. Haywood boasted in the first I. W. W. convention: "We have not got an agreement existing with any mine manager, superintendent, or operator at the present time. We have got a minimum scale of wages and the eight-hour day, and we did not have a legislative lobby to accomplish it."[2] They were out to fight and get what they could.

In 1905 this group of western miners, with their new American Labor Union, joined with Daniel De Leon and the remnants of the old Socialist Labor Party, together with several other leaders and minor unions, in a convention at Chicago that called itself the Industrial Workers of the World and was bound together by the common hatred of the American Federation and "pure and simple trade unionism." The group consisted mainly of socialists from the Western Federation of Miners, under Sherman, who was elected president; Socialist laborites, the so-called "impossiblists" or "fanatic Jesuits" of the socialist tradition; a small handful under De Leon; and revolutionary unionists under Haywood and Vincent St. John of the Western Federation. Personal squabbles split off Sherman and the Miners in 1906; and in 1908 De Leon and the advocates of political as well as revolutionary economic action were excluded by the so-called "bummery crowd," which left the I. W. W. in the hands of Haywood, St. John, and the revolutionary direct actionists.

The successive quarrels and splits that mark the history of the organization are unimportant; they merely signify the disgust with which

[1] Brissenden, *The I. W. W.*, 42.
[2] *Proceedings*, 1st I. W. W. Convention, 154.

the strong central leadership of the business unions was regarded by these rebels. The subsequent history of the I. W. W. is well-known: how they organized that class of homeless and womanless migratory workers which the capitalists' need for " a good labor market" has called into being in the Northwest, and found among the wandering agricultural laborers, the miners, and above all the lumbermen, staunch supporters in their campaign for livable conditions. They have even invaded the East, coming into Lawrence in 1912 and other textile centers after the unorganized unskilled have been driven to revolt. The men they have appealed to have been the men no other labor organization considered worth while—the very lowest of the low. But their principles forbade any efficient organization; their fields do not stay organized, and although aided by persecution they have not gained nor are they likely to gain any considerable membership. They claim at the present time only 70,000 members, nearly all in the Northwest, and this number is far in excess of their real strength. Brissenden estimates that the government figure of 200,000 probably represents the number of those who at one time or another have carried I. W. W. cards. But it is not upon their membership, but upon discontented and desperate workers driven to sudden revolt, that the I. W. W. depends for its fighting strength.

Despite its analogies to French syndicalism, despite the international relations upon which they have in the last decade prided themselves, the I. W. W. was a purely indigenous organization, born of the union of the Western pioneering atmosphere and a fully developed capitalism. And despite its elaborate and detailed social theory, which it has of late years worked out on foreign models, the I. W. W. can scarcely be said to have a philosophy or even to be descended from Marxian forbears. Its leaders indeed started with a smattering of the great socialist, and have latterly developed their genealogy; but they stopped with the class struggle. Of economic determinism, of collective state ownership, to say nothing of the intricacies of surplus value and the other dogmas of the Master, in which every true socialist is at home, the average Wobbly lumberjack knows nothing and cares less; but that there is a big fight going on and that he must see that his side wins, that is perfectly obvious. And the typical Wobbly, when he says "class struggle" and the "overthrow of the capitalist," means it in a sense in which few revolutionaries have ever meant their stereotyped phrases. A struggle is an active physical combat, an overthrow is a real crash; it is not merely a persuasive labor lieutenant to the captain of industry, with his "You've got my sympathy," or a tiresome political campaign with an efficient bureaucracy. As Carleton Parker so well explained, the I. W. W. movement in the rank and file owed its popularity to deep-seated and instinctive needs of the migratory worker, and not at all to the carefully developed industrial departments and technique of future production which the leaders developed.

The only immediate result on the Federation was the half-hearted attempt, since abandoned, to organize the unskilled among whom the I. W. W. worked into local or "federal" labor unions. But the indirect influence has come through other channels. Besides their tactics of the general strike and sabotage the I. W. W. gradually developed an interesting syndicalistic social theory, in which the political state was to be abolished and industrial unions were to take over all the functions of production and government—the typical syndicalistic economic federalism. Many of the younger and more intellectual leaders have also occupied their time with elaborating the plans for such direct control of production by the workers, and the I. W. W. has been a pioneer in emphasizing industrial education and training with a view to eventually "capturing" and administering the means of production. These leaders have come to feel that their aim can best be achieved, not in a miscellaneous rabble such as constitutes the rank and file of the Wobblies, but through the older business unions and the orthodox labor movement, which has recently been exhibiting remarkable signs of transformation. Hence many of them have come to favor an educational propaganda through the "coffin societies" themselves, and the now celebrated policy of "boring from within"; and in the process their earlier views are of necessity being modified. They believe that a steady and prolonged training and education in responsibility is required before the workers can ever hope to capture industry, and that training they see possible only in the unions of the A. F. L. They also do not utterly give up the ballot as an instrument of transformation. It was for this reason that De Leon left the I. W. W. and set up a rival I. W. W. in Detroit, since renamed, the Worker's International Industrial Union; he had come to desire above all the discarding of political representation and the organization of workers along industrial lines, and he could not but feel that sabotage and destructive methods were the worst possible kind of training for the eventual management of industry.

These influences, which may foretell a turning of the extreme radicals back into the regular labor movement and towards the building up of a trade unionism which shall be far more than business unionism has hitherto been, readily join forces with the tendencies we have already observed within the heart of business unionism itself, and serve but to hasten its change. It is to the outcome—to the New Unionism, as it already is and as it appears likely to become in the near future, that we must now turn our attention.

12. THE GROWTH OF CLASS SOLIDARITY AND THE NEW UNIONISM

THE progress of the industrial revolution has at length reached the point where common class interests are tending to break down particular group interests, and weld the labor movement into one great whole; or, to be more correct, where particular group interests can no longer reach their realization without combining into larger and mutually interdependent groups. This, of course, is a generalization, and like all generalizations it has many exceptions: there still are and probably for some time will remain a certain number of groups which, either by reason of the purely technical persistence of a considerable degree of skilled craftsmanship, or for some other special reason not germane to the labor movement as a whole, preserve the skilled craftsman's aristocratic sense of elevation above the general struggles of the mass of the laboring classes. But all indications point toward a marked tendency in the labor movement, taken by and large, toward the replacement of wage-consciousness by class-consciousness.

The primary cause, of course, is the technological one of the progress of invention; the introduction of machines everywhere to replace the simple tool of the manual laborer. With the increasing strength of the business union and its consequent greater demand for wages, the employer will be more and more driven to supplant processes depending upon skilled workmen with elaborate and intricate machines that work automatically; and it is highly probable that as the union reaches a position where it will be able to regulate the introduction and assure the retention, in some other capacity, of the workers, and the employer seeks gain in increased production rather than in discarding workers, the unions will not only permit but welcome new labor-saving devices. For it is, of course, not the new machine itself, but only the fact that its introduction in the past has so often led to a dismissal of most of the workmen, that has led to the hostility of the worker. This advance in technique will, on the whole, slightly raise the skill required by the lowest grade of unskilled labor; machine tending requires the exercise of slightly more intelligence than ditch-digging or wheeling barrows. But on the other hand all the higher branches of skilled craftmanship will give way to the common level of the machine tender; and though the minimum be raised, the reduction of the whole body of workers to one common rather low level will result. The knowledge of processes and of the designing and construction of the machines will come more and more to be concentrated in the hands of the highly trained technological experts forming the major portion of the management group. An example of the resulting economic condition was given recently in the trade of glass blowing, which had from its inception remained in the hands of a highly skilled, highly conservative, and typically business union of hand workers. About 1906 a machine for blowing bottles was widely introduced, completely disrupting the bottle-blowers' schedules and plans and reducing them at one stroke to an only moderately skilled union. In many industries the exigencies of the war operated in a similar way, and only the strength of the unions and their ability to control the situation was able to save their ruin. But even where such unions are able to secure very favorable terms, every such occurrence brings them more and more immediately into contact with the rest of the labor movement as it destroys their special monopoly of skill. To put it concretely, although the locomotive firemen, to save themselves the back-breaking labor, are demanding the introduction of mechanical stokers on all the larger engines, it is indisputable that it is much easier to secure a strike-breaker who can stoke a fire with such a device than one who knows just how to place a shovel-full of coal where it will count most. And this sudden identification of interests with the less skilled labor everywhere, even where it does not give rise to strong industrial unions, leads inevitably to coöperation and joint action with the unskilled.

In addition to this purely technological reason for the growth of class solidarity, there is another and economic one. With the increasing organization of labor the employer too has been driven to organize; for, as we have already seen, any general collective bargaining presupposes an employers' association with which to conclude agreements. On the other hand there are many economic forces tending toward centralization of industrial enterprises. In addition to the desire to avoid through price agreement the evils of competition, and of the natural tendency toward the formation of single great monopolies or trusts in the basic industries, there is the necessity of great modern corporations seeking further credit and capital in the large banking houses, in Wall Street. Mr. Veblen's keen analysis has revealed how the typical figure of the present age is no longer the captain of industry who built up a great business, but the investment banker who sits in his counting-house, loans money to the industrial enterprise which he considers profitable, and is able through his control of credit to hold the entire country in the hollow of his hand. Even where there is no agreement between competing enterprises, the fact that their stock is pretty much owned by the same individuals is a quite effective guarantee against excessive differences of policy and attitude. Thus, while the traditional Marxian prediction of the concentration of all wealth into the hands of a very small group seems as far from verification as ever, if there has not actually been a great increase in the number of investors, it nevertheless remains true that the control of wealth is daily passing into fewer and fewer hands; and the great army of widows and orphans is gradually awakening to the fact that high finance is conducted for the profit of those who control, and not for that of the small investor.

Hence organized labor is facing a greater and stronger organization of capital which also is forgetting its competitive differences in the common class-consciousness. And recent events have revealed how strong that class-consciousness is and how determined a stand it is going to make. In the face of such opposition the laborer is driven to forget the petty differences that divide him from his less skilled brother, and to join hand and soul with him in the great struggle against the capitalist. When the power of the Steel Trust lifts its head, and Western Pennsylvania takes on the air of a country at war, conservative and radical, skilled craftsman and common laborer, A. F. L. executives and Amalgamated Clothing Workers, all forget their differences and band together against the common foe. And, from present indications, the necessity for such concerted action is going to become more and more frequent.

Partly as a result of the above two tendencies, partly, perhaps, as their cause, there is the increasing prevalence amongst the workers of the Marxian theory of the class struggle and of the corresponding fact of general class-consciousness. The old preambles written back in the eighties and nineties under the influence of Stewardism are becoming meaningless to the worker brought up in a modern environment; he needs stronger meat than the conciliatory phrases of that era. As a sign of the times, for instance, the Firemen's Brotherhood in 1918 expunged that section of their preamble that declared that the interests of employer and employee were identical, and substituted for it the aim to make them so— a pious hope in place of a now obvious misstatement. Marxianism as a whole, as we have seen, the American worker will not accept; but the experience of the Western Federation of Miners and the I. W. W. and the great increase in socialist strength in the Federation proves that he will eagerly embrace the theory of the class struggle and class consciousness. He is especially apt to do so if he finds the employers, whom in all his opposition he has hitherto rather secretly admired and envied, on their side through concerted action and political instruments endeavoring to bring that class struggle very close home to him in all its bitter reality.

The first outcome of these tendencies has been the growth of industrial unionism. Business unionism depends upon the development of bargaining power. To develop this to keep pace with the increased strength of the employers and to get rid of the competition of the unskilled industrialization has been imperative. But industrialization, meaning the formation of unions embracing the unskilled as well as the skilled, the complete organization of industry, can mean very different things. It can mean, as it means to some of the I. W. W., one big union of all the workers, in which unskilled predominate; in this sense the Knights of Labor was an industrial union. Or it can mean the organization of all the workers in a particular material such, as metal or wood, as it means to the German industrialist and as is represented in this country by the Metal Trades Department of the A. F. L. Or it can mean, as it meant to De Leon and the Socialist Laborites, the organization of workers according to the tool they use. And finally, it can mean the organization of workers according to the product and the productive unit or plant.

It is indeed a question just what constitutes an "industry." Some industries, like mining, clothing making, or meat-packing, stand out clearly and unmistakably. It is in these that industrial unionism has already proceeded furthest. Others, like the work of the machinists, are very hard indeed to classify; do the machinists belong with the metal trades if, say, they are employed about mines, and do the metal trades, strictly speaking, constitute an industry at all? These questions seem to preclude the possibility of an absolutely simple and clear-cut division of the basic industries; and, as a matter of fact, all theoretically complete schemes of the industrial state do include either an extensive system of transfers from one union to another, or a subsidiary persistence of trade lines within industrial ones, and some such solution would seem necessary as industrialization advances.

But the significant point is that the form of industrialism that the development of business unionism forces is necessarily the last type mentioned. Business unions exist to fight or bargain with employers; hence they are inevitably developing in conformity with the employers' organization, which is that of productive units or plants. From the earliest days the workers have been led naturally to parallel the masters, growing in scope as the latter grew; and hence today their very function excludes the possibility of their organizing along the lines of the one big union, the material, or the tool. For the tool today has become the entire factory in all its ramifications.

The importance of the fact that it is this particular type of industrialism and not one of the others that is developing, is profound. For while conceivably one of the other forms of organization might be successful as a labor trust for the selling of labor, none other could possibly serve as a basis for production, and hence none other could possibly release the second or social strain of labor in productive and socially advantageous channels. Only the union organized around the plant as the basis could possibly enter into and share or assume the control of industry.

Some writers, notably Selig Perlman in Commons' *History of Labour in the United States*, have divided industrial unionism into that of the skilled and that of the moderately skilled. These are not really two types, but merely the result of the impulse to industrialism meeting varied technological situations. The A. F. L. has always stood for what it called craft autonomy, and in 1901 at Scranton took a firm stand against industrial unionism. But nevertheless it was forced in 1908 to recognize the Structural Building Trades Alliance, which had been since 1897 endeavoring to form a national organization of the highly effective local Building Trades Councils which dealt as a body with contractors and builders, and formed it into the Building Trades Department of the A. F. L., followed in the same year by the Railway Employes' Department, in the next by the Metal Trades Department, and in 1912 by the Mining Department. The latter is a true industrial organization, brought about by Moyer, president of the Western Federation of Miners, which had joined the A. F. L. the preceding year. The building trades are also organized industrially, with autonomy over the building trades sections and authority to charter new ones. But the railway unions went furthest when in 1912 they abandoned their original purely advisory plan with voluntary membership for a federation of federations with a convention, salaried officers, and full authority.[1] These ten A. F. L. railway unions, it may be added have from their union acted in close harmony and concert with the four brotherhoods, so that while each preserves its autonomy, for all practical purposes the railroads are organized on an industrial basis and in important crises act as a unit.

The principal function of the departments so far has been to decide jurisdictional disputes, that bugbear of craft unionism; and in the settle-

[1] A. F. L., *Encyclopedia*, 431, 432.

ment the opposition to "dual unions" and the almost invariable preference given to unions of the strong "basic trades" in the industries has
gravely compromised the official A. F. L. doctrine of craft autonomy.
Thus the woodworkers were in 1912 absorbed by the strong carpenters
and joiners, and the steamfitters by the strong plumbers; and the
A. F. L. convention practically gave its official sanction to the new industrial principle of basic trades.

In addition to these industrial combinations of the strong craft unions
the principle of joint action and blanket agreement, particularly spon-
sored by the Metal Trades Council, in which a number of craft unions
in an industry join in their demands and threaten a common strike, has
received considerable vogue, not only in the steel strike, but also in the
Northwest, in Portland and in the Seattle strike of 1919. The A. F. L.,
despite the fact that its strongest union, the miners, has from its beginning in 1890 been completely industrialized, has for so long opposed
industrialism with craft unionism that it is necessarily loath to change
its professions, but no one who is not blind can fail to see the gains for
the industrial idea that are daily being made in the heart of the Federation.

All of these considerations taken together have made for the rise of
a new and more radical form of union—an industrial union which has
come to feel that the tactics of the traditional business union have secured much for the worker, and cannot be dropped or discarded as the
intransigeant revolutionary would desire, but that at the same time
they are in themselves by no means sufficient to secure for the worker
that security from unemployment and that practical equality of position
in society which has from the beginning been his great aim. This new
unionism differs from the revolutionary unionism of the I. W. W. and
the radicalism of the socialists in its perfect willingness, nay, in its conviction, to serve the workers' ultimate interests through developing to
its fullest extent the machinery of collective agreements with the employers' associations. But it also differs from business unionism in
working with a clear prescience of whither its business tactics are taking
it, and with the realization that in the interests of society as a whole,
and of the workers as the major part thereof, the policy of group individualism is inadequate and must be superseded. It thus admirably
combines, in a manner as suited to the present situation and state of
the industrial arts as was that of Stewardism in the seventies and eighties,
the two strains of group advantage and social idealism, making the
second spring naturally and continuously out of the first, and uniting

in one policy the advantage of the individual group and that of society as a whole. And, because this new unionism seems so well adapted to the exigencies of the present situation, and because it seems a natural growth out of and not an impatient revolt against and away from the main body of the orthodox business labor movement of America, and, finally, because it seems fully in accord with the present tendencies in labor in the other parts of the industrial world, it seems wholly probable that, allowance being made for different situations in different industries, the new unionism represents the prevailing tendencies in American labor today, and will in the future assume increasing importance.

The general causes of the rise of the new unionism, the progress of the industrial arts and the increase in the strength of the capitalists, have been supplemented by other more immediate factors. Perhaps the most striking, in its way, is the gradual realization that the era of rapidly rising prices since 1914 has forced upon the workers that no matter how successful they may be in raising wages, when the entire labor movement has successively struck and the capitalists have added their private profit, their real wages and their standard of living have not materially altered. Consequently they have been led to search for some other alternative. It is, of course, not true, as the press delights to point out, that the worker gains nothing from strikes for higher wages; he does gain materially for the time being, and that is all he has hitherto been in a position to take into account. But it is true that as the community becomes more and more completely industrialized the gain of the single group becomes less and less, until, theoretically, if all consumers were wage-earners, the added cost to the consumer would precisely balance the added wage. And long before that state is reached, the employer by multiplying his increased labor cost five or ten fold, (which seems to be the popular figure these days) can bring about the same result, and thus hasten the struggle. Thus as a direct result of the war a large body of workers has become convinced of the futility of wage raising as industry approaches complete organization. But, unlike the professors of economics whose theories they have thus finally come to accept, they do not advance to the further orthodox inference that since raising wages availeth naught there is nothing for the worker to do save to work harder and persist in thrift until he too can become a capitalist. They propose instead to work for a gradual abolition of the wage-system itself, with a view to eventually controlling the industries. It is significant that bodies seemingly as far apart as the radical garment workers and the conservative railroad brotherhoods have both come to the same conclusion, that the raising of wages is a mere temporary expedient.

Added to this result of the war experience has been the disgust that the more reflecting workmen have felt at the failure of the present management of industry to meet the test of war and of the universal lessening of output in other lands and consequent greatly increased demand here. The complete collapse of the railroads under war pressure, and the incontestable proof that government control, whatever its eventual merits, not only did not end in complete disaster but was even able in many ways to improve the efficiency of the public service, coming, as it did, very shortly after the scandalous revelations of the methods of high finance on the New Haven, the Rock Island, and many other systems—revelations which "the public" is prone to forget but which the workers remember—this situation produced in the railway workers, whose pride in their work and whose craftsman-like habits are proverbial, a natural disgust with capitalistic control, and an assertion, in the popular Plumb Plan, that if they were only allowed to they could show the country how its railroad systems really ought to be run. And the coal miners, in the face of the tragic maladjustment of production. to demand and to distributive facilities, in the last few years, have assailed in strenuous terms the inefficiency and waste of the present management. A story is told of an English shipyard during the war where the workers, angered at the profiteering and delaying methods of the owners, took over the contracts themselves and delivered them long before the specified time. This spirit is of course by no means as yet general; indeed, the counter-charge of the employer, that the prime cause of his inefficiency is the failure of his workmen to do all that they might, is probably not utterly devoid of truth. It only makes plain, however, how the worker is becoming unwilling to continue working for his employer's profits.

There is, moreover, with the growth in strength consequent upon the war, an increasing desire for some more efficient means than the old collective bargaining for the translation of existing power into industrial control. Collective bargaining is at best diplomacy and armed peace; it is a form of treaty making between distrustful and suspicious armed groups, usually occurring at the conclusion of or on threats of a strike, and very rigid and irresponsive to changed conditions and needs. What more natural than to replace the collective agreement, arranged between envoys at relatively long intervals, with a standing body or board with legislative rather than mere treaty functions, a board on which both

employers and employees would be represented and which would provide for continuous adjustment rather than intermittent conflicts—
which, in a word, would aim to prevent strikes by making them unnecessary rather than settling them after they had arisen? This is the
change which has been, more or less fully, introduced into the clothing
trades, which has been proposed by the railways, and which is effected
in various forms, more or less sincerely and well, of shop organization.

One other tendency, not directly due to the war, has operated to bring
matters to a head. This is the growth in interest among the more intelligent workers and their leaders in problems of production and industrial control. As a result of our increased insight into the springs of
human actions, and the abandonment, under the influence of pioneers in
social psychology, notably of Mr. Graham Wallas, of the older over-
intellectualized conception of human conduct for a realization of the infinite complexity of the human mind and the great variety of mysterious
traits or ways of acting we call instincts, the intellectual leaders of the
workers on the one hand, and the trained employment managers of the
companies on the other have come to realize the necessity of giving the
workers some opportunity to release their inheritance of productive
force and energy. The increasing mechanization of industry and the
reduction of the skilled laborer to the mere machine-tender demand a
substitute for handicraft work as a channel through which creative
energy can function, and both leaders and employers are more and
more seeking this channel in control of the processes of production.
Hence the growth of shop-committees to share in the administration
of plants and to supervise conditions. The employer for the most part,
it is true, is fostering the various forms of so-called "industrial democracy," among which a complicated system modeled upon the federal
government is probably most popular, both because of the increased
interest and production this effects and because he hopes thereby to
keep out the dangerous national union. But the more far-seeing worker,
even when he realizes the impossibility of such shop organization ever
supplanting the large trade union, sees also that the worker is through
such participation in the control of industry, meagre as it may be, developing habits of thought and interest in methods and problems of
producion that will be invaluable for him if, as the worker hopes, he
eventually acquires a much more important control over industry. He
knows the employer is deceiving himself if he believes he can thus bribe
the worker to forget his own interest; but he also knows the employer
is unwittingly giving the worker training the union most probably could

not now give him, and that the business activities of the unions need supplementing along just such lines as the shop-committees indicate.

Together with this interest in the control of production there goes an interest in industrial education and training, which finds expression in the United Labor Education Committee of the New York needle trades, the Workers' University of the Ladies' Garment Workers, such enterprises as the Boston Trades Union College, established by the Boston Central Federation, and the Seattle Labor College of the Seattle Federation; and the Workers' Education Bureau, designed to coördinate all these agencies. Everywhere efforts are being made by leaders to provide training in industrial technique to labor leaders, and the workers themselves, where long hours do not make this impossible, and expert advisers and industrial engineers are being consulted by executive committees. The demand of the capitalists that at all costs production must be kept up and the public efficiently served are being met with specific proposals for increased efficiency and production that hardly meet with the capitalists' approval, but do indicate that the whole country has been driven by the war to think in terms of social production, social consumption, and social needs.

These especial factors have united with the general tendencies of the development of business unionism, as outlined in Chapter 10, to produce a new type of union with a new type of leader—a type approached both by hitherto conservative business unions, like the railroad brotherhoods, that have come to transcend their own aims and functions, and by radical and socialistic organizations like the clothing unions: the industrial union participating in the control of industry, the democratic, responsible union for production. Let us examine a few of the specific indications that such a unionism is really developing in the American labor movement.

First of all there are the railway unions. Since the seventies there have been in existence four powerful organizations of the skilled workers on the railroads, the Engineers, the Firemen, the Conductors, and the Trainmen. They have been the aristocrats of the labor world. They have been too conservative to join the A. F. L. For a long time they refused to adopt a "protective" policy; they would not even threaten to strike. They have built up the most elaborate system of benefits of any American unions, a system supposed to insure obedience and docility. They have elected the most conservative leaders and kept them in power for long periods. They have not troubled themselves about the other workers on the railroads, the switchmen and the section-gangs and all the rest. They refused to aid them in their strike on the Gould system in 1886. They have not had a real strike themselves since the Burlington strike of 1888. They have preserved the typical attitude of the small business man, as well they might, for after the July, 1920, award of wages their pay runs from 2500 to 3500 dollars a year.

Yet in the summer of 1919, when various plans of railway reconstruction were being proposed and talked of, by an overwhelming majority in a referendum—over 90%—they voted to advocate and if necessary enforce a proposition for government ownership of the roads and for operation by a joint board of employees, management, and government officials—a plan rightly considered as radical as any proposition yet put forward by any of the extremest unions, and differing not in essentials from the theories of the I. W. W. and the Communist Parties.

How is this change to be explained? The answer is simple. About ten years ago the less skilled workers were, through the foundation of the Railway Employe's Department of the A. F. L., seriously taken in hand and brought together. The Brotherhoods had been making agreements and acting in closer and closer harmony. During the summer of 1916 they coöperated in agitating for and securing the eight-hour day from Congress. And then came the war, government control, and the mushroom growth of the organizations of unskilled like the shopmen and the maintenance of way men. For the first time all the railway workers were brought together in dealing with government labor agencies. All of these things led to a close harmony of purpose and attitude between the fourteen railway unions, which has resulted in a virtual industrial federation—an industrialism that by virtue of the persistence of highly skilled crafts on the railways does not resemble the homogeneous industrialism of the miners, for instance, but is none the less a genuine industrialism. But government control meant more than merely bringing the workers together for self-protection; for perhaps the first time in their experience the aim of their labor was to produce a service to the public and to the aims of the nation. For the first time all pretense at competition was given up and efficiency and economy of service made the prime consideration. And, for the first time, and in return for loyal and productive work, the employees' contention was recognized that to produce well they must be furnished with the means and the conditions of good production. President Garretson of the Conductors told the Senate Interstate Commerce

Committee that the majority of the men had previously been advocates of private control, but that the experience of government control
had led them to change their minds.[1]

But the railway workers had not been blinded by generous wage
awards to an uncritical acceptance of Government ownership on the
old lines. Wages, in fact, were not advanced to meet the increased
cost of living. From May 25, 1918, to October 1, wages for the lower
paid workers were raised fairly adequately; aside from an advance to
members of the brotherhoods in April, 1919, nothing more was done,
in spite of the rapidly mounting cost of living. In 1920 wages had advanced 73% over the pre-war level, and the cost of living was rising
from 100 to 114%. And none but the brotherhoods had received any
advance since the armistice. No, the Railroad Administration was
not perfect. In the summer of 1919 the workers were very far indeed
from being satisfied with it, as the general complaints and the shopmen's strike indicated. Only President Wilson's plea that Mr. Pal-
mer's anti-profiteering campaign be allowed to bring down the cost of
living saved the country from a railroad strike then.

Instead of urging the continuance of the Railroad Administration, so
soon as the armistice was signed the leaders of the fourteen unions got
together with their joint counsel, Mr. Glenn Plumb, to work out a practicable business plan for managing the railroads with all the benefits for
public service of centralized control, yet without the dangers of bureaucratic inefficiency so real to every American. These officials knew
nothing of any radical philosophies or plans for the control of industry
by the workers. They had never heard of the British national guild
movement. Officers of railway unions are too busy handling the business affairs of the men they represent to waste any time on radical
social theorizing. But they realized that the old system of railway
management in this country had broken down, and they were going to
devise a new one to propose to Congress. They carefully considered
the condition and the needs of the railroad business, and they gradually
and thoughtfully worked out a new plan. This plan was presented to
the Senate Interstate Commerce Committee in February, 1919, long
before any other constructive proposal, as a business proposition that
would protect and further the interests of all concerned, stockholders,
employees, and general public.

This plan, though it received little publicity, was considerably talked
about by the employees themselves. At the same time discontent at

[1] *American Labor Year Book*, 1920, 65.

the failure of the Railroad Administration to effect another wage adjustment was rapidly growing. Men were becoming restive and were liable to strike without authorization from headquarters. The officers resolved to take a referendum on whether they would willingly strike for the Plumb Plan, in the hopes that they might thus secure its passage by Congress, or at least use it to effect some wage increase—for at this time the men who devised the plan, and Mr. Plumb himself, were very dubious about the reception it would get from their own men. And they secured in the referendum an astounding surprise. The railway workers had been thinking over the Plumb Plan, and they had come to favor it—to favor it enough to strike for it—over 90 per cent of them.

The public and the capitalists were horrified. "Bolshevism" was the only term fit to apply to such a revolutionary proposal. Lenin or the I. W. W. must be back of it. So ran the press editorials, and the leaders, who probably knew no more than the editors of Bolshevism's economic program, were frightened. They feared that public opposition would overwhelm the workers, and so they immediately shifted their attack to other ground. Mr. Gompers, fearing the wave of economic reaction sweeping across the country, drew back in alarm. And Congress passed the Esch-Cummins Bill, after a hard struggle on the part of labor to prevent an anti-strike clause.

The essence of the Plumb Plan is production for service—efficient service of a public utility for the public welfare by public servants who are given responsibility for that service and are rewarded as that service is successful. The country rejected the Plumb Plan in favor of the old methods of collective bargaining and sound business principles. The railway workers are willing to accept the decision, to take all they can get in wages from the wage board of the Esch-Cummins Act and then, when the government has withdrawn its support of the stockholders, to strike for more, and get it. That they are none too well satisfied, however, with the officials who failed to enforce their demand for the Plumb Plan was revealed by the outlaw strike against them in the spring of 1920. They have not forgotten the Plumb Plan. Nor has the labor movement as a whole, when even the hand-picked delegates of the A. F. L. convention, against a vigorous opposition by Mr. Gompers and the whole Executive Committee with the exception of Mr. Frank Morrison, can vote by a large majority to support and demand it.

Once again the efforts of the workers to allow their second motive— the strain of social idealism—to come to the front have been defeated by the hostility of the public. It evidently still prefers a labor trust that will raise wage as high as it possibly can—and it certainly has the power to raise them pretty high. But the railroad workers have still the Plumb Plan, and when they offer it again they may strike for it and secure it.

Or take the coal miners. They have long been—since 1890—structurally the model of an industrial union, a model to which even the I. W. W. can only point with admiration. But in policy they have been the very type of business union, highly conservative and proceeding by collective agreements and the rigid keeping of contracts. The anthracite workers have been operating since the strike and settlement of 1902–3 with a system of permanent boards of conciliation; the bituminous workers, facing a highly decentralized group of competing employers, have made individual and regional agreements interspersed with frequent strikes. Soft-coal mining is highly competitive, production depends largely on fluctuations in the market conditions, and the price must be high enough to enable the least efficient mines to make a profit, which of course results in exorbitant returns from the better equipped mines. Under the Fuel Administration some attempt was made to secure organization and continuity of production; production for the relatively steady public demand was made the aim, not production for the highly unstable market. The miners of course benefited by anything that increased the most highly prized desideratum of their life, continuity of employment. As a result of this war-time experience with the possibility of greater efficiency, and of another motive than private profit, and, to some extent, as an imitation of the similar British movement, the rank and file of the miners became disgusted with the old methods of business unionism and of business inefficiency, and voted overwhelmingly, in their convention in March, 1919, and again in their special convention in the fall, for the nationalization of the mines under democratic control, and for a thirty-hour week, five days of six hours each, to prevent the annual employment of only 233 days out of the year. The inefficient and fluctuating management of the bituminous mines is the special grievance of the workers, and they have employed experts to investigate the whole field and reveal just where the system of private competition has proved itself wasteful and harmful to worker and to public.

The miners, then, seem at last to be waking to the possibilities of the use of their extensive power as an industrial union to secure an actual control over the industry. It is highly significant that in the negotiations in the spring of 1920 between the United Mine Workers and the anthracite operators for a renewal of the agreement expiring in 1920 the claim of the operators that the breakdown of the coal supply is due primarily to the inefficency and slacking on the job of the miners was met with detailed and imforming analyses of the entire industry which completely turned the tables upon the operators and established their inefficiency and their pursuit of profits as the real cause of the trouble. It is merely another instance of the importance that production and the service of the needs of the community has been assuming in the workers' minds.

But the most advanced, the most highly developed, and the most interesting example of the new unionism is to be found among the clothing workers. Ten years ago the making of garments was still carried on under the most primitive sweatshop conditions in the slums of our great cities; the garment trade was without rival as an example of the horrors to which modern civilization in its insistence on cheap commodities can descend. Today sweatshops have been abolished, the workers have the 44-hour week, a living wage, a permanent board of conciliation, and are advancing towards the abolition of unemployment and the eventual control of the industry. This result has been obtained wholly by the efforts of the workers themselves in their spontaneous and sustained revolt against conditions as they were; they could have come about through only the loyal coöperation of all, but the outstanding figure and spokesman of the movement has been the brilliant leader of the Amalgamated Clothing Workers, Sidney Hillman.

It is not the place here to relate in detail the series of great strikes and lockouts that were the outward mark of this transformation. It is rather to analyze the changes in ideas and philosophies, and to attempt to appraise the tendencies that have been revealed. For nowhere has the labor movement more clearly grasped the underlying realities of the present industrial situation and its probable future developments than in these garment trades.

Although the International Ladies' Garment Workers does not differ greatly in either spirit, attitude, or achievement from the Amalgamated (the union of workers in the men's clothing trade), the latter organization has indisputably led the way since 1914, and it occupies today the center of attraction in the eyes of all interested in the labor movement, largely because it possesses Sidney Hillman, although where it leads the Ladies' Garment Workers are not far behind.

The Amalgamated was formed by those workers whose delegates were shut out of the 1914 convention of the United Garment

Workers, an A. F. L. union of the approved business type with a membership among the overall workers and not much elsewhere. The Amalgamated elected as President Sidney Hillman, cutter in the Hart Schaffner and Marx shops in Chicago and representative of the workers in the shop agreement that firm made after the great strike of 1910. That epoch-making agreement had caused the workers, and above all Hillman, to organize themselves and to think and act in terms of their shop, the productive unit, not of the union formed to sell labor. It comprised fellow-workers democratically elected by all the employees in the shop, not from several skilled crafts to the exclusion of all the rest. Hillman organized the Amalgamated on analogous lines.   It became a true industrial union and took in all who worked in or about the shop, clerks and draymen as well as cutters and pressers. In contradistinction to the old United Garment Workers, it requires a referendum for every important decision. The Executive Board is elected by referendum; no strike can be either called or settled without one. And it stands definitely for peace in the industry, not armed peace marked by frequent battles and truces, but long time agreements for the establishment of permanent legislative bodies, Joint Boards and Boards of Arbitration with impartial chairmen in each field, and it is working for a national agreement of the same nature. This plan has met with unqualified success wherever it has been put into effect; the only trouble has come from individual employers who refused to enter into the general agreement, but these have nearly all come into line, until now there are but four large plants in the country that have no agreement with the Amalgamated. It can truly boast that it has brought law and order and peace into an industry where during the last generation there has been very little of anything save strife. And the peace it has brought is not the peace of stagnation—a long persistence of unchanged conditions; it is the peace of active growth and advance, going forward to a new gain for workers so soon as an old one has been consummated. The impartial chairman of the Chicago district, Professor James H. Tufts, has laid down the epoch-making principle that the workers are entitled not merely to the maintenance of their standard of living but to an actual raising of that standard. It is the peace which eliminates friction in the process of change, not the peace which prevents that change.   The New Unionism thus distinguishes itself most sharply from the revolutionary unionism of the I. W. W. or the Western Federation of Miners, which refuses to make any agreements at all. It is the substitution for guerilla warfare of progressive legislation.

To the old demand for equality of condition it has replied with a practical leveling up of wages—an equalization hastened by the necessity in a rising market of raising the poorest paid most. Though the craft divisions are preserved for administrative purposes, there is no longer the wide gulf between the highly skilled and the less skilled. The old system of piece-work, resulting in the terrible sweating conditions and at times the sixteen-hour day of the old rule, has been abolished in favor of the weekly wage on the basis of the 44-hour week— secured as the result of a lockout by the employers on armistice day. And to the demand for security and continuity of employment—a demand which because of the highly seasonal nature of the clothing trades is especially pressing—it has voted, in its 1920 convention at Boston, for the establishment by the employers of an unemployment fund—a fund to be used to support workers during slack seasons, and indirectly a tremendous incentive to the employer to arrange for continuous production in his industry. For the Amalgamated has at length openly expressed the underlying notion of the worker everywhere, that unemployment incident to fluctuations in the market for profit has nothing to do with the worker, and that he must be supported by the employer in dull periods just as the machine and the factory are supported, no matter what the demand for goods. The worker who engages in a particular industry must be supported by that industry, either by continuous employment if the employers care enough to arrange it, or by an unemployment fund contributed by them if they don't. Every other union, if it were strong enough, would make just such a demand, and every other union as it grows stronger will make it.

At the same convention the Amalgamated voted to establish coöperative institutions—also under way by the Ladies' Garment Workers— for the distribution of clothing, and a coöperative bank; it is significant that this step has been paralleled by the railway brotherhoods.

But the most significant factor of all in the new unionism is its growing interest in production. Hitherto radical movements have like the I. W. W. advocated sabotage and the "conscientious withdrawal of efficiency" as a weapon against the capitalist. The Amalgamated, largely under the influence of Hillman and his fellow officers, has steadily kept in mind its eventual aim of taking over complete control of the industry and complete responsibility for production, and is constantly working toward that goal. The organization of the union, built up as it is about the shop and not the craft, concerned as it is with shop conditions and shop practices, cultivates a direct sense of responsibility in and consequently responsibility for the production of clothing. In the Boston convention the question of the establishment of standards of production—measurements of work and requirements of output—came up for discussion, and though the old slavery of the task system of the sweatshops still rankled in the minds of the workers, and there was a good deal of opposition, a substantial majority for the grading of all workers into certain classes and their demotion if their weekly output fell below that of their class, with a consequent decrease in wages, was secured by Hillman's appeals. This system of standard had already been established in the large Sonneborn shops in Baltimore, instituted by the workers and under the workers' control; and Hillman, Schlossberg, and the other officers were firmly convinced of its value—a value not to the worker alone, in preparing him and educating him for the assumption of greater control, but above all a value to the industry, and to the industry as a public service. Mr. Hillman said: "We officers understand that the principle of our organization is to deal with the employers so that the rights of our people will always be protected. But it is not our purpose to protect them against work. Employers demand safeguards against decreased production when we demand increased wages. And we stand for production; we want shorter hours to give you more leisure and more money to ensure better living conditions, but I refuse to be a party to a vicious campaign of labor against production. The greatest enemies of our organization are those who speak against production. For such a policy would ultimately be our downfall." [1]

And to prove the sincerity of this attitude, the officers have succeeded in enforcing discipline upon their members,—a disciplinary power freely granted them by vote, and not a discipline assumed by them to keep their authority—and upon that bane of the clothing trades, the minor labor official who is seeking to aggrandize himself at the expense of the workers and the employer. Several such were recently tried and removed in New York; three were expelled from the union. In Chicago, where the collective agreement is much older, the "bad" leader is almost unknown. A New York shop recently suffered badly from sabotage: the officers investigated and gave the employers permission to dismiss the entire force. In other days this would have meant at once a general strike. No leader would employ such tactics if he were not sure of the support of his followers, and if he were not firmly impressed with the importance of production.

[1] *New York Evening Post,* May 13, 1920.

For Hillman and the Amalgamated, while they are radical—even revolutionary—in their advocacy of the overthrow of the capitalistic system and the control and administration of the means of production by the workers—the body is quite solidly socialistic, and voted its sympathy with the Russian Republic—do not consider that the Revolution will usher in the millennium. In fact, they do not pay much attention to the Revolution at all. They are too busy trying to develop in their workers the habits of responsibility, the technical knowledge, the genuine ability, to assume under collective agreements greater and greater control of the industry as it is now. They would not welcome any responsibility placed upon the worker before he is ready for it. But their every move is always made, not only in the light of its immediate beneficial effect, but also in the light of its influence in educating the worker for the assumption of greater responsibilities. They do not disclaim political action, they consider it necessary as the legal system is outgrown; but they are not national socialists, they look forward, with the miners and the railroad workers, and with far greater foresight and realization of the burdens involved than either, to the eventual national ownership of industry with democratic control through the unions.

The Ladies' Garment Workers has not yet secured the permanent establishment of collective agreement machinery, as has the Amalgamated. Agreement with employers' organizations still comes at the end of the strikes and runs till new strikes break out; and shop strikes are frequent. The 44-hour week, and the substitution of weekly wage for piece-work has been effected in imitation of the Amalgamated; and the union is trying to build up an "American standard" psychology amongst the week workers so that they will give a day's work for a day's wage. But the union has not yet taken the momentous step of compelling its members to live up to standards of output.

But in all other particulars, in democratic organization, in industrialization, in general philosophy and spirit, it closely approximates the men's clothing union. And since 1910 it has had a permanent organization with the employers, the Joint Board of Sanitary Control, that has eliminated the sweatshop and greatly improved working conditions. And it is just as much interested in production, and the social value of learning its technique. It has employed production engineers to devise more efficient methods. Both it and the Amalgamated have done remarkable work in the education of their members, in genuine Americanization.

These few outstanding examples of the New Unionism by no means exhaust the number that might be cited. There are very few unions indeed that have not in their rank and file come to demand something more than the traditional aims and methods of business unionism. What the future will bring forth, no one can say; but it is difficult to understand how these tendencies, born as they are out of technological conditions dependent upon the progress of the industrial revolution, can fail of eventual fruition.

To summarize, the aims of the New Unionism, then, are: 1. To secure the greatest possible bargaining power through industrial organization, as a means to the attainment of further ends. 2. To work for the ends of business unionism as temporary and immediate expedients, higher wages and shorter hours. 3. To secure continuity of employment and an assured position in the industrial system. 4. To prepare themselves to assume a larger and larger share in the control of industry, and hence, in accordance with the double strain, to train themselves to think in terms of production and industrial technique, and of social responsibility. 5. Thus to realize the old democratic ideal of an approximate equality of status and remuneration together with differentiation of function, of liberty of fulfilling their creative impulses through the directing of their own activities, and of fraternity and coöperation in the social community.

And, to serve this newer tendency, that has been in progress much longer in Europe than in this country, there has arisen a new social philosophy—a philosophy of economic and industrial federalism which under various names—guild socialism, syndicalism, democratic control, industrial democracy—is coming more and more to express the aspirations, not only of the more thoughtful workers, but also of the intelligent and professional classes everywhere. It is utopian—all social philosophies are utopian, none more so than the dreamings of the economic liberalism and individualism which is still the orthodox philosophy of today. It portrays an ideal which in its very definiteness is too selective and limited to include the rich and complex fabric of human existence. Like all such utopian ventures, it must not be taken too literally; its value lies rather in the illumination and clarification it can furnish to the particular and specific problems of economic organization and industrial technique than in the immediate practical possibility of ever realizing any such social structure, or, indeed, in the desirability of doing so if we could. The main features of the ideal commonwealth— its great industrial units of workers banded together to produce commodities through a democratic organization, with a central governing and adjusting body composed of representatives from all industries, either alone or in connection with a political congress of consumers— these are familiar today to all well-informed people. The details remain just as vague as the main lines are distinct; and critics to the contrary notwithstanding, that really doesn't matter. For the significance of such a vision is rather its imperative force, its driving power when burned into the hearts and minds of the workers throughout the lands of the world. Whatever of approach is ever made to such an ideal can not depend upon the theoretical working out of an abstract plan into the very last detail. If it needed such a lesson at all, the world learned it in the celerity with which the Russian revolutionists forgot most of the Marx they ever knew and faced realities. It can only come as the result of patient, laborious, and repeated experience with the concrete problems of particular industries, and of harmonizations and adjustments between conflicting interests worked out in the very toil and moil of economic life—in a word, it can come only as the result of some such educative process as the New Unionism seems to be developing.

PART II

GROUP RESPONSIBILITY

14. GROUP RESPONSIBILITY—THE PROBLEM

In our examination of the present industrial situation we have seen that society today is rapidly approaching a state wherein it is economically organized into a number of great industrial groups, groups essentially monopolistic and as yet at least socially quite irresponsible. In contrast with this prevailing state of affairs it has become apparent that coincident with the formation of these great groups, society has developed an increasing need for efficient and continuous service from each of these component groups.

The history of the growth of these groups has revealed a double tendency: a tendency to think solely in terms of particular group interests, to the exclusion of the interests of other groups or of wider interests; this tendency has been called group individualism, and has been explained as the old traditional philosophy of individualism and economic liberalism revised and brought up to date through the substitution of the modern unit, the group, for the older and original unit, the single human being: and a tendency to be concerned with social problems, social needs, and social aims, and to merge group interests into those of the community as a whole. Both tendencies have become accentuated of late, group interest leading to huge industrial struggles in which those not directly concerned suffer almost as much as the participants themselves, and social idealism leading to class-conscious revolutionary efforts at the alteration of the structure of the economic regulation of industry. And between them both tendencies threaten the complete overthrow of the industrial system as we know it today, the first through a catastrophic break-down of the actual technique of production itself, and the bringing about of a chaotic state somewhat resembling that which the war effected in Central and especially East Central Europe; the second, through a radical overturn of the legal and economic structure through which that industrial technique is controlled, which has its parallel in the situation obtaining in Russia after the November revolution.

With the second of these tendencies, and with the dangers it presents, we do not purpose to deal here; for in America this danger is remote indeed. There is in this country no problem of an extreme social idealism that might exemplify here the strong as well as the weak points of a fanaticism which, like that of Cromwell and that of Lenin, verges upon the theocratic rule of the chosen vessels of the Lord. The problem of social idealism in America is not the problem of reconciling its too-zealous impulses with the patient and realistic appreciation of the psychological needs of the prevailing situation. The American problem of social idealism is rather how to fill what at present appears to be a yawning, gaping void.

But the first of the tendencies presents a quite different aspect. The experience of the nation in the post-armistice days, the many strikes and industrial conflicts that threatened the continuance of certain very vital public utilities, and the certainty that when the era of business prosperity subsides such strikes will become much more serious and bitter; (for it has always been in the face of a reduction in wages during a business depression that, as in 1877, in 1885–6, and in 1893–4, labor has fought most fiercely) and the even more serious prospect of probable future increases in wages to higher and higher levels, perhaps in collusion with the employer, have made it imperative that some way be found out of this general group individualism to a group social responsibility. Numerous attempts at devising some such plan for securing the accountability of labor groups to society as a whole have been put forward, ranging from the official A. F. L. solution of forthwith giving the workers everything they demand to the official pronouncements of chambers of commerce to declare all strikes illegal and enforce production at "reasonable" wages by the strong arm of the law. Despite the generally interested nature of the loud heralding of "the rights of the public to uninterrupted and efficient service" by press and business man, the emphasis thus placed on efficient production not only serves to illuminate a problem of the utmost consequence, but it can also hardly fail to have its effect upon the workers themselves in transforming them in their eyes from useless "hands" to necessary public servants. Unfortunately if such an emphasis becomes too patently subservient to the interests of the employers, the workers may unwisely but quite naturally be driven all the further into their own group individualism.

This state of affairs has already given rise to a new social theory, that of "pluralism." It has been developed both by legalists seeking to make jurisprudence conform more closely to the social interests it should serve, and by economic utopians in search of a new social order. This theory, while exceedingly interesting and illuminating, unfortunately has not as yet given much practical knowledge that will enable society to meet the problem of securing social responsibility in the component groups that make up the community. And the basic reason for the inadequacy that has hitherto in greater or less degree marked the theories of the pluralists has been the practical non-existence, under any theory of individualism, be its unit the man or the group, of any such concept as social responsibility.

To the individualist there is but one kind of social responsibility—it is the responsibility of the government to those who have elected it, its responsibility to dispense justice, to protect from external aggression, and, in general, to furnish certain services to individuals. It is a responsibility in typical utilitarian vein to serve the greatest good of the greatest number. In America, in France, and in practice if not in theory in England, the individualist theory is, in the terms of the Declaration of Independence, that governments exist to secure the rights of individuals, and endure only so long as they do secure them. They are responsible to the people for thus securing them.

Of course, in the very limited sphere of activity that the government was supposed and permitted to serve, the individual had a reciprocal obligation and responsibility. He was obliged to assist in the defense of the country, he was obliged to contribute taxes to the support of the government, and he was obliged to refrain from that interference with the rights of other men known as crime. But aside from this very definite and rigorously circumscribed obligation, the individualistic theory recognized no such thing as obligation to society. Society, in so far as such a concept of the whole as distinct from its constituent parts is at all comprised in the individualistic theory, has, in the vast range of social activity known as economic, only a responsibility to keep each man free from intrusion by his neighbor; there is no reciprocal responsibility on the part of the individuals to do anything for society.

This being the case, it is not surprising that the apologists for group individualism and pluralism similarly tend to overlook the question of the responsibility of their groups to society. This comes out in the case of Mr. Laski, who favors a society composed of economic groups, the differences between which are to be adjudicated through impartial courts whose establishment and maintenance he regards as the essential function of the state. This plan, in strict conformity with the individualistic theory, and with the liberalism of which he is so able an advocate, recognizes perfectly the obligation of the state to keep one group from infringing upon the prerogatives of another; the court is the best instrument for securing a careful determination and adjustment of rights. But his plan disregards, and his courts hardly touch, the important question of the determination and the fulfillment of duties and obligations of the groups to that collective whole called society.

On the whole, then, it must be confessed that of those pluralists who approach the problem from the standpoint of jurisprudence, Mr. Laski, while giving an admirable survey and analysis of the present situation, and clearly revealing the large measure of irresponsible power or "sovereignty" that resides today in various groups, economic and otherwise, against which, to say the least, the government, as the organized instrument of society as a whole, finds it exceedingly inopportune to proceed, nevertheless does not offer any clearly defined program for meeting such a situation, and does not in fact seem to regard it as a situation which particularly needs to be met otherwise than by a recognition of its existence and an adjustment of legal theory to *fait accompli*. M. Duguit, the great jurist of Bordeaux, can not be accused of falling into the same error; but, it seems to the candid reader, however great his admiration be for the glowing ideal M. Duguit holds out of a society of functional groups whose sole thought shall be of the service they are rendering to the community, and whose only rights are those privileges granted by the community that it may be the more efficiently served, the French savant has, after the way of legalists, and especially of French ones, rather overlooked the psychological nature of man and the obstacles it presents to a realization of such an ideal.   Between M. Duguit's wholly admirable but rather remote ideal and Mr. Laski's penetrating analysis of a not entirely admirable state of affairs, the social observer, and, it may be, the practical statesman, desire some intermediate step, some method or at least some faint indications of how to formulate a method for the passage from the one state to the other.   Jurists, great as their ability may be, do not and perhaps should not be called upon to descend to such practical considerations.

The economic reformers have, it is true, given more of consideration to this important question of how the admittedly group individualistic society of today can be brought nearer to the admittedly desirable and necessary society in which groups are actuated by a sense of their social responsibility; but, after the manner and wont of radicals, they have been too prone to consider it entirely in the light of conditions that are to obtain after The Revolution, a light which, however theoretically interesting, hardly suffices to illumine the gloom of these pre-revolutionary days. Syndicalists, guild socialists, economic federalists of all sorts and varieties, have in general taken one of two courses: they have assumed that in those idyllic times after The Day there will be an impartial and wholly just central authority or state, which will enforce social interests on any particularly recalcitrant and self-seeking group; or, if they be very radical indeed, and very much incensed against the state, they have assumed that with a central authority entirely abolished men will just naturally prefer the good and interest of all to their own private group interests, and will not think of using their economic power to aggrandize themselves at their fellows' expense. Both types assume that the real class solidarity and cohesion necessary to bring about The Revolution will naturally persist after the great enemy who has called it forth is utterly overthrown and vanquished.

Now these claims may possess considerable of truth, but at the same time they betray the characteristic faults of too great utopianism—a one-sidedness bred of undivided and earnest vision, an impatience with irritating details like human nature born of an abiding faith in general principles, and a consequent tendency to slur over the real and vital problems. Moreover, they remain strictly hypothetical, dependent upon The Revolution for their verification. Unfortunately the problem will not also obligingly wait. Let us, therefore, proceed to an examination of the problem as it presents itself to society at the present stage of its development, without reference to possible future transformations, and let us take it up as it is phrased by the two schools of social control and of free development, of socialism and anarchism, if you will, or of autocracy and liberalism, if you so prefer.

The most natural and probably the first formulation of the problem of securing social responsibility in the groups comprising the community is that which regards it as one of enforcing, by the government and through suitable penalties, the efficient functioning of groups from without. This is the recognition by law that groups are legally responsible to the will of the majority who control the government. It is the instinctive reaction of the irate householder who, finding himself unable on the eve of winter to obtain coal and all the miners out on strike for higher wages, quite naturally wants to send somebody "to make 'em dig coal." Now this way of approaching the problem would certainly be revolutionary, for the very basis of our civilization has been that a man had the right to do what he likes with his own, whether that own be labor or property. And when such an outcry is raised against, say, the packers, and the same householder grumbles, " The government ought to make 'em put their prices down," the law in all its majesty intervenes and protects the sacred rights of property against even the duly elected Congress and President of the United States, which cannot confiscate property "without due process of law." To recognize, then, that the majority can thus legally and effectually enforce production of commodities which may be assumed to be necessities, is to alter profoundly our legal and economic system and to deny that a man may do what he likes with his own.

But assume that this radical procedure is adopted; the assumption is far from rash, for chambers of commerce, editors, and a considerable portion of "the public" is already quite willing to enforce production—upon labor unions, at least—what can we say of its efficacy and its probable results? How will it operate to secure that steady and efficient production that society needs?

It is a comparatively simple affair to enforce the will of a majority upon a territorial unit; the world has just finished with a tremendous example of just such enforcement, though, to be sure, it is somewhat of a question whether the results in central and eastern Europe represent the will of the majority of the Allies. Military power, bullets and machine guns can generally accomplish it, or the mere threat and certainty that they will be used. So long as it is a question of preventing a minority from doing something, and is thus essentially a problem of suppression and repression, the majority can eventually have its way. But when the desire of a majority is to compel the minority to do something positive, the outcome is far more dubious. Thus it is comparatively easy to suppress a Sinn Fein government in Ireland, but all the power of the British Empire had a hard time of it to compel the Irish people to obey and live under a British government. Quite similarly it is simple, if you have enough power, to force Germans out of France and to force the cession of Alsace-Lorraine; but when it comes to getting as much coal as you want, or as large an indemnity, you find innumerable annoying obstacles in your way.

And when the problem shifts from a territorial minority that can be conquered in a military sense to a minority which is a functional group, the difficulty becomes even more acute. To force a functional group to do something positive which they are resolved not to do is a task to test the ability of the firmest dictator. As the old adage has it, "You can lead a horse to water, but you can't make him drink." The Germans found it out in Belgium, the Northerners found it out in the South, and the French are finding it out in Germany.

Of course it is possible to secure results of a sort if you are determined enough. Most miners would rather mine coal than be shot, and if you have enough bayonets coal can certainly be got out. But such methods, though undoubtedly entirely possible, are not of a nature to prove widely practicable. Entirely apart from any psychological considerations as to whether a majority of Americans would permit the adoption of such tactics, it seems, on the face of it, that as a remedy for the insufficient or inefficient production of coal it would not in the long run be practicable. This is admittedly a very extreme case, but it is crucial, for it makes plain that mere power to enforce the will of a majority upon a functional group is not the only, and perhaps not the most important, element necessary for the securing of social responsibility.

In fact, the greatest contribution of the pluralists like Mr. Laski is just this fact of the ultimate " sovereignty" or ability to resist compulsion resident in groups. The same householder who wanted government to apply pressure to the miners and the packers, whenever he desires a remedy for a certain ill, immediately thinks first of all of "passing a law against it. " He is unaware of the profound truth the liberals have recognized, and which the socialists and other apostles of "social control" have not yet learned, that there are many, many things that legislation and direct social control cannot effect. Bismarck found it out when the Catholics and the Social Democrats beat him and forced him to go to Canossa. The Bolsheviki are finding it out; and the American Congress would find it out if, for instance, it passed a law breaking up the family. It is a commonplace that the prohibition of liquor belongs in the same category; if there be anywhere a large minority seriously desirous of a drink of whiskey, no army of inspectors can prevent them from getting it.

It would seem that the efficient production of commodities is to be placed in the same category of actions which no legislative fiat can effect, and government authority can enforce only with the utmost difficulty. For while the mere working—the mere tending of machines— is quite possible to enforce by sufficient penalties, the efficient production of a large supply is infinitely more difficult. Sabotage—not the sabotage of destruction, but the sabotage practiced by conservative business unionists as the "deliberate withdrawal of efficiency"—sabotage and lowered output is bound to result. The French government, by calling all railway workers to the colors and making striking a court-martial offense, succeeded in crushing the great railway strike of 1910. And forthwith the French railways lapsed into a most woeful state of inefficiency. Accidents would happen; cars would turn up hundreds of miles from their proper destination; men would insist on obeying every rule in the book literally when a little discretion might have prevented a wreck or a tie-up. And in this case the government, by waving the flag of German invasion, applied an exceedingly powerful patriotic motive as well as mere force. The government was indeed vindicated; but it still remains a question whether the country as a whole would not have been infinitely better off had the demands of the strikers been granted.

It is significant that in those countries where the greatest restrictions are placed upon the labor unions and upon strikes, like France, Italy, and Spain, revolutionary unionism employing sabotage and violence is most strong and dangerous. It is a tenet of the American tradition that repression of grievances, whether those grievances be just or whether they be unjust, is the sure road to revolt; and the candid observer of history is forced to admit that there is considerable evidence in its support. It may then be fairly predicted that recourse to the enforcement of the will of the majority upon a functional group, even if it were successfully effected, would but drive union activities underneath the surface, to break out in sporadic revolts.

Moreover, to be at all successful, the method of repressing and enforcing responsibility implies the presence of an impartial state—a state in which all concerned, both parties to any grievance, can repose the utmost confidence that it will decide questions and adopt policies only after the most painstaking and unbiassed research, and that its decisions will be based on premises which all parties admit to start with. The present government, in all criminal and in the overwhelming majority of civil cases, is such an impartial adjudicator. The few exceptions are the faults and dishonesties inevitable in any human institution. And our criminal and civil law is accepted as just by the parties whom it most concerns.

But when it comes to a question of the economic interests of groups, it is just as unquestionable that the present state is certainly not impartial. With the presence in the economic fabric of various great conflicting interests, it is too much to ask any human individual to preserve a frigid impartiality. When, for instance, there come to trial men who do not accept the basic hypotheses upon which the present state and the judge who loyally supports it proceed, that judge can not be impartial. It is like asking a loyal and patriotic citizen to judge impartially of the reports of the enemy's atrocities. Human nature, save in very rare cases, simply is not cast in such heroic mold. The best the state can do in the face of conflicting economic interests is to side with that side which the individual judge thinks right, and endeavor, so far as in him lies, to be fair to the other side.

Precisely an analogous case is that of any international tribunal, any supreme court of a league of nations whose decrees are to be enforced. Where disputes of minor importance are to be brought up, it is easy to be impartial, and firm in integrity; but where vital national interests are concerned, where "national honor," that illusory but highly important entity, is at stake, no international court can possibly be expected to render absolutely just decisions, and hence no international police to enforce peace is as yet at all possible.

It must be admitted by detached observers that even the highest courts in the land are today dominated by conflicting class interests, that judges of different antecedents necessarily proceed upon different hypotheses, and that, for instance, while a judge whose social philosophy derived from Herbert Spencer and one who got his from Karl Marx can be trusted to agree perfectly and to render a quite just decision on the merits of a plea to grant retrial in a murder case, they will of necessity differ radically in their interpretation and application of the Fourteenth Amendment. In the middle of the last century the United States Supreme Court undoubtedly enjoyed a much higher reputation for impartiality than it has throughout the country today; yet at the present time there are few so blind as to deny that during the whole slavery struggle the Supreme Court was anything but impartial. When the supposedly impartial court handed down its crucial Dred Scott decision, almost the entire North absolutely rejected it, and six years later by force effected a sweeping reversal of its principles. Is it reasonable to expect that the passions aroused by economic conflicts, just as bitter and vital, are to be calmed by an impartial state, a state which claims, and probably sincerely believes, that it is acting for the best interests of the entire community? The Dred Scott decision was not enforced, and it is dubious whether any decision today that seemed as unrighteous as that one did to the North could be enforced.

The possibility of enforcement appears to be dependent upon the confidence which those to be coerced have in the essential impartiality of the government. That confidence and that impartiality, as regards economic interests, are certainly lacking today; nor does it seem at all possible that in any post-revolutionary state they would be present to any greater degree. Certainly Russia and Hungary, the only two examples we have to date, do not seem to have advanced especially on "capitalistic" governments in their impartiality towards men of all economic interests and faiths.

Moreover, even if it did exist, it would be well-nigh impossible to convince the workers of such an impartiality so long as the enforcement of responsibility meant first of all and primarily the enforcement of responsibility to the employer, and deprived the worker, to the open glee of the capitalist, of the only weapon he possesses to advance his own interests. With such a complete coincidence of the employer's interest and the assumed interest of the community at large, it is difficult to see how the unionists could regard the enforcement as a matter of good faith.

In fact, the employment of coercive means for the enforcing of responsibility is exceedingly apt to increase resentment at the selfish "public," and to provoke far more of disorganization, inefficiency, discord, and group selfishness than it could possibly eradicate and suppress. As a single instance, the passage of the Kansas law to prevent strikes resulted in a great strike of miners who had not before dreamt of striking at all. This could hardly be considered a successful increase in productivity in a public utility.

Moreover, if the method of enforcing responsibility is to have any success, it must succeed by educating the workers to a position in which they will not need the actual application or even the threat of force to secure their obedience. If the average citizen needed a bayonet to keep him from breaking the criminal statutes, those statutes could not fairly be called practicable. And it is quite apparent that the issuing of injunctions broadcast, the quelling of strikes with troops, and other tactics of a like nature, however successful they may be in preventing open industrial warfare, are scarcely methods likely to result in the education of the worker toward social responsibility. It is indeed the worst possible course that could be adopted to effect such an end.

Thus our general examination of the first of the two suggested lines of approach to the problem has resulted in the conclusion that though the enforcement of responsibility is perhaps ultimately possible, its employment is fraught with so many perils and difficulties that it is exceedingly dubious whether, save in cases of extreme emergency, and as a measure of the very last resort, it would prove in any sense practicable; and that it is certain to result in defeating the very aim toward which it is directed, the ultimate development of an attitude of social responsibility in place of the present group individualism. If there is any other possible method of achieving this end, it is certainly deserving of the most careful examination.

But let us proceed to consider several more concrete proposals of those who pin their faith in the enforcement of responsibility through the political government. Though for obvious reasons not often advocated as a permanent method of settling anything, the means most popular and most frequently employed in practice has been the injunction. This is a legal instrument, devised in an age when labor unions were yet undreamed of, for protecting property rights from irreparable injury for which there is no remedy at law. It was invented to restrain parties in dispute about title or damages to property from interfering with the property before the courts had passed on the title. It has since, in contradiction to many fundamental legal principles, been expanded in scope to enforce criminal law and to abridge personal rights and liberties. It is not a criminal, but a civil instrument, which means that the offense in disobeying it is contempt of court, and that offense requires no jury trial. The penalty for disobeying it is not great; but the value of the injunction as a means of preventing a strike lies in its power to nip such a movement in the bud; it introduces delays into a situation where every movement counts. Hence it has been frequently employed by the employer everywhere to crush strikes and labor activity; and its complete identification with the employer and the capitalist serves to render it all the more damning and odious in the workers' eyes when employed in behalf of "the public."

The injunction as a method of enforcing social responsibility is thus liable to every disadvantage to which any method of enforcement is subject, it has none of the possible advantages of other methods, and in addition it has the special demerits of a very doubtful foundation in legal principles and of being applied without investigation of any sort by a single judge. It is a method to which organized labor is already bitterly opposed. It is the very height of the "public's" attitude of peace at any price; for it is adapted to secure nothing but immediate peace, and the price is continuous warfare.

Another proposal is that of incorporating the unions and making them liable at law to keep their contracts and to pay damages in case of non-fulfillment. This proposal overlooks the absence of any means of the union going into bankruptcy if it finds performance of the agreed services impossible. It has the additional disadvantage of making the responsibility exclusively to the employer, and providing no stimulus whatever to the growth of social obligation. There would be no social control over the nature of the contract; it would be the apotheosis of business unionism with all its faults. It seems, indeed, as though the unions will increasingly observe their agreements without any such elaborate safeguards, if our conjectures as to the New Unionism be at all verified. The making of union funds subject to damage suits could only result in the carrying on of union activities with very small funds—in a word, in the introduction into business unionism of the tactics of the I. W. W.: violence, destruction, and "striking on the job."

But the remedy most popular just now, and which is indeed infinitely preferable to the other suggested, is that of compulsory arbitration. It recognizes the obligation of the labor groups to the community as a whole, and it also recognizes the reciprocal obligation of the community to the labor group to see that it secures fair treatment. Under an impartial administration, an administration whole-heartedly devoted to the welfare of every member of the community and hence whole-heartedly devoted to the welfare of the workers also, such a plan of enforced responsibility, if greatly aided by other conditions, might have a chance of succeeding. But where can an impartial administration which shares the workers' aim of practical equality and security of position for every member of society be found, and could such an administration, strictly speaking, be impartial? Moreover, the very fact that such a body would legally have the power to prevent a strike so prejudices the worker against it that it could hardly attain the universal confidence necessary for success. And it is excessively undemocratic; it entrusts to a small body of men who it assumes will "do the right thing" absolute power. It asks the workers to hand over their only weapon, and promises they can get what is good for them without it. The workers, already sadly disillusioned as to the promises of government authorities, are not going to do any such thing. It may well be benevolent, very benevolent and paternalistic, but it is despotism nevertheless. No body of men is good enough to entrust such momentous power to. The American worker, even if he thought that from their hands he would receive precious gifts, instinctively would reject such offerings and though it cost him much would prefer to rely on his own exertions. Hence, as an expedient for the enforcement of social responsibility, compulsory arbitration is not successful; where it has been tried, in Canada and in Australasia, it has either been discarded or remained a dead letter. Both workers and business men, in centering their attention upon the strike-prevention side and overlooking the arbitration features, are probably not very far wrong.

Foreign experience has proved that such a board of arbitration has an equalizing effect upon working conditions: it tends to raise all workers to a single standard, and hence is of great benefit to the lower class of sweated workers. But that standard, upon which all decisions are made, becomes fixed and stationary; and the workers, growing in power and vision, become intensely dissatisfied with the whole scheme and strike anyway. When the workers once decide to strike,—well, the whole dubious impracticability of enforcing decisions upon them is brought home. Any system which allows things to reach the stage in which the workers are resolved to strike is a foregone failure.

Yet if compulsory arbitration is not the answer to the problem, it has nevertheless within it the germs of great good. It can become, with certain modifications, an immensely valuable educative instrument; and it can, if administered with sympathy and integrity, do much to secure that social responsibility at which it aims. To achieve such an effect, its compulsory features must first be entirely abandoned; only thus can the all-important confidence of the workers be obtained. The success achieved by Canada's arbitration act has been due entirely to the virtual abandonment of the anti-strike feature. Then, it must cease to be a judicial tribunal and become an administrative and legislative council, in which not a judge or arbitrator alone makes decisions, but in which the democratically elected representatives of the two parties are allowed to act together. The Kansas Industrial Court plan is fundamentally wrong, not only in its compulsory features, but even more in regarding its function as judicial. Its crowning folly is to be governed by the rules of evidence—a provision making intelligent decision by the industrially inexpert judges almost impossible. For a court is essentially retrospective; it interprets past agreements and standards, and exists only to settle disputes after they have once risen. Industry demands instead a council that will erect new standards, that will plan for the future, adjust rates and scales and conditions as need for their change arises, that will eliminate the causes of disputes before they are generated, and, in general, administer and legislate for the industry. The Industrial Court has all the faults and all the pitiful futility of the International Court of Arbitration at The Hague; a court without a legislator and an administrator is a monstrosity. But for such a genuine coöperative administration of industry, such a council would needs be made up of experts in that field, with perhaps an impartial chairman representing the interests of the consumer. And so we have arrived, not at compulsory arbitration, but at something very different indeed—something very similar to the boards and councils in the men's clothing trade, and just what the new unionism stands for. And enforced responsibility—it has vanished in the process.

Thus none of the specific methods for enforcing social responsibility contains anything to alter the conclusion that such enforcement is of highly dubious practicability, and the most promising of them, on being followed up, leads to an entirely different method. We are thus driven to a further examination of the very bases of political and social obligation, and to a search for the reason why men obey "authorities."

The question of group responsibility can not be settled, as the irate householder thought, merely by making a law against it. That may be necessary. But that alone is bound to be hopelessly inadequate. The question of responsibility depends ultimately on the grounds on which men obey constituted authorities of any kind, political, religious, economic. These have never been adequately determined, and it is probable that until our social psychology has made such more progress over its present crude state they never will be. But one thing at least is certain: that the police power of the state, its power to enforce its will, or the will of those who have captured it, is not the primary basis of political obligation. If not the active consent, at least the passive assent of those governed is essential to the continuance of that government. Men must feel that it is to some extent representative of their desires and purposes, at least sufficiently representative to keep them from going to the exertion of throwing it off. In large measure this feeling of assent and acceptance is the result of habit and the inertia of established ways and customs persisting after their most efficient work is done—habit drilled into the individual from his birth by every instrumentality of education and social life.

Political obligation is thus at bottom the result of education and trained habituation. All the agencies of collective existence are constantly impressing upon the individual the importance of law and order, the importance of observing the ordained social rules and regulations. Hence the normal individual is so habituated and trained to act in conformity with certain standards and rules that he simply does not think of anything else. The normal citizen does not break the law, and he fails to break it, not because the police would prevent him, not even because he is afraid the police will get him if he does, but simply because he has formed the habit of obeying the law. Why he formed the habit is immaterial; it may have been because of the fear of the penalty, it may have been because of religious tabus and the fear of future torments, it may have been because he came to recognize as good certain moral ideals, it may have been because everybody about him obeyed the law, or it may have been because of a mixture of all these. The important thing is that these are all differing means, more or less efficacious, toward the education of the individual and the development of moral habits, moral ways of acting. Man obeys constituted authority because he has been trained to do so; the best way to secure his obedience is to employ the best way of educating him in habits of obedience and response to social rules. Anything that will develop in him fixed responses to social demands is bound to lead naturally to his becoming a good citizen; anything which, even though like the bayonet of the tyrant's mercenaries it secured present acquiescence in the will of the government, does not so tend to develop moral habits of social response, is at best but artificial and must be applied continually and with increasing intensity to secure that social response that has not become habitual.

All groups thus tend to educate their members into habitual response to the chosen *mores* or codes of those groups: the doctor acts in accord with medical ethics, the lawyer in accord with the standards of his profession, church members in accord with the customs of their particular sect. Nowhere is this habitual response to the demands of the group stronger than in the case of labor unions; and this same habituation is rapidly growing among the entire body of workers as a class. This habitual loyalty is also, in the average individual, directed toward the nation or community as a whole in certain channels which from long custom have been impressed upon all men: in the field of legal regulation, patriotism, and the like. It has not appeared in the field of economic production, because society has not here recognized any standard of production for social needs, any production for the sake of "the public." Since the triumph of economic liberalism business and industry have been divorced from every thought of social responsibility. It has not as yet occurred to any one to expect it. The business man has not had such a principle in his code, the trade unionist certainly has not, and until very recently no one even expected it in the name of the "public" or the community. We had all been taught that the correct thing was to obey the law and do as well as we could for ourselves in a business way. We succeeded in this fairly well because there were very few laws in the realm in which we were advancing ourselves that we could disobey. We never thought of our responsibility to the community because we did not realize the necessity of social obligation.

Today in a crude and blundering way we are beginning to recognize this necessity if our civilization is not to crumble away; but we are not at all used to the thought, and we are very prone to follow our old habits of group individualism.

The problem of the social responsibility of groups, then, it is clear, is not fundamentally a problem of how to enforce a new standard and aim upon groups that have become accustomed to far different ones. It is not what kind of a law we can pass against group individualism, how we can put down its now unpleasant manifestations. Such a view is superficial in the extreme. The problem of group responsibility is at bottom a problem in the education of the entire community toward the adoption of a relatively new social principle—new, that is, to those brought up in the chaotic competitive system of individualism and economic liberalism, though in reality as old as Plato, who wrote his wonderful *Republic* about it. It is to develop a new habit of mind, a new way of responding to our social environment, a new way of thinking and acting—or to rediscover an old one.

If the problem thus be at bottom, as in truth most really important social problems are, a problem of education, then the immediate question is, what means are the best for so training ourselves? When economic groups follow their own interests too exclusively, the solution we must seek must be approached always with the educative value of whatever measures we adopt in the foreground. If we contemplate the use of force on refractory bodies of men, we must employ it solely as a means to our larger end of educating those bodies in habits of social responsibility, else we shall have sacrificed permanent good for a brief temporary respite, and have bought immediate peace at the price of an unending succession of further wars. Force applied for the sake of the immediate attainment of our object is autocratic and can get us nowhere; but force applied in the process of education is often essential. This must be our final answer to those who advocate the immediate suppression of strikes.

The problem with which we set out has thus in essence become one of education in the broadest sense, of what social institutions and what measures of social control will best seize upon the social aims and social responsibility already present or still dormant in the labor movement and increase and foster them. The problem is thus not the simple one of devising a new law or a new government instrumentality; it is immensely more difficult than that. It implies the necessity of a psychological change of attitude and a moral change of heart in the various conflicting groups of present day society. It implies a gradual turning away from the old and a turning toward the new. To those individuals looking for panaceas to cure at one dose all the ills of society, to those reformers who imagine that legislative enactments can in themselves bring social salvation, to those optimistic radicals who believe that the destruction of any institution, even though it be the great institution of the "capitalistic system" itself, can bring about the millennium and create on earth the New Jerusalem—to such men the problem may well appear insuperable as they hurry off to their far easier tasks. But if our industrial civilization, dependent as it is upon the efficient functioning of all its component groups, is to continue as an industrial civilization, some solution must be found, and that at no very remote time. That some solution will be found, those who as a result of the last six years' brutal futility are not grown profoundly pessimistic over the entire body of mankind will be confident. But that solution is not going to be easy. We have as yet discovered hardly any fragments of a solution. It is only as political invention and social philosophy, doffing their gay but useless holiday garb of optimism and complacency, descend to the economic field where the battle for the future of the world is now being fought back and forth and there patiently, persistently, and painstakingly labor and experiment at the tremendous task, that the body of society, grown sick with the cancer of malignant and self-centered irresponsibility, can ever hope to be healed.

14. THE PROBLEM AS AN ESSAY IN EDUCATION

In this final chapter, having envisaged the problem of the attainment of group responsibility as essentially a problem in education, the most that can be done is to point out certain tendencies in the social situation that make that problem seem a not wholly impossible task. It will thus be a stock-taking of resources rather than an attempt, even the slightest, at a formulated method, a stock-taking based on what evidences of social responsibility have appeared in the history of the American labor movement and of its attempts at organization, and on the forces and tendencies at work in the present industrial and economic ferment which seem to be making for the education of industrial groups in habits of social obligation.

In general, it would seem that in every situation which is to develop and train responsibility five factors are necessary, five factors which, though in varying degree, must nevertheless to some extent all be present to make the process truly educative and productive of responsible habits. The first of these is a situation in which coöperative endeavor is absolutely essential to the fulfillment of individual purposes. This is apparent in all cases of team-work, where the individual, to fulfill his private purpose of winning and winning ıor his team, must coöperate effectively with the other members. The desire to make brilliant plays cannot lead such a team member to neglect this coöperative effort, because no play can be really brilliant if it neglects the essential quality of aiding the work of the team. The futility of attempting coöperation where this necessity for mutual aid and assistance is lacking is obvious.

But not only must this social action be necessary; the individuals, by group opinion or by some system of rewards and penalties, must be held responsible for the performance of the tasks which, within their power of accomplishment, it is their portion to perform. No matter how necessary the coöperation of the members of a team may be, unless they realize that necessity, hold individual members to a strict accountability for their actions, and create such a sentiment and group opinion that offenders against it are promptly censured and lose caste and group standing, that team will never be a success. The necessity for coöperation must be present, and it must be consciously present, crystallized into group opinion.

But it must not only be present in the group at large; every individual member must have a clear recognition of that necessity, and a clear knowledge of just what is expected of him. The man who can not do team-work is the man who does not recognize that team-work is necessary, and does not realize the part he must play in the actions of his group. When his individual responsibility is clearly brought home to him, it is usually as though a new light had dawned upon his mind; the transformation is at times surprisingly rapid. Mr. Thomas Mott Osborne has recently given some most astounding demonstrations of the possibility of thus awakening in those who previously had had the least sense of responsibility of any in the community, the professional criminals, a very real and a very strong sense of responsibility to the group when they are placed in a situation where their coöperation is required and expected.

Such coöperation, moreover, must be a mutual attitude of give and take—the responsibility can not be directed solely to the group without a recognition of a reciprocal obligation toward the members. In a team the individuals are required to give their best to the team's aims, but in return they demand that the rest of the team stand by them. A member who feels that his fellows are not playing fair with him—not giving him the opportunity to do the best he can, not supporting him and giving his own advice and opinions careful consideration—such a member will not be loyal to the team. Loyalty can not be one-sided; it can not thrive unless it is mutual. As directed toward persons it is an inheritance from feudalism and chivalry, and in its original form the loyalty of the vassal to the lord imposed upon the lord an obligation to protect that vassal. In the more modern form of loyalty to a group, it necessarily imposes upon that group the obligation of protecting the loyal members. This mutual responsibility is well expressed in the saying of Solon which, significantly enough, has won great popularity in the ranks of the labor movement, "An injury to one is an injury to all."

Finally, for the development of social habits of response, there is necessary a dominant and clear group purpose—a common group aim, not in any sense superseding or contradicting the private aims of the members, but become a very part and parcel of those individual aims, merging imperceptibly into them and extending them further. It is for the sake of this group aim that coöperation is necessary; it is to the attainment of this group aim that men are loyal, that they play their parts, and unite with their fellows in mutual loyalty and coöperative endeavor. It is where this group aim is clearest and most appealing, as in the desire of an athletic team to win a contest, or in the desire of a great army to win a war for a high ideal—defense of hearth and home, overthrow of autocracy, securing of national independence—that the situation develops the strongest sense of group loyalty and responsibility.

Such is the situation that must prevail if habits of social responsibility are to be developed and fostered. It is, to some extent of course, present in every group and community of men; that is what Aristotle meant when he said, "Man is by nature an animal who forms states." The ability of men to respond to group aims and group ends is what determines his existence in society, and is in turn reciprocally determined by it. Social responsibility is thus something inherent in the very nature of mankind; without it he would not be man. It is not, as egoistic and individualistic theorists have argued, something totally alien to man's nature, something artificial that can only be evoked by appealing to the motives of self-interest through reward and punishment. Fortunately our better knowledge of the springs of human action has overthrown so erroneous a view.

Such a situation prevails within the labor union, and has succeeded remarkably in breaking down the old attitude of irresponsible individualism in favor of a real and habitual group activity. A dominant group purpose, coöperation absolutely necessary to attain it, the conscious realization of the necessity of this coöperation, the recognition by the individual of what he must do to help attain it, an attitude of mutual loyalty and responsibility—all these are present in the struggle of groups to better their social and economic position. This has perhaps been the chief social value of the labor movement to date—its profound educative influence on the development of a social spirit within the group. And in time of war—in the recent great struggle—somewhat of such a situation has been approached in the community as a whole, between as well as within groups. In war-time there is a dominant national purpose, an intense necessity for coöperative endeavor, and the nation largely recognizes this, calls for loyalty, receives it, and truly seeks to protect all its members. This fact has not only proved the possibility, under certain conditions, of evoking this general sense of social responsibility in groups and individuals who otherwise seem wholly to lack it, but it has led many, who felt the value and the thrill—for such coöperation includes as by no means the least of its advantages a very general emotional satisfaction—who rejoiced in the presence at last of national solidarity, to believe that such solidarity marked the birth of a new spirit that would continue to function in time of peace. These optimistic—or perhaps, since they are our militarists, we had better say pessimistic—individuals utterly overlooked the fact that the war situation is intensely artificial, that it is sustained by the most vicious and insidious of propaganda, that it tends, if continued for any length of time, to destroy the nations that indulge in it, and to sacrifice upon the altar of futile greed the very nation whose solidarity it may achieve. The war "spirit of service" was for the most part genuine enough, and it is highly revealing as indicating the potentialities resident in human nature hitherto unsuspected by most men of today; but it cannot continue into the weak piping days of peace because the situation in peace time is, or has been to the present, a very different situation from that in time of war. The former is not a situation calling for education in social responsibility; the latter is.

But let us examine more closely this social situation in time of peace. What elements does it contain of the situation in which social responsibility is developed?

In the first place, the development of industrial technique and the consequent division of labor and integration of society have made a considerable degree of group coöperation absolutely essential. When the industrial revolution was just starting, and the theories and habits upon which we have acted ever since were first developed, this was not at all the case; but especially of late years such coöperation and reasonably efficient service of community needs has become a matter of the utmost necessity for the continuance of that industrial revolution and the civilization it has created. Thus the first factor in the situation is certainly present today.

There has been, moreover, in the recent decrease in productivity throughout the world directly attributable to the war, an increasing realization of the necessity of holding groups responsible for community service. The present agitation in favor of the extension of the idea and the attitude of the public utility, and the stress laid upon the needs of "the public" in addition to the demands of struggling workers and employers, whatever its motives may be, and their sincerity is certainly in many cases highly dubious, can not fail to have a very beneficial effect in hastening this realization. Unfortunately, as yet industrial groups are not organized upon a basis which permits the performance of these socially expected responsibilities; and those upon whom the ultimate control of production now depends legally and to a great extent actually, the employers and the "capitalists," are not yet comprised within this demand for social responsibility. The public conscience is quick to rebuke striking miners, but it quite overlooks the inefficient methods and the exorbitant profiteering of the coal-operators, which are socially even more undesirable. As the brilliant English economist R. H. Tawney says, "To recommend an increase in productivity as the solution to the industrial problem is like offering spectacles to a man with a broken leg, or trying to atone for putting a bad sixpence in the plate one Sunday by putting a bad shilling in it the next. . . . A functional society would extinguish mercilessly those property rights which yield income without service. There would be an end of the property rights in virtue of which the industries on which the welfare of whole populations depends are administered by the agents and for the profit of absentee shareholders." [1]

Accordingly, there is a general lack of recognition by industrial groups of any social obligations, a lack of recognition bred of a century of business philosophy. Where this responsibility has not been demanded by public opinion and social custom, but has rather been expressly discouraged and overlaid by the competitive business principle of making profit, it is not surprising that industrial groups have not given voice to much sense of social obligation. Yet the persistence of the second strain throughout the labor movement, its return again and again after repeated rebuffs and in the face of deep public hostility, as well as the remarkable response which the recent demands for efficient production have met—a response that has gone much further than the protectors of "the public" dreamed or desired it would, to the demand for the total reorganization of industry upon a more efficient basis of serving needs than private profits—the rise and spread of the New Unionism, all betoken the readiness with which the worker is willing to meet this social obligation half-way. If this second strain leads the workers, as in England, to champion a social order which will be an advance from an acquisitive toward a functional society, if it becomes the conscious aim of the labor movement in their struggles upward from the depths into which the industrial revolution hurled them to create a new and more harmonious society, as indeed it has always been their more or less articulate endeavor, then there can be no question as to the attitude which those as yet preserving the calm of neutrality in the industrial struggle must assume.

As yet there is little answering sense of responsibility by society to the single group. Our whole political theory, in fact, has deprecated "class legislation" and "group interests" and demanded that every social measure must work for the benefit and advantage of the entire

[1] *The Hibbert Journal*, April, 1919.

population. On this ground all laws designed to benefit and protect certain groups, giving them privileges and rights not accorded to all members of the nation, such as minimum wages, limitation of hours, insurance and pensions, and the like, have been vigorously denounced as "class legislation", as though it were not to the benefit of the community as a whole for its members to enjoy improved conditions. It is difficult to reconcile this attitude, however, with the perfect willingness to protect certain industries and special classes through the tariff— especially since the argument in its favor has been precisely this one, that the prosperity of the small group redounded to the benefit of the community as a whole, and since the particular application is in this case much more dubious than in the other. Nevertheless the community is gradually coming to a recognition that it has a duty and an obligation to its component groups, especially to the most oppressed and sweated of them, as the enactment of much "welfare legislation" betokens. The hostility, however, with which the impartial representatives of "the public's" interests at Albany regarded such legislation in 1920 makes it plain that "the public" which supported those representatives certainly has still far to go before it recognizes its full obligations.

And finally, in time of peace there is very little common national and social purpose. The recent efforts made to replace the war purpose of "making the world safe for democracy"—a purpose very powerful indeed, and quite sincere if you interpret "democracy" according to its differing meanings for different individuals—with the peace aim of "securing the supremacy of American Business," are bound to be a failure, because no one is much interested in the supremacy of American Business except the American business man. Such an aim can scarcely serve as the rallying cry of a real national solidarity. Yet for all that there does exist a very powerful social motive in civic feeling and patriotism—a motive usually latent, but capable in time of crisis of sweeping everything before it.

From this examination, then, we can conclude that there certainly do exist tendencies favorable to the creation of a situation in which social responsibility can and will be developed, but that the modern organization of industry for the most part fails to foster them if it is not actually hostile. The problem, then, becomes two-fold: in order to create a situation in which habits and standards of social responsibility will be naturally developed and will increasingly function, it is necessary, first, to create favorable social conditions through the modification of the present economic and legal system of controlling and administering industrial production and technique, and secondly, it is necessary to build up the new attitude of expecting and granting social responsibility in production through actual educational propaganda, in school, in press, in every means of social training, supplemented, where necessary, by the judicial application of social pressure as an instrumentality of education. Both of these methods must be employed simultaneously, because neither is possible alone.

What, then, are those changes in the social structure which appear likely to lead to a situation more favorable to the development of habits of social response? It is at this point that the average radical reformer of society fails, and fails miserably. There is no single system of utopian reform adequate to meet the infinite complexity of even the industrial side of modern civilization, to say nothing of the multitude of non-industrial factors that must be considered. No plan, no theoretically elaborated ideal social structure, however great its value and importance as a spur to new achievement—and as such a spur the creation of utopias is admittedly an invaluable function of the human spirit—no "solution" or panacea, can be propounded as a practicable program of accomplishment. The value of such imaginative constructions of the spirit lies in the light they throw upon practical problems, in the illumination and clarification of purposes and standards that can be applied as criteria of future achievement, and in their utility as regulative ideas, ideals to inspire men and to be worked toward until in that very process of realization they are themselves modified, readjusted to new needs, and transcended. Just such an ideal is the picture of a society in which all component groups coöperate toward a genuine social purpose, each contributing its share to the enhancing and enriching of the whole, each sympathizing with and making its own the aims and interests of its fellows. It stands as the type of social organization that contemporary conditions demand. But the realization of such a society, nay, any progress whatever toward it, can come about only through the patient and laborious application of intelligence to the specific social and economic problems, through experiment, through trial and error, mayhap through failure and success.

Nevertheless our examination has resulted in the emerging of several general principles, which, provisional as they be, still may serve to indicate the general trend which the reorganization of industrial life must take if it is to create a situation in which social responsibility will thrive and wax strong. In the first place, we must conclude that for such a situation to result, both the present business unions and the industries of which they are a part must in some way be organized upon a basis of production to serve the needs of the community. This may mean "Whitley Councils" of a sort, joint councils of the employers and employees in an entire industry invested with administrative powers; it may mean the development of shop committees and plans involving the coöperation of employer and employee in the actual business of production. But it must also comprise some method for the regulation of the profit motive through the salutary influence of an awakened public opinion that will demand service, and will allow reward only for service well done. Or, it may mean in certain industries, like the railroads and the mines, actual government ownership and industrial management, with direct public participation in the control, as tentatively outlined in the Plumb Plan. In fact, it does not seem probable that without the elimination of the profit motive, and of domination by the market, any organization of industry can ultimately insure the supremacy of the motive of public service. But such a thoroughgoing reorganization is not yet applicable to very many industries, and if it come, it can come only as the result of a gradual and somewhat prolonged education in responsible power through less complete participation in the control of industry. The railway workers, coöperating with the railway managers, could, it seems probable, assume such control today, and with not too great transitional disorder transform the railroad system from the servant of the shareholder and of the expert in high finance to the servant of national distribution; but it is difficult to point to many other industries where today a like ability exists.

Whatever method is evolved will necessarily be adopted slowly and with considerable hesitation; our knowledge is at present entirely inadequate to justify more than a purely experimental point of view. What does appear certain, however, is that the steps that are taken must come with the coöperation of and grow out of the present organizations of labor, and that they must secure at least the consent and honest acquiescence of the employer. The attempt at any ill-advised plan of "public ownership" in accord with the strict Marxian theory, which would antagonize both the ousted capitalists and the existent labor organizations, hallowed through the struggles and achievements of the past, would necessarily fail miserably. The nation can not stand any more post offices. The most fruitful path, on the whole, would appear to be the sympathetic fostering of the spirit of the New Unionism wherever it appears, and a cordial willingness on the part of employer and government to meet it half-way and coöperate with it. To many, such is the bitterness of the economic conflict, and so irreconcilable appear the attitudes of both parties today. Such a cordial coöperation seems utterly impossible, and they see hope only in a cataclysmic revolution. This may indeed be true; but there are few who would not be loath, in this ostensibly free and democratic land of America, to be compelled to admit it. Whether it is so or not will depend largely upon the employers and the public and the attitude which they adopt. Organized labor is determined to have what it wants, a secure and equal position in society, and it is going to change the entire nature of our state and our industrial civilization to secure it. It will be the part of wisdom for "capital" and "the public" to accept this fact and aid labor to secure its aims with as little friction as possible. The employer, like the British aristocrat, and, it now seems, like the British capitalist, must realize when it is time to retire gracefully from the lid of the kettle when the pressure gets too great. He must be willing to give up what he has hitherto regarded as his inalienable rights—the right to run his business as he pleases, and the right to make just as much profit as he pleases. There are many individual employers who are quite willing thus to assist in the revocation of their own privileges, for they realize that social advantage must in the long run take precedence over their immediate private interests; and, may we not add, they have the example of Russia to edify them if they do not.

But if the unions and industry in general must be reorganized on the lines toward which the New Unionism is working, there must also be a recognition by society of its reciprocal obligation to the groups it expects to serve its needs. The old theory that government exists only to serve the interests that are common to all citizens, and which under those conditions included only the administration of justice and the public defense, must be revised in accordance with the present situation in which the interests of groups have become inextricably intertwined. This taking into account of the manifold special interests of various industrial groups may even extend to the provision for industrial representation in the central legislative body, as a measure to secure the adequate social consideration of group interests. In any case, there must be social guarantees of a reasonably equal status and position, with minimum and possibly maximum determined, the latter through a graduated income tax, and effective provision against unemployment. In other words, the society must guarantee the main aims of the workers, stability and security from want. This also, to judge from present tendencies, does not seem a wholly impossible development.

Finally, industries must be definitely held responsible, both employers and employees, if that distinction remains, to the performance of their social function efficiently and well, with the expectation enforced through a rigorous public opinion, of securing a response. Group individualism must cease to be the dominant philosophy, the habits it has engendered must cease to control, and "public" and government alike must expect and demand efficient functioning.

What are the prospects that in such a changed social situation economic groups would respect community interests instead of regarding merely their group advantage, would merge the two into one? There would indeed be created a situation in which group responsibility might naturally arise and flourish, and the obvious obstacles presented by the present situation would be removed; but what would be the chances of its actual development? There are several considerations which make it appear that they are not unfavorable.

First, there is the probable psychological result of the change within the union itself. The union has already altered the workers' dominant attitude from one of individualism to one of group coöperation; the worker now thinks not merely in terms of his own interests, but also in terms of the group interests that he identifies with his own. This is certainly a change significant enough. The old pioneering self-reliance has been supplanted. by a confidence and a reliance upon group coöperation, in itself a profound psychological change. But the purpose of the union has remained individualistic; at best, it has been expanded to take in the working class. As in the process of development and reorganization this purpose changes and comes more and more to emphasize production, as the New Unionism betokens, it will find the men to whom it appeals accustomed more and more to think in terms of coöperation; it will face the problem, not of creating an entirely new type of response, which problem, difficult as it is, the union has already accomplished in organizing the frontier American, but rather of extending the scope and applicability of the old one. The task before the society that proposes to bring about such an extension of previously acquired habits is not, apparently, so great as the task it has already accomplished in producing a relatively unfamiliar habit of response within the union.

Moreover, another important psychological trait will come to the aid of the coöperative one. There exists a tendency, an impulse, an instinct, a way of acting—call it what you will—that impels men to creative and productive endeavor, to desire to do what they

do well. At present the habits and training in coöperative group action
run directly counter to this impulse; the union bids the unionist work
so as to get the most wages, even at the expense of sabotage and inefficient production. With the industrialism of the union and the participation in and emphasis on the processes of production, this creative
tendency or impulse will directly coincide with and reinforce the tendency toward efficient functioning as a social organization, and the
two most powerful tendencies in the life of the worker, the instinct of
workmanship and the desire to make money, will strengthen instead
of as at present negating each other. This is already appearing in the
new unionism of the railway workers, the miners, and the clothing
makers.

There is still another reason for believing that social responsibility
will develop in the situation we have described. The chief source of
dispute between groups at present, between skilled and unskilled workers, between workers and capitalists, is the disparity of social position
between them. The lower group desires to rise to the level of the higher,
the higher wants to keep above the lower. The increasing tendency
towards a more equal social status of all members of society, one of the
developments of union organization, the gradual movement already
considerably advanced toward the equalization of income, to which
the war, in lowering the salaried and professional classes almost to the
level of the wage-worker, has powerfully contributed, will remove one
of the chief causes of group dispute. The intense longing for "equality" is important and strong only in a situation in which there is great
and obvious inequality, just as it never occurs to any man to proclaim,
"I'm just as good as you are," unless in some particular he obviously
isn't. In a society of relatively equal citizens, such as the development
of the labor movement is tending toward, and such as the three general
principles we have formulated would tend to bring about, men would
probably be too busy improving and developing their qualitatively and
individually different excellencies to worry much about small quantita-
tive differences. Class and group bitterness and rivalry finds little
food in a farming community. Such a society would probably even
tolerate without bitterness and probably with much pride the greater
rewards it accorded to those men obviously expert in fields where they
could appreciate genius and skill, even as today the very workers who
bitterly rail against the "capitalists" and the "plutes" take great pride
in the immense incomes of their well appreciated movie stars, and
cherish no rancor against (striking bedfellow!) Mr. Henry Ford.

And finally, economic groups do not exist in vacuo, but have their place within nations which are very much indeed collective wholes. Though the groups are not as such very consciously part of the nation, the individuals who compose them certainly are. Every unionist is a citizen of his country as well as a member of his own group, and if it came to a genuine conflict between group and patriotic motives, would probably follow the latter. The way in which the employers have utilized the patriotic motive to their own advantage is notorious, and shows how influential that motive is. If systematically thus misused, it will fall into disrepute, as it has in some European lands where the throne has been wont to rally the workers to its support through rumors of foreign aggression. But intelligently and honestly applied through a social agency, it can be made to stimulate powerfully the sense of social obligation of a disgruntled group.

So far patriotism has not been very successfully used in developing group responsibility, and it does not appear as though it could well be, because responsibility, while ultimately to society, has been legally and actually first of all to the employer and to his interests. The worker knows that submission on his part will increase profits and dividends, but he does not see how it may also benefit the community. He thinks that better conditions for himself and his fellows will benefit the community just as directly, and probably more. But if industry is organized for production, with coöperative participation in the service of human needs as its expected and wonted aim, if the producers thus came to coincide completely with the consumers, so that they could feel that the government really represented them because they were society, then the solidarity of the class would be merged with and not antagonistic to the national solidarity or patriotism.

Moreover, there remains the possibility of developing the national purpose itself so that instead of being fitful and largely bellicose it might take its place amongst the nations of the earth in the performance in that larger field of some especial task. There are numerous non-economic and cultural aims that might together furnish a sufficient national and civic purpose for the efficient functioning of groups to serve. It would indeed seem as though the preservation and the enhancing of all the values of Western civilization would in itself be a sufficient purpose, when once the supreme need is made apparent, for such a socially responsible activity. If men are willing to forsake all they hold dear and risk life itself to defend that civilization, it would seem as though when once they realized that it was menaced with just as dangerous internal disorganization they could be led to do what on the whole they want to do anyway.

Nor, in estimating the chances of such a situation calling forth a social response, must we overlook the influence of individual men who are convinced of its necessity—the influence of outstanding personalities and leaders like Sidney Hillman. When conditions are ripe one such leader can work wonders in crystallizing sentiment and giving the impetus to the formation of new habits and attitudes.

Nevertheless, after all these factors are taken into consideration, it is evident that some form of force will always remain necessary, just as among individuals complete anarchism is not and does not promise soon to become a very practicable social arrangement. In the situation as reorganized this force may well be employed as an educative measure. When so employed, however, against groups and not individuals, to be ultimately of any avail it must be employed to develop habits of social responsibility and never simply as a means to the attainment of social peace at any price.

The most effective social pressure is the force of public opinion—not public opinion as voiced by the editors of newspapers, but the real and genuine feelings and attitude of all the members of society. It is significant that even under present conditions it has proved infinitely more efficacious against the selfishness of economic groups than any scheme of police power yet devised. A law against a strike is quite apt to provoke it; an overwhelmingly adverse public opinion is bound to result in its failure, and probably to prevent its outbreak. Hence it is that all the competent investigators of the system of compulsory arbitration have declared against the compulsory features and have, like the President's Industrial Commission, preferred to rely solely and entirely on the public opinion following upon full publicity.

But if a group should still, in the face of such a united public opinion, prove obstinately recalcitrant, it will be necessary and under such conditions quite possible to proceed to apply direct pressure. There are untold possibilities in the use of economic ostracism, for instance, when employed by a constituted authority and supported by the weight of a great public opinion against the group ostracised. There are in fact such possibilities in it that it is difficult to conceive of a group even compelling in order to further its own interests the mere threat of such an action. It seems as though the employment of such severe measures might, in a society organized primarily for production, bear somewhat the relation to the prevention of group depredation that capital punishment does to the prevention of every man murdering his neighbor: a relation which, though present, can hardly be said to enter appreciably into the situation.

These considerations must not, however, be allowed to induce a too confident optimism. The pathway to a more socially responsible society is not easy; and long and arduous will be the journey, many the slips and failures. These suggestions do not, of course, point to any "solution," sinple or complex. There is no "solution," in the sense of a formula, however elaborate, that can be applied to the concrete material, any more than there ever is a "solution" to the complex human problems of society. They may, however, serve to illuminate the problem; and after all the important consideration is that the problem, the necessity of developing within society a sense of mutual responsibility for the efficient functioning of those tasks which the members of society, be they individuals or groups, have as their chosen duty to perform, be clearly recognized. The important thing is that the problem be clearly envisaged in its full setting, and worked upon patiently through long experiment. When once its importance is fully realized, the nation will have already gone a long ways, a very long ways, indeed, towards eliminating its consequences.

And thus we return, as men have so often returned, to the guiding light of the best Greek thought about society, and to Plato; for what is our ideal state but that heavenly city in the sky where each group does its work harmoniously and joyously, and what is that which we have been calling "the sense of social responsibility" but that saving virtue of Justice which is both the product and the prerequisite of a well-ordered social life? True, the philosopher need in our state no longer be king, and keep the groups in their proper relation, for we have discovered that the regulative power of Justice in the state arises through being just in small things; but he will be all the freer to revisit the ideal realm whence he has brought us his vision, that he may return with new insight and new illumination to assist in the eternal ideal progress of the quality and texture of the life of the spirit.